EMBERS OF CHILDHOOD

EMBERS OF CHILDHOOD

First Arcade Edition 2019

Originally published by Plumley Press under the title *Embers*

Arcade Publishing books may be purchased in bulk at special discounts for sales promotion, corporate gifts, fund-raising, or educational purposes. Special editions can also be created to specifications. For details, contact the Special Sales Department, Arcade Publishing, 307 West 36th Street, 11th Floor, New York, NY 10018 or arcade@skyhorsepublishing.com.

Arcade Publishing® is a registered trademark of Skyhorse Publishing, Inc.®, a Delaware corporation.

Visit our website at www.arcadepub.com.

10 9 8 7 6 5 4 3 2 1

Library of Congress Cataloging-in-Publication Data

Names: Biddle, Flora Miller, author.
Title: Embers of childhood : growing up a Whitney / by Flora Miller Biddle.
Other titles: Embers
Description: First Arcade edition. | New York : Arcade Publishing, 2019. | "Originally published by Plumley Press under the title Embers."
Identifiers: LCCN 2018059764 (print) | LCCN 2018061576 (ebook) | ISBN 9781948924016 (ebook) | ISBN 9781948924009 (hardback)
Subjects: LCSH: Biddle, Flora Miller. | Whitney family. | Whitney Museum of American Art. | Art patrons—United States—Biography. | Arts administrators—United States—Biography. | BISAC: BIOGRAPHY & AUTOBIOGRAPHY / Rich & Famous. | BIOGRAPHY & AUTOBIOGRAPHY / Women. | BIOGRAPHY & AUTOBIOGRAPHY / Personal Memoirs.
Classification: LCC N5220.W64 (ebook) | LCC N5220.W64 B53 2019 (print) | DDC 973.91092 [B]—dc23
LC record available at https://lccn.loc.gov/2018059764

Jacket design by Erin Seaward Hiatt
Jacket illustration: George Macculloch Miller

Printed in China

Embers of Childhood

Growing Up a Whitney

FLORA MILLER BIDDLE

ARCADE PUBLISHING • NEW YORK

CONTENTS

continued

Acknowledgements

Mark Donovan first edited every page, every word, as I wrote and rewrote. His intelligence, sense of humor, and professional skill, enhanced by his knowledge and understanding of material and author, helped immeasurably to shape and hone my story. His belief that it was a worthwhile project gave me confidence to persevere. I'm deeply admiring of and grateful to Mark.

Annabel Davis-Goff, whose writing I love and respect, encouraged me to go further and deeper, and to make the story chronological, which I did. She thought that I should show it to our friend, the wonderful writer Susanna Moore, who offered to read it and make suggestions. Susanna's offer became three close readings. She corrected grammar, chose apt synonyms, shifted events and paragraphs around. Her distinctive hand decorated page after page. Susanna gave her brilliant mind and loving heart to my book. Endless thanks for her extraordinary generosity.

Besides her inestimable gift of time and expertise, Susanna introduced me to her splendid agent, Stephanie Cabot. I'm so very grateful to Stephanie for her tireless efforts to sell my book.

My daughter, Fiona Donovan, a gifted writer and teacher, gave me invaluable ideas and encouragement. She also gave precious time to proofread this book, an extremely generous act for which I thank her profoundly.

These and others read all or parts of my book, and I thank them for their useful comments, among them Barbara Ascher, Mary DelMonico, Linda Donn, B. H. Friedman, Rob Ingraham , Phyllis Levin, James Mairs, June Levin Roth, Dorothy Ruddick, Will Schwalbe, Jeannette Seaver, Susan Seydel Cofer, Patterson Sims, Andrew Solomon, and Adam Weinberg.

Many thanks to Anita Duquette, head of Rights and Reproductions at the Whitney Museum of American Art, for arranging to have my father's watercolors photographed.

It was a pleasure to work with Julie Rubenstein, my former agent, who helped with an earlier version of the book.

Michael Russem, of Kat Ran Press, has been endlessly patient and kind. He has designed and produced my book. I admire and appreciate its elegance so very much.

Prologue

A sense of security, of well-being, of summer warmth pervades
my memory. That robust reality makes a ghost of the present.
The mirror brims with brightness; a bumblebee has entered the
room and bumps against the ceiling. Everything is as it should
be, nothing will ever change, nobody will ever die.

VLADIMIR NABOKOV
Speak Memory

Today, July 29th, is my mother's birthday. Once again, as
often before, I wish I could speak with her. There's so much
that I want to ask her; so much I'd like to tell her. First, I
would tell her how much I loved her—I never told her in
words.

*

My mother's name was Flora Whitney Miller. Her second
husband, my father, George Macculloch Miller, was called
Cully. My older half-brother was Whitney Tower. My half-
sister is Pamela Tower, and my younger brother is Leverett
Saltonstall Miller. I myself am Flora Macculloch Miller.
Many servants, both black and white, who tended to us over
the years, were also part of our family. We lived in Aiken,
South Carolina, in Joye Cottage. It was my first nest, and the
one that means the most to me in my long life; a touchstone,
origin and symbol of that part of me that is deep inside.

In the summer, we went to the Adirondacks. We bathed in the cool lake, warming ourselves by a fire after catching fish for dinner or picking raspberries for a pie, lighting a kerosene lamp as darkness drew family and friends together. Our sadness each September as we left that paradise was linked to losing our freedom. We knew, even if we couldn't conceptualize it, that we would be returning to a more restricted life. For me, life elsewhere was never as pure as life in the Adirondacks; good and evil never as unambiguous. Surely, childhood should be a time for growth, for inventive play, for vivid sensations, for security, and for the certainties of good and bad. Just as surely, it fails to give us everything that we need—whether from the human failings of parents and caregivers or the disasters of war, poverty, famine, and disease. How can I not feel grateful for the values of my own childhood? Separated from the hurly-burly of a great city, we lived in a gilded cage with all material comforts, surrounded by protective adults, unaware of hunger and the many forms of suffering that exist almost everywhere in our world. What was the effect of growing up in such a rarefied world? When did the Good and Evil I learned from the adults around me, and from the Episcopal Church and its prayer book, become real to me?

Thanks to my upbringing, I developed a rosy view of life. It included a belief that I was lucky to have been born at that particular time, in that place, to that family. For many years, I loved and idealized my childhood in Aiken, but when I married and had children, doubts began to surface. Had some of the prejudices I'd hardly noticed as a child, prejudices that I thought I'd rejected, stuck to me after all?

As I envision my mother, other characters crowd into

my thoughts. I wonder if, in grasping their elusive identities, perhaps I will better understand my own. As a child, I didn't know how valuable these people were to me. They were simply part of my life and, like most children, I took them for granted. At times, as I write, these people open their worlds to me; at others, they remain obscure, reluctantly yielding their secrets. Although some have died, they all remain with me.

PART I: HISTORY

CHAPTER 1

Ancestors

I don't remember my parents ever telling me that I would need a marketable skill—it would have been an outlandish idea. Among the many subjects we discussed at meals, tea, or cocktails (politics, the war, hunting, fishing, riding, school, friends, travel, clothes, family, proper behavior, romances, movies, books, religion), money was never a topic.

Money was a mystery to me for years. My mother had grown up with absolutely no idea of the value of money. It must have seemed limitless to her—and in her parents' family it had been, less than two generations earlier. With a Whitney father and a Vanderbilt mother, my mother was born an American princess. What does this way of life mean to a family? To a community? We weren't the only ones. Most of the people I knew growing up were alike in class, religion and income. My parents may have been at the top of the heap, but the philosophy was the same. "Money-grubbing" and other disdainful references to a life of hard work made labor seem vulgar. Even talking about money was in bad taste—and we never did talk of it. Unaware of the source or extent of our uncommon comfort, we had no shame of it.

Doing research in the Seventies for B. H. Friedman's biography of my grandmother, Gertrude Vanderbilt Whitney, I learned the sources of my family's wealth, and began to wonder how it had filtered away. There had once been so much money! What happened? Admittedly, there were a number of 20th-century societal and economic factors: the graduated income tax, established (through the Sixteenth Amendment) in 1913, made it difficult to maintain enormous fortunes through several generations. My great-great-great grandfather, Cornelius Vanderbilt, had made the original money. As B. H. Friedman wrote:

> Now, after these three generations, the energy which the Commodore had directed into creative productivity was being channeled largely into custodianship . . . To their Dutch Protestant tradition of industry and piety there had already been added a sense of Puritan prudence and social service.

Caretakers who do good don't usually increase large fortunes. Entrepreneurs do that. To backtrack: the first Vanderbilt of whom I know is a farmer, Jan Aertsen van der Bilt, of the manor of Bilt, near Zeyst, Holland, who, in the mid-seventeenth century, emigrated to Flatbush, New Amsterdam. Jan's grandson, Jacob, bought a large acreage in Stapleton, Staten Island, where farmland was less costly. Jacob's grandson, Cornelius Vanderbilt, and his wife Phoebe Hand, a strong, well-educated woman of English descent, raised their family there. Cornelius Vanderbilt, Jr., was the fourth of their nine children.

At eleven, this Cornelius was over six feet tall, with dark blue eyes, a hawklike nose, strong mouth and chin, and a mop of wild blond hair. This youth, already outstanding for his ambition and vitality, was to become the Commodore, named thanks to his large shipping interests. A bold, canny entrepreneur with limitless energy, he was especially attractive to women, as have been many of his descendants.

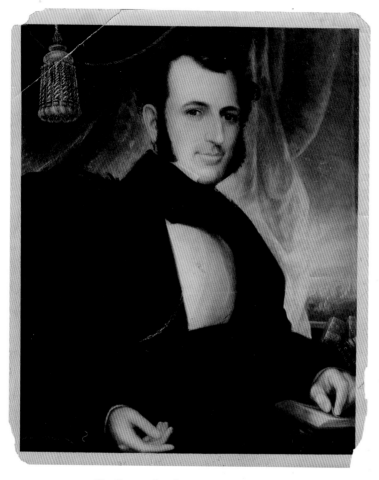

The Commodore, by Henry Inman, 1837

The Commodore was respected by bankers and businessmen for his clear vision, toughness, and courage—and for sticking to the bargains he made. On the other hand, his speech and habits were crude—he swore like the docker he'd once been; he chewed tobacco and spat. In the elegant drawing rooms where Mrs. Astor and Ward McAllister were beginning to define and regulate a young American society, Cornelius was considered impossible.

His rejection rankled, and in order to gain a place in society he built, in 1846, a large town house at Washington Place in Manhattan. His loyal wife and cousin, Sophia, who'd been his hard-working partner as they began their rise, refused to leave their comfortable home in Staten Island, so he committed her to a private asylum for a few months until she agreed to move into their new house. Sophia died in 1868, and, at 75, Cornelius married another cousin, Frank Armstrong Crawford, a thirty-year-old Mobile, Alabama belle. In 1877, after ten years of marriage and much hard work, he became ill. Ready to die, he calmly said farewell to his wife, children, and grandchildren as thousands gathered outside the house in a deathwatch. As his wife led the group in singing his favorite hymn, "Show Pity, Lord," he requested that Grand Central Depot, the icon of his success, not be draped in mourning black.

Starting with virtually nothing but character and ability, the Commodore left at his death more than $100 million. Of this, $90 million went to his oldest son William Henry; the remainder to his other nine surviving children. It was the Commodore's intention to create a dynasty, and by keeping his fortune intact, he did just that.

A superb caretaker, in nine years William doubled the fortune to $200 million—more than $2 billion in today's money. At his death in 1885, William's eldest son, Cornelius II, hard-working and intense, became head of the family. Besides taking over the business, he was much occupied with charity, becoming a trustee of major hospitals, universities, and churches. As head of the executive committee of the Metropolitan Museum, he donated many paintings to the Museum, including Rosa Bonheur's popular "The Horse Fair."

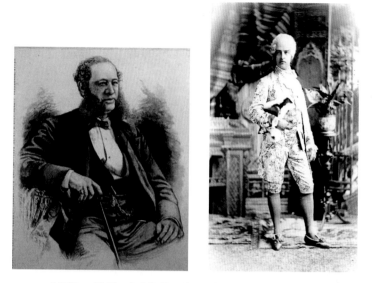

LEFT: *William H. Vanderbilt, President of New York Central Railroad.*
RIGHT: *Cornelius Vanderbilt II dressed as Louis XIV*

Despite this cultural largesse, the Vanderbilts weren't accepted by longer established wealth until March 26, 1883, when Cornelius's brother, William K. Vanderbilt, gave a costume ball for the opening of his new mansion, designed by William Morris Hunt, at Fifth Avenue and 52nd Street in Manhattan. Miss Caroline Astor, daughter of the leader of the exclusive "400," planned a quadrille for her friends to give at the ball. When William's wife heard about it, she told a mutual friend she was sorry she couldn't invite Miss Astor to her ball, as her mother had never paid her a call. At last, Mrs. Astor saw fit to call on Mrs. Vanderbilt. The ball was described on page one of the *New York Times* as "most extravagant." In photographs, Cornelius is dressed as Louis XIV in fawn-colored breeches trimmed with silver lace, and a diamond-headed sword, while his wife, the former Alice Claypoole Gwynne, holding an electric torch above her

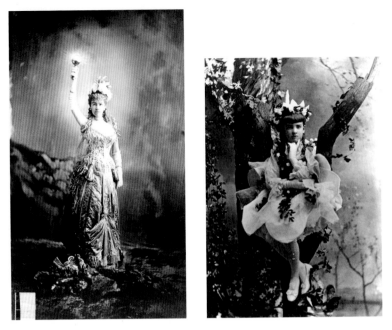

LEFT: *Alice Gwynne Vanderbilt as "Electric Light"*
RIGHT: *Gertrude Vanderbilt as a rose*

head as "Electric Light," wears white satin trimmed with diamonds, and a headdress of diamond speckled feathers. (Edison had made the first light bulb only four years earlier, in 1879, and newspapers had recently published impressive images of the Statue of Liberty, about to rise in New York Harbor.) Their eight-year-old daughter, Gertrude, photographed perched in a tree, was a rose, in pink tulle with a satin overdress of green leaves. Four years later, when the Social Register replaced Mrs. Astor's List, the Vanderbilts were included. When Cornelius Vanderbilt died in 1899, each of his five children inherited about $7 million from a fortune already decreased by division, and an increasingly evident lack of entrepreneurial energy in the men of the family.

In 1896, Cornelius's twenty-one-year-old daughter, Gertrude, married the Vanderbilts' neighbor across 57th street, Harry Payne Whitney. His fortune was smaller than hers, but he could trace his lineage back to Turstin the Fleming. Turstin had followed William the Conqueror into England and is mentioned in the *Domesday Book* of 1086 as an extensive landholder in Hertfordshire and the Marches of Wales. In the seventeenth century, his family moved to Watertown, Massachusetts, where the men became successful leaders. Harry's father, William Collins Whitney, made the move into the bigger arena of national politics and business. He was over six feet tall, with large dark gray eyes; sharp, well-formed features; straight brown hair and a soft moustache. At Yale, his friend William Graham Sumner later judged him *easily the man of widest influence in our Class and perhaps*

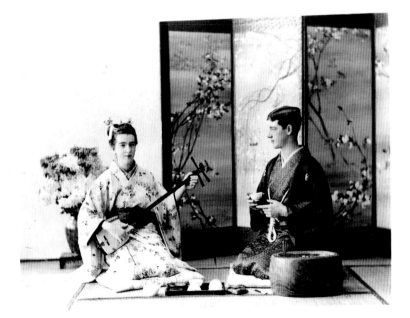

My grandparents, Harry and Gertrude Whitney, honeymoon in Japan, 1897

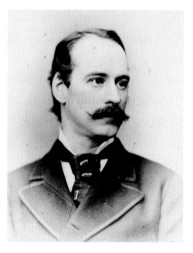

William C. Whitney

in the College. After Yale and Harvard Law School, he practiced law in New York City, counting Cornelius Vanderbilt among his clients. In 1869, William married Flora Payne, sister of his friend and Yale classmate Oliver, and daughter of Henry B. Payne, one of the wealthiest and most powerful Democrats in Ohio, later to become U.S. Senator. Of the many Floras in my family, Flora Payne Whitney was the first. Unusually well-educated for a girl of that time, Flora had traveled in Europe, North Africa and the Levant, pursuing her many interests, including science, archaeology, and languages. She had also attended an experimental seminary for women taught in Cambridge by Louis Agassiz. I have the two notebooks she kept, including high praise from Agassiz. When I leaf through the pages of fine script in which she describes the large variety of *Flora* and *Fauna* of which she made elegant, precise drawings, I realize how gifted she was. All her life, she wrote letters and diaries that reveal her grasp of current events, sense of humor, and emotional and intellectual depth.

William Whitney soon became deeply involved in Democratic politics, fighting successfully against Tammany and the Tweed Ring as Corporation Counsel of New York City, eventually becoming Grover Cleveland's Secretary of the Navy (1885–1889). He was successful in modernizing the fleet and eliminating corrupt bidding and contracting practices at a time when the Navy represented the country's primary security and power.

Harry Payne Whitney was Flora and William's oldest child (their first, Leonore, died at birth). *Never came a baby into the world more wanted, with more love ready to receive him, than our Boy,* wrote Flora. And indeed, Harry received everything they could give him. At Yale, he earned a Phi Beta Kappa key, was on the board of the Yale Daily News and a member of He Boule, Psi Epsilon, and Skull and Bones. He seemed destined for great things. Very much like his father, he differed from him in one important way. As B. H. Friedman and I determined,

> William C. Whitney had to work, had really to struggle, in his early years for his money. . . . Though Harry had all the advantages of two exceptionally distinguished parents and their great wealth, he had been better prepared for the leisurely sporting life of a gentleman and the custodianship of wealth than for a committed career from which he could receive satisfaction.

Although he enrolled and took classes, Harry never completed Columbia Law School; never took the Bar exam. He became instead a sports hero, often in newspaper headlines. He was captain of the Big Four, the Meadowbrook Club polo team that, in 1909, won the America Challenge Cup, held by England since 1886. My mother remembered Oakley Court, the castle her parents rented in England, and the

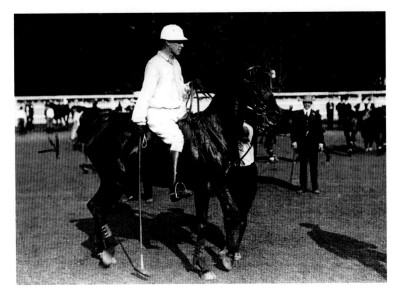

My grandfather on his polo pony Royal Diamond,
at the Philadelphia Country Club, c. 1913

excitement of the games, of receiving and being received by
the King and Queen. Winning other big matches in America and England, her father and his teammates went on to
triumph again in 1911 and 1913. Later, no longer able to play,
he raced his powerful 75-foot schooner "Vanitie" nationally
and internationally. And always he raced horses, often leading all owners in earnings. His "Regret" was the first filly to
win the Kentucky Derby. These activities led to lots of social
life and lots of drinking.

Late in his life, Harry invested in the Mammoth Oil
Company, the subsidiary that held Harry F. Sinclair's lease
on the U.S. Navy oil reserves in Teapot Dome, Wyoming.
The political scandal, while not implicating Harry, was a
blow to both his pride and his investment portfolio. Con-
cerned about his childrens' inheritance and wanting to
recoup his money, he revived his long-unused but once

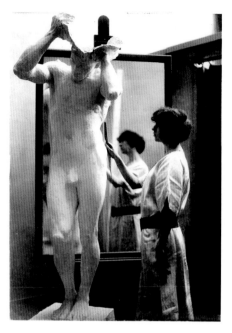

My grandmother working in her studio

estimable abilities, and discovered and developed Flin Flon, an extremely productive mining property in northern Manitoba, Canada. His shares of Hudson Bay Mining and Smelting (the successor to Flin Flon) made a spectacular recovery after the worst effects of the Depression. In his will, made shortly before his death in 1930, the principle of primogeniture remained in force when he left his son, Cornelius Vanderbilt Whitney, twice as much as he did to each of his two daughters.

Harry's wife, Gertrude Vanderbilt, had different interests from her husband's. Although they loved each other and had three children together, they often lived separate lives. Gertrude became a sculptor who sought and often won large commissions—she made the "Buffalo Bill" in Cody, Wyoming, and an immense "Columbus" rising from the harbor

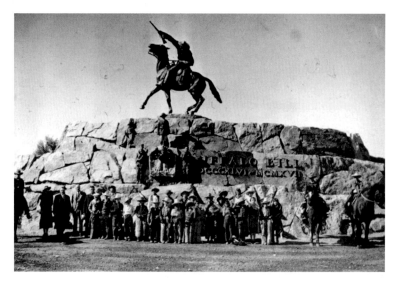

Dedication of Buffalo Bill, by Gertrude Vanderbilt Whitney, Cody, Wyoming, 1924

in Palos, Spain. She had studios in Paris, Long Island, and at 19 Macdougal Alley in New York's Greenwich Village, then center of the small American art world. Realizing that her friends in the Village had no place to show their work in a New York obsessed with European art and culture, Gertrude bought the building adjoining hers at 8 West 8th Street to make the Whitney Studio where she invited artists to have exhibitions. She bought work from each show, and added more buildings at a time when American art was becoming more recognized and accepted. In 1931, Gertrude converted the original buildings to make inviting spaces with fine American furniture and rare textiles, and opened the Whitney Museum of American Art.

With her husband's help, Gertrude provided the funds for the entire Museum. By 1942, however, when she died, the Museum was already exceeding her financial capacity. With the loss of entrepreneurial energy, with taxes, divorces, and many children, the family fortune had shrunk. My parents weren't good caretakers of their money. My talented father, George Macculloch Miller, had had little money of his own to begin with and wasn't motivated to earn more as my mother's inheritance enabled them to live very comfortably. As partner in the architectural firm of Noel & Miller and a gifted amateur artist, his designs for buildings and his watercolors were beautiful, but not profitable. Their business affairs were looked after by his stockbroker brother and an office manager. Through generosity to their children, bad investments, and continued support of the Whitney Museum—an embodiment, really, of Flora's adored mother, Gertrude— the money was further diminished. At her death in 1987, my mother's estate was tied up in land and houses. My siblings and I had to sell most of her properties and possessions to pay estate taxes, which is when we lost our share of the Adirondacks.

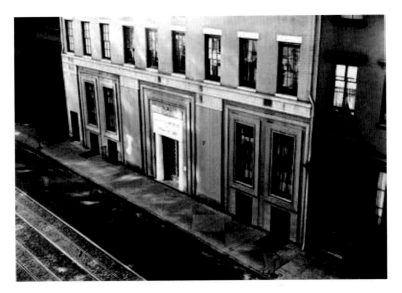

The Whitney Museum of American Art on West 8th Street, c. 1931

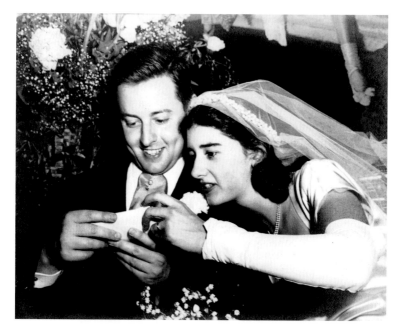

With Mike Irving at our wedding, June 7, 1947

Money is still an uncomfortable subject for me. My first husband, Michael Henry Irving, was kin to both the Duponts of Delaware and Washington Irving. Like my father and my brother Lev, he'd gone to St. Paul's School. At Harvard he'd been a member of the Porcellian Club with my brother Whitty and then served in the Navy during World War II. After graduating from the Columbia architectural school, Mike became a gifted architect who never lacked for work. He took pride in the money he earned, and in the buildings he designed, including our own attractive modern home. We led a normal suburban life—different from my childhood and, to me, preferable. Mike worked long hours; I too was busy with our four children, community activities, and my increasing involvement at the Whitney Museum. We had a full-time housekeeper until our last child was in school, then part-time house-cleaners or baby-sitters. Over the years, I taught myself to cook and to care for the children, mostly with pleasure, and fully believed that it was a better way to live. My mother paid for our children's education, and gave me unpredictable sums of cash from time to time. I don't have an extraordinary fortune, but I've never earned my living. This seems to me wrong, but it's too late to change. Financial inequality is an itch, and I've tried to scratch it in various ways—but I haven't repudiated the money I've inherited.

My descendants will earn their own money.

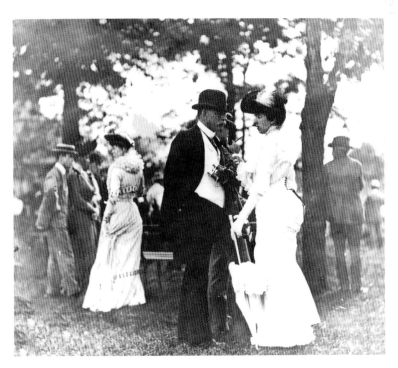

William C. Whitney and his daughter-in-law,
Gertrude Vanderbilt Whitney, at the races, c.1900

CHAPTER 2

Aiken

My great-grandfather, William C. Whitney, had followed his friend, Thomas Hitchcock, to Aiken, South Carolina, in the 1880s. These two men led Aiken's growth as a center for sports, with horses at the core. They bought over eight thousand acres of forestland—the Hitchcock Woods—for the enjoyment of their families and friends. William's first wife, my great-grandmother Flora Payne, died in 1893, and William, then only fifty-five, married Edith S. Randolph. He enlarged the small country inn he'd bought in 1896 from a Charleston woman named Sarah Joye and it became their home. Less than two years later, though, Edith broke her neck while riding under a low bridge, and died fifteen months later. William was devastated. For the rest of his life, he immersed himself in horseracing and breeding, often in Aiken. For his stable of thoroughbreds, he constructed a mile-long racetrack with training stables where he wintered his racehorses and trotters. Both this track and the first polo site, Whitney Field, have been in use ever since. No cars were allowed, only horses. The two partners saw to it that the soft clay roads of Aiken stayed unpaved, as some still do today.

After its introduction to the United States in 1876, polo became a bit like football is today—popular, with well-known stars. Through the 1930s, as many as 40,000

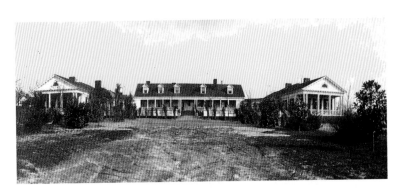

Joye Cottage, c. 1900

people came from New York to watch the big matches at the Meadow Brook Club in Long Island. As Nelson W. Aldrich says in his book *Old Money,*

> There is no sport that more graphically illustrates the means and objectives of Old Money's ordeals. The man on horse-back is a primal image of command and self-command, grace and power united . . . Polo is the most difficult game on earth, requiring the horsemanship of a Ghengis Khan, the antici-patory sense of a hockey player, and the hand-eye coordina-tion of a pool shark; to play it well therefore, one has to have always—past perfectly—played it . . . the entrepreneur cannot learn it without looking ridiculous.

At one time, there were sixteen polo fields in Aiken. William C. Whitney's son, my grandfather Harry Payne Whitney, became a ten-goal player—the very top—and kept up the tradition of polo in Aiken, attracting first-rate teams with their stables of horses for major tournaments and their attendant social events.

Court tennis is the world's oldest racquet game, played by European royalty and clergy from at least the thirteenth century. In 1902, in Aiken, William built one of only seven

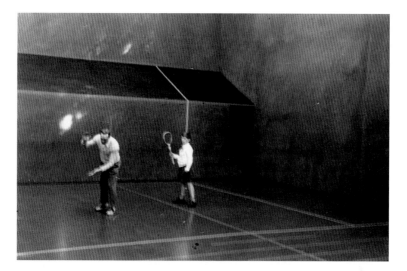

My brother, Lev Miller at his first court tennis lesson

courts in the United States for this challenging and complex game in which the ball can be played off both walls and roof. Only men were allowed inside, except during matches when women, too, could watch players from all over the country. My father took me to see the court's intriguing interior with its overlapping planes of walls and roof in the 1960s, only when he was sure no one would be around. Our voices bounced against the narrow, high walls like the hard leather balls in a game I could only imagine: men in long flannel trousers racing from side to side, sweating, yelling in impassioned, echoing barks. Whitney also donated land to complete the first golf course in Aiken, the Palmetto Golf Club—in those days, the greens were made of sand. His own squash court, adjoining Joye Cottage, later became home to the Aiken Day School—my school—from 1932 to 1957.

In the search for relaxation and pleasure after his lucrative public life, my great-grandfather was a strong influence

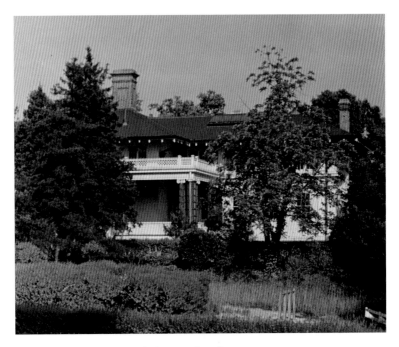

Squash Court at Joye Cottage, c. 1900

on Aiken's developing character. His daughter-in-law, Gertrude Vanderbilt Whitney, characterized him in words that apply to his gifts to Aiken as well as to many other facets of his life. He experienced, she said,

> a sheer joy in giving things, not because of a philanthropic or altruistic urge for publicity, or to impress, or to obligate—but because he simply derived joy out of making people happy. When they were happy, he was happy.

*

Cornelius Vanderbilt Whitney was the middle child and only son of Gertrude Vanderbilt and Harry Whitney. Barbara, the youngest child, was a lovely, generous soul, although troubled for much of her life. This may have begun when she was very young and her parents abruptly fired her nurse, Lizzie. Barbara's aching distress at losing her beloved mother-figure wasn't recognized as traumatic—in today's psychologically aware environment, she'd surely have been treated for her distress. The oldest child, Flora, was my mother. The strongest and most stable of the three, she was the closest to their mother and the only one not afraid of their father, who adored Flora. He was extremely hard on Cornelius, whose nickname was Sonny. In one story I heard later from his granddaughter, Nancy, Harry mocked and humiliated his son in front of his friends on the tennis court, going so far as to hit him with his racquet.

As a father, my Uncle Sonny patterned himself unconsciously on Harry. Like his father, he was bright, but unfocused. Despite his reputation as moody and difficult, the women with whom he was involved couldn't resist his charm—let alone his name and fortune. When he was at Yale, a young woman brought a much-publicized paternity suit against him. Infatuated by many women, he married four times. With his first wife Marie Norton (later married to Averell Harriman) he had two children, Harry and Nancy. Harry was a tall, boisterous man with great charm and talent, whose bi-polarity became destructive to his work and his family life. Sonny's second wife, Gwladys Hopkins, was a spirited beauty from Philadelphia. Their daughter Gail, wild and lovely, died of cancer in her twenties when Sonny was about to sail for Europe with his next wife, ignoring Gail's pleas to visit her. With his third wife, singer and evangelist Eleanor Searle, he had a son, Searle, who Sonny also undermined and neglected. His fourth wife, Marylou Hosford, had four children with her first husband and a daughter, Cornelia, with Sonny. This marriage survived. Cornelia is an artist who, keeping her distance from her parents, has maintained a good relationship with them. Sonny forbade most of his children and grandchildren to visit the Adirondacks; only Marylou's children were allowed. My mother, who'd once been so close to her brother, finally renounced him. My cousin Nancy, though her heart had been hopelessly wounded by her father, retained the rapturous spirit I remember so well in the lakes and forests of the Adirondack Mountains. Conversations with her often harked back to her father's injustice and meanness. In turn, Sonny's children found parenting an almost insurmountable emotional challenge.

CHAPTER 3

Flora & Cully

"Baby Sweetheart" was the caption beneath my mother's first newspaper photo. She had everything, it would seem, to guarantee a happy life. Beauty, brains, grace. Although she was often lonely, she loved the trips to Europe, and to England for hunting and polo. She spent one miserable summer in Newport with her very strict grandmother, Alice Vanderbilt, widow of Cornelius II, when she was thirteen. Alice and her husband, Cornelius Vanderbilt II, had raised their children—with only partial success—to be disciplined, religious, and studious. Flora had broken her ankle and the rest of her family had gone abroad, leaving her with Alice at The Breakers. Flora described it in her diary:

> For lunch there was Grandma, Aunty, Uncle, Mamma, Papa, Cousin Ruth, Aunt Florence, Mabel Gerry, Barby [*Flora's younger sister*], and me. It was the horridest lunch I was ever at. They gossiped and talked stupid things all the time. Oh how I wish we were back in New York.

Everything she did that summer seemed to be wrong. She'd never been told that boys weren't allowed in her room or that it wasn't proper to wander freely to the beach or to town by herself. Her parents, Gertrude and Harry, had always trusted her to know how to behave. But not

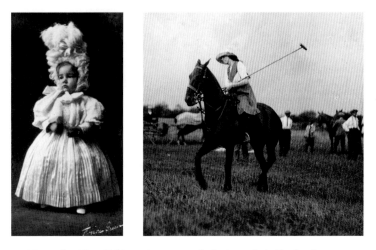

My mother Flora Whitney in 1899, and playing polo in England, c. 1910

Alice Vanderbilt! Almost every morning at breakfast she'd say, "Flora, please come up to my room in a few minutes," and Flora would clutch her curly head, wondering what she'd done to offend her grandmother. "You know you mustn't ask Tommy and Douglas into your room, child. Now don't ever forget again," Alice would warn with a cross expression. Flora still couldn't move around easily because of her ankle, and the boys would visit her in her room. Once they hid under the bed when they heard familiar footsteps outside. As the door opened, Alice noticed a boy's straw boater on the floor. "And how did that get in here?" she asked. "Oh—Annie brought it over, just as a joke, to see how I'd look in it." For days, Flora felt bad that she'd told a fib, but she was afraid of her grandmother. She was miserably homesick for her parents. Later, after her ankle had healed, she escaped one evening after bedtime to join her friends at a nearby house. She was having such a grand time that she forgot how late it was—when she returned, the house was locked for the night. She crept

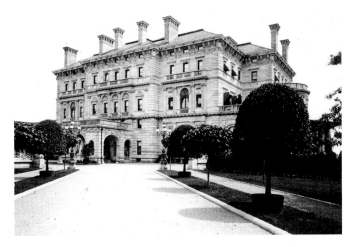

The Breakers, c. 1900

around the enormous mansion, trying every possibility, and finally climbed a fire ladder by her own bedroom. Luckily, she'd left her window open, and crawled in without being discovered.

Flora's mother Gertrude had often rebelled against her own mother's strictness, bitterly criticizing her in her diaries, as she did when she was nineteen, in 1894. Here's a bit from Gertrude's diary of that year, when Alice didn't want her to spend so much time with a girl of whom she disapproved:

> You think you can twist me round your finger, and let me tell you that the only thing you have succeeded in making me do is in telling you less and less about myself and my affairs. . . I am old enough to make my own friends. Because I have seemed to agree with you is no sign that I did. I used to think it was my duty to do in almost everything as you wanted me to, now I think I am old enough to do more as I want and I am going to speak my opinions hereafter and not only think them . . . Other children tell their parents almost everything. I never did . . .

Despite the retinue of servants, Flora's parents' lives were quite disorganized. While they traveled, while Harry pursued his sporting activities, while Gertrude worked on her sculpture or her Museum, their three children were left to nurses, governesses, and other servants, many of questionable capability. At a time when most children were brought up strictly, the young Whitneys and their small group of friends were on the wild side—there's a hint of it in the journal my mother wrote in 1912 when she was fourteen:

> JANUARY 1: After supper, Jimmy, Douglas (her cousins), Sonny (her brother, two years younger) and I locked ourselves in the room downstairs and smoked sigorates. It's great, I love it.
>
> Stayed in house all afternoon and read my bad books *The Memoirs of Jacques Casanova*. They are terreble. They are in the left of the libery as you go in bound in blew.

It is no wonder that my mother's spelling was creative. In the fall, she often remained in Long Island or Newport long past the beginning of the school year, and later she'd sometimes go with her parents to England or France. Although she attended Brearley, the girls' school in New York where her mother had been a top student, she was often absent; in 1912, for instance, she was only there for one day in an entire semester.

In many photographs of my mother, her wide eyes are downcast; her expression puzzled or sad. Although no wrinkles mar her smooth forehead, her thick black eyebrows are permanently knitted as if she questioned her place in the world. Unlike her mother, who wrote lengthy journals delving deeply into her emotions, she learned early to avoid self-examination. Perhaps it was too frightening, with the new awareness of Freud's emphasis on sex as the basis for human drives. Activities and friends filled

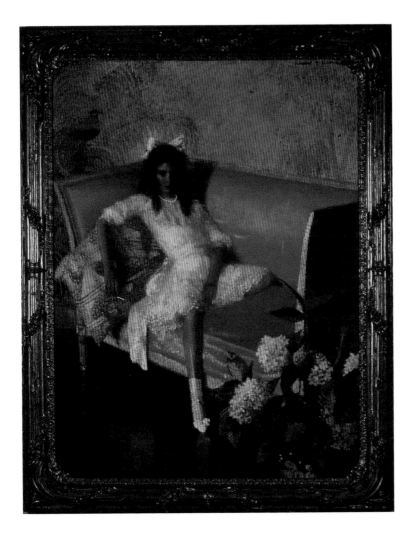

Flora Whitney, by Howard Cushing, c. 1911

Mum's days and nights until late in her life, when television took the place of companionship. Still there were empty times, when she was sick or alone, and I suspect she had doubts about some of the choices she'd made. A newspaper clipping from 1925, reviewing an exhibition in New York, praised a bronze sculpture by my mother, *Crisis*, that I'm looking at now: a young woman sits hugging her knees to her chest, her head resting on her folded arms, in an attitude of doubt and sorrow. The reviewer wrote that Flora Whitney planned to become a professional artist like her mother. I wonder if she regretted giving up this goal. My grandmother, who'd had a strict upbringing, had early on decided on a less conventional life for herself. Much as she loved her daughter, in the intensity of the search for her own identity and potential, Gertrude taught Flora more about manners and customs than ethics and morality. Despite (because of?) my mother's chaotic upbringing, she survived and flourished. Although frequently absent, her mother and father adored her, and gave her more attention than they did her younger brother and sister. For instance, in the winter of 1914, she lived in her own apartment in Paris with a sympathetic governess while her mother lived and worked in her nearby studio. Flora wrote:

> We went to see Mamma's studio. Then went to the school I am going to, to see about my lessons Wednesday and Saturday mornings. Had lunch with Mamma at her studio. It's awfully nice . . . I loved my first day in Paris.

Besides lessons in ballet, riding, piano, and sculpture, Flora attended church, and roller-skated in the Tuileries. She met Gertrude's friends and went to art exhibits, operas and plays. Shopping in couture houses was a new delight:

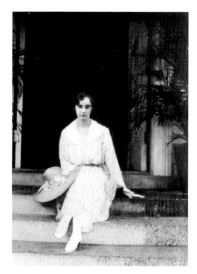

My mother, Vogue, *c. 1916*

After lunch I went to Poiret's with Mamma. I helped her choose dresses . . . Mamma got 2 coats and 16 evening dresses, suits and afternoon dresses. I loved all of them. Then we went to get my clothes. I got 12 dresses, one suit (blue), 3 hats, and 4 coats. I love them all . . . I had a fine day.

For Gertrude, and later for Flora, dressing was a big part of presenting themselves to the world. Gertrude's favorite designer, Paul Poiret, evoked in both his salon and his clothes "an Arabian Nights atmosphere of brilliantly colored, sometimes shimmeringly metallic Turkish trousers, kimono blouses, turbans and high aigrets, tassels, embroidered floral and avian decorations, Persian brocades—in short, a world of exotic fantasy very close to Gertrude's." (Friedman) It must have been enchanting for a sensitive, imaginative young girl like Flora. When she traveled to Italy with a cousin who criticized the bright pink suit she wore on the train to Florence as silly and unsuitable, Flora only

Gertrude's bill from Poiret, 1914

laughed at her cousin's conservatism. In worldly ways, she was sophisticated beyond her years; often isolated from her schoolmates, she was less comfortable with children her own age. When she was older, she bought clothes from Balenciaga and Chanel, who continued Poiret's tradition of sensuous fabrics and liberating, elegant designs. Her hats were made by Paulette—feathered, sequined or veiled. Both she and her mother chose to adorn themselves in the avant-garde; exquisite, and daringly festive.

In a sculpture Gertrude made of her daughter in 1919, grief infuses Flora's face and posture. Her fiancé, Theodore Roosevelt's son Quentin, an aviator in France during the first World War, had just crashed and died. Nothing in her childhood had prepared her for such a loss. The English nineteenth century poetry she and Quentin had recited to

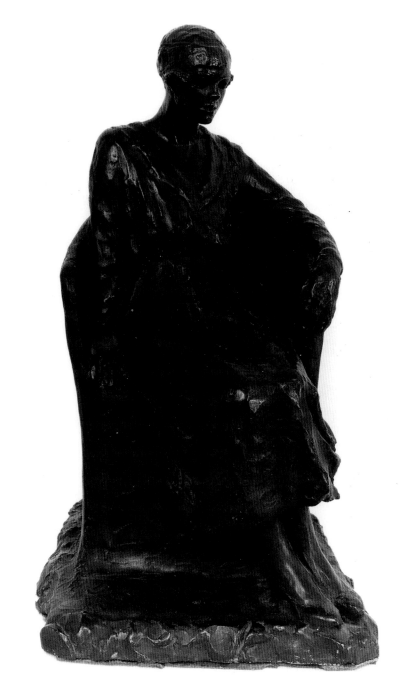

Sculpture of my mother by Gertrude, 1919

each other was deeply idealistic, although death was certainly present in the poems of Keats, Shelley, and Coleridge that she marked in her books as a schoolgirl. Beauty, truth, love, and even premonitions of death saturated Flora's and Quentin's moving letters to each other. Her blue-bound copy of Keats's poems falls open here:

> When I have fears that I may cease to be
>   Before my pen has glean'd my teeming brain, . . .
> And when I feel, fair creature of an hour!
>   That I shall never look upon thee more,
> Never have relish in the faery power
> Of unreflecting love!—then on the shore
> Of the wide world I stand alone, and think
> Till Love and Fame to nothingness doth sink.

Thomas R. Coward, who later became a distinguished publisher, and who had always loved Mum, wrote to her soon after Quentin was killed:

> Why are you, you? And what constitutes your appeal. I think it is partially your being a child with a woman's sophistication and cleverness. And then, of course, you are a delight to look upon and to hear. That voice!
> I believe utterly and entirely in your humanity, your generosity, your inability to be mean or petty, your fineness of perception—in a word your essential bigness of soul. If I had time I could relate that to the queer streak of the child in you which is so fascinating. It is at once your greatest charm and safe-guard.

Although sorrowed by her loss, in 1920 my mother married Roderick Tower, a man she'd met through Quentin, following him to the oilfields of California. She tried her best to adjust to his peripatetic life, but they were temperamentally unsuited, and after five years, with two children, they separated and divorced. In the divorce ruling, custody

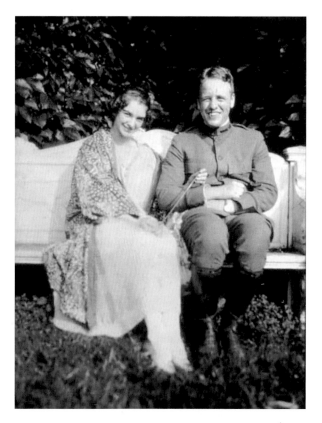

My mother and Quentin Roosevelt, 1918

was to be shared: Pam, at four, would live with her mother; Whit, at two and a half, with his father. As the two children were extremely close to each other and to their mother, the separation was traumatic.

Living in California shortly after the divorce, Whit was badly cut when he stepped on a rusty nail. Penicillin wasn't discovered until World War II, and when his second toe became infected he developed osteomyelitis. The toe was amputated, the wound cauterized, and the toe reconnected, leaving him with a grotesque tiny toe on his left foot. My mother and Pam had moved to Los Angeles during this

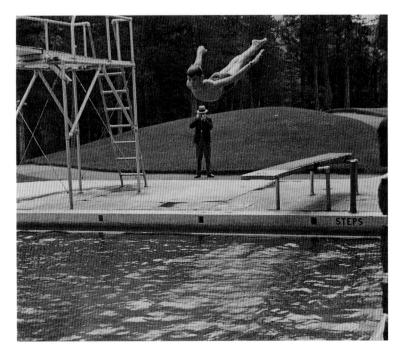

My brother Whit Tower doing a swan dive, c.1938

time, and when they went back to Long Island, Whit went with them. From then on, both children lived with their mother. Whit struggled to overcome a severe stutter all his life, which perhaps originated in his terrifying early experiences of loss and pain.

As a child, I was less aware of Whit than I was of Pam; he went to boys' schools, he was busy with athletics. He didn't often ride. Tall and very thin, he had a lively sense of fun and a crooked, winning smile. At his schools, he was a remarkable swimmer, and as an adult he became an outstanding sports journalist and essayist, publishing prize-winning books on horse-racing. His many close friends included his two ex-wives and a number of girlfriends. Since their early childhood, Pam had felt responsible for her brother, wanting to help him feel secure and happy in his work, romances, marriages, and divorces. Pam's love for Whit has meant as much or more to her than many of her other relationships. And Whit depended on his sister, knowing she'd always listen, understand, support, and love him.

When my parents found each other, my father had never married. Their letters contain the joy of first love. My mother wrote,

> Haven't been so happy in months and months and months. Stayed in bed all morning and drifted on a lovely pink cloud. I hope he lets me stay there just for a little while.

In 1927, Flora's mother, Gertrude, was researching ancient Egyptian sculpture in preparation for designing a monumental statue of Christopher Columbus in Spain. When Flora sailed to join her in Egypt, my father wrote quickly:

> Oh it's so hard to have you go my dear one. But of course when one can look forward to seeing you and seeing you and seeing you in only a month one should be grateful and patient— and I am, dearest. My 'tummy' is all going round inside first because you're leaving me and next because I am so happy at the thought of marrying you. Take care of your precious self— don't smoke too much please—in fact don't do too much of anything dear bad one.

That winter, they married in Cairo—Flora's ring was an elephant hair, later encased in gold—and spent their honeymoon sailing up the Nile on an Egyptian dahabeah.

My mother was beautiful. When she smiled at me, I was filled with happiness. When she asked me about school or riding—when she had the time to do that—I expanded like a

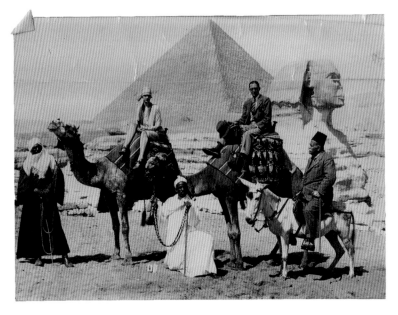

My parents on their honeymoon in Egypt, 1927

Japanese paper flower in a glass of water. When she hugged me, I felt as if I were melting into her soft body. When I was sick in bed with a cold, she'd come to my room and read aloud to me, perhaps Kipling's "The White Seal." I didn't understand much of it, but I loved it because I loved her so much.

She had two or three close women friends. "Auntie" Helen Clark seemed a bit tame for Mum, but I liked her, partly because she gave me one of my first horses, an old chestnut polo pony, Redbank, and partly because she encouraged me to write stories with her and my mother. Phyllis Preston, "Auntie Phy," definitely wasn't tame. A dark beauty with the girlish body fashionable in the twenties, she bewitched everyone with her slinky clothes and graceful walk. I now realize how sexy she was—a firebrand in their

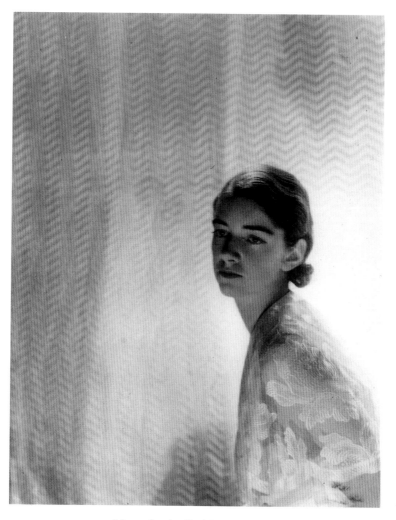

My mother, by Cecil Beaton, c. 1932

relatively staid community. She and Mum shared secrets; they giggled like young girls. In my memory, though, most of Mum's friends were male, and they loved her in a different, more sexual fashion.

Despite her captivating aura, my mother was shy and uncertain—she hadn't inherited the ambition, energy, and idealism of her mother—but she was fascinating, with her wide smile and husky, beguiling voice. Her delicious smell was a hint of lily of the valley and tuberose. Not tall, not excessively thin or glamorous in the manner of a flapper, she was warm, with scarlet nails on long tapered fingers and black curls tumbling over pretty flowered shirts. She had no hard edges. She lavishly powdered her upturned nose, rouged her cheekbones, and wore bright lipstick on her wide mouth. Her huge hazel eyes were fringed with long eyelashes below abundant eyebrows. She wore flowing silk dresses, well cut trousers and shirts, and trim French suits. We were moths to her flame, circling, wanting more and sometimes getting singed—not that she burned us knowingly. She didn't realize, perhaps, how much we needed her attention. How much we minded when her mind and heart were elsewhere.

*

My father's background was different from that of my mother. He'd inherited some of the furniture in Aiken and New York; fine old American Empire chairs, a desk, a bed. My mother's share from the ballroom of her parents' house at 871 Fifth Avenue were pieces of Louis XV furniture. Her own taste ran to the modern and exotic: ivory chairs from India, curtains trimmed with monkey fur, an African zebra-wood desk. My father was more interested in things with an aura of history. A chronometer in a polished wooden box was the first thing you saw when you entered the front hall of Joye Cottage. It sat on the hall table, and you could count on it to keep the correct time. My father loved its precision. It had been passed down to him—GMM, as my father signed his architectural drawings and paintings; initials which

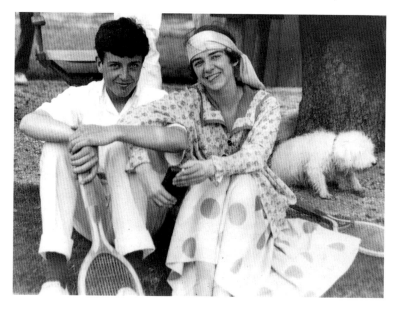

My mother and her cousin Douglas Burden, c. 1916

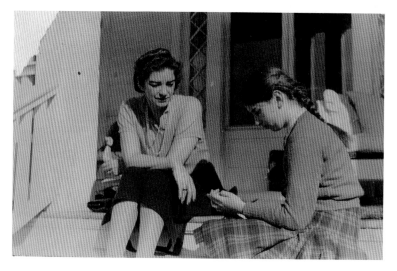

With my mother on the porch in Aiken, 1941

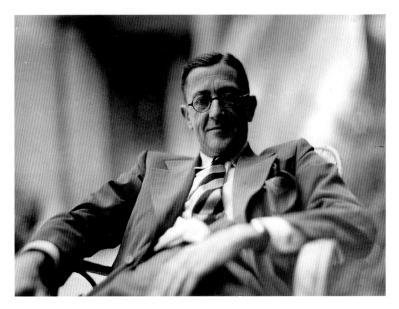

My father, G. M. (Cully) Miller

adorned a succession of cars, suitcases, and stationery—from his great-great-great grandfather, George Macculloch, who was born in 1775 in Bombay, where his father worked for the East India Company. Orphaned at nine, George had grown up in Edinburgh with his Scottish grandmother. She had high ambitions for her promising charge and arranged for his excellent education, which included fluency in German, French, Spanish, and Italian. Despite the Napoleonic wars, he traveled widely in Europe. Macculloch's young wife-to-be, Louisa Saunderson, was fifteen when they had their first child. After the second child was born, the couple married and emigrated to Morristown, New Jersey, where they built an imposing brick mansion, Macculloch Hall—now a museum—and quickly became community leaders in business, politics and education.

Like most children, I was uninterested in my ancestry, or

the history of the chronometer that now sits in Lev's front hall in Florida. Now I wish I'd asked my father more: why did George and Louisa Macculloch delay their marriage so long? Was it customary for young couples in Scotland to ascertain their fertility before marrying? Did George's ambitious grandmother disapprove of Louisa? Was her first pregnancy an accident?

Of my father's relations, I have few memories, although his brothers, Larry and Lindley, sometimes came to visit with their families, and their sons became our friends. When I was eighteen, I spent a night with his aunt, Edith Macculloch Miller, in Boston. Aunt Edith, an erect lady with crisp lace around her neck, served me wafer-thin lemon cookies with pale China tea. With her faded blue eyes, she wisely penetrated my shyness to find a yearning for acceptance. She left me one of the pins given to my great-great aunt, Miss Murray, by General Washington, being a miniature of Washington set in pearls and with his hair. The fearless Mary Lindley Murray, of Murray Hill in New York City, had entertained Lord Howe, the British commander, at a tea party while the rebel General Putnam made good his escape from New York. The pin or locket was given to her in gratitude for saving Washington's army. To succeed in such a risky venture, what pluck, intelligence, and charm she must have had! Such stories gave me a more estimable pride that was different from the well-hidden self-importance I felt through being connected to my mother's more prominent Vanderbilt and Whitney relatives.

Although I felt that he adored me, my father often seemed remote. Perhaps he found it difficult to imagine the interests of a small child. He often seemed at a loss how to talk to me. In lieu of conversation, he'd take my little hand

and lay it flat on his own, then his other hand, then mine again, and we'd flip the layers, bottom to top, over and over again. I was so serious—how in the world was he to make me laugh? He whistled very well; lively tunes to amuse us, but we took his whistling for granted. It was just one of the things that fathers did. When I try now, not a sound emerges, and his tunefulness seems miraculous. At holiday feasts when we were all together, he sang in his true, sweet tenor voice *In the wintertime, in the valley green*; *Bye, bye, Blackbird*; and many tunes by their friend, Cole Porter.

> When I walked along the Bois de Boulogne,
> With an independent air,
> You could hear the girls declare,
> He must be a millionaire
> You could hear them sigh
> And hope to die
> And turn and wink the other eye
> At the man who broke the bank in Monte Carlo!

Tall, with straight black hair parted on the side, in his fashionable British-tailored jackets, he cut a fine figure. His long face was usually tanned, and behind horn-rimmed spectacles his blue eyes gazed at the world with interest and curiosity. We were amused by, and proud of his inventions, which he drew in great detail in the manner of Rube Goldberg, who was one of his heroes. Some were actually made: a long, silver cigarette box, for example, divided in four, with four colorful package covers behind the glass lid; Chesterfield, Philip Morris, Lucky Strike, and Camel. My father, however, ordered a special brand called M & M for himself and Mum: flat cigarettes with gold tips made with Egyptian tobacco. I liked the rich, penetrating smell that clung to my

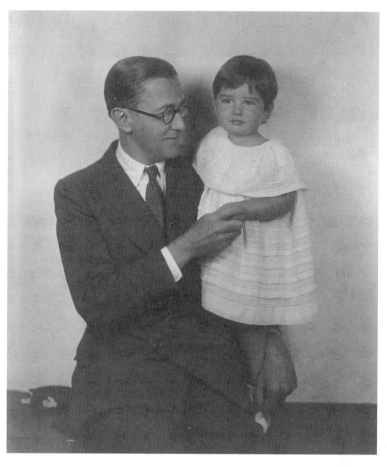

Daddy and me, 1930

father's clothes and skin. When he kissed me, my nose tickled. He designed elegant monograms for the family's cars,
for his handkerchiefs, and sometimes for his friends. A mal-
formed hip kept him out of World War I, but despite his
limp, he played tennis well and was a nimble dancer. All the
ladies wanted him as a dancing partner, and not simply for
his dancing. My father was charming. When I was a bit older,
I saw that he was different from other men. He made people
laugh, and he was considerate, always finding the time to

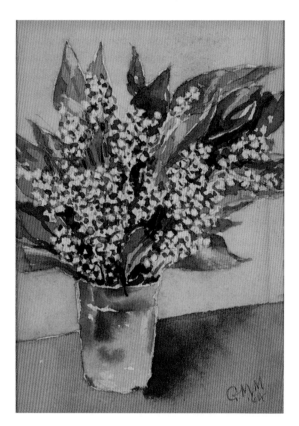

Lilies of the valley, by my father

speak to the youngest, the oldest, and the least attractive.

My father painted very well. In a long white smock, palette in one hand, he painted portraits, landscapes, or still lives of flowers, fruit, bottles. We weren't supposed to disturb him when he was painting, but sometimes we'd catch glimpses of him from the garden by the pool, through the open door to his studio, which he reached by going down a long flight of steps, then through the dark and—to me—frightening rooms of the Spooky Wing. The smell of oil paint and turpentine from his studio mingled with the scent of flowers and mown grass. When he wasn't in the studio, he painted little watercolors on side tables or in his lap, sketching in pencil or ink.

He wrote illustrated verses: jingles, he called them. Often about ladies, they'd now be considered politically incorrect, but we found them very funny.

Only later did I understand that these glimpses of his work and, most of all, his ardor and joy, had beguiled me with the idea of art. In 1958, at thirty years old, I was living in Connecticut with my husband Mike and our four children when I became a trustee of the Whitney Museum of American Art. Under my mother's leadership, the Whitney had moved from its original home in Greenwich Village to 54th Street, next to the Museum of Modern Art, in a building

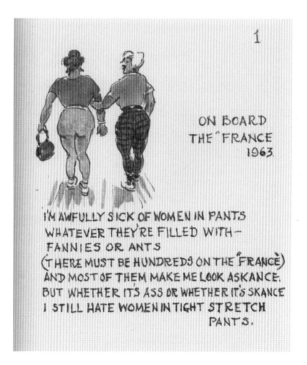

Jingle by Cully

designed by my father's architectural firm. Enthralled by my grandmother's vision of a museum for American artists, who had been mostly ignored by American collectors and institutions, I soon realized that the Museum needed more money to survive. My mother and grandmother had paid the Museum's expenses, but I knew that I couldn't; instead, I could work. One day a week, I sat behind the desk in the lobby, chatted with visitors and tried to answer their questions. Soon I progressed to sorting artists' files, with their intriguing letters and sketches. Talking with curators, artists and collectors was thrilling. I saw only the positive side of this new world of creativity, and longed to be a part of it. Life at home was rewarding too, of course, but I looked forward all week to my day at the Whitney. When my husband joined the board in 1962, we shared the excitement of the Whitney's expansion, with Mike as Marcel Breuer's associate architect on the present building at Seventy-Fifth Street and Madison Avenue.

The meetings were different, now: more formal, more about money. My father was on the board, too, and I wish I'd kept the amusing sketches he made at meetings on envelopes, pads, and scraps of paper. Never mean, they were skillful caricatures of the new Whitney supporters. With a few strokes of his pencil, he captured their elegant suits, their intent expressions, and their tense attitudes when financial matters were under discussion. Directors and curators came under his scrutiny, too, looking determined or sometimes puzzled by the new ways. Perhaps unconsciously, with his artist's eye and hand, he foresaw some of the problems we were later to face, when trustees accustomed to running things their own way came up against the free ideas about art espoused by the Whitney.

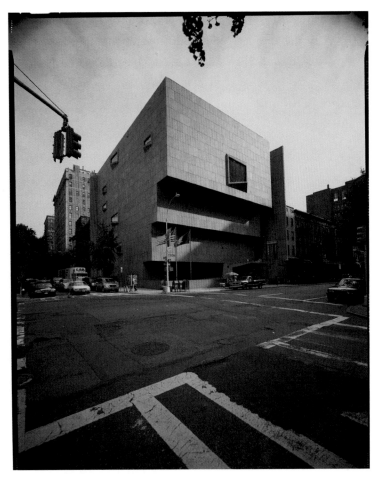

The Whitney Museum of American Art on Madison Avenue

I wasn't aware that I was absorbing my father's message; that I was learning what an artist sees and does. How I wish that I'd told him how grateful I am.

*

My father was happiest when using his imagination. Above all, he was happy when he was painting. He was content in his life, and in himself—more so than anyone I ever knew. Some inner balance, enabling him to love and support my mother in her fluctuations and flirtations, girded and sustained his humor and affection. He was her rock, her constant companion, her ever-fervent admirer.

I have my father's sketch of my mother, lying with a book by a lake in the Adirondacks, wearing her glasses, bathing suit shorts and a loose sharkskin halter top with no built-in support (she rarely wore a bra, and if she did, it was a weightless wisp of netting). In another sketch, she is sitting in her mother's Paris garden, by then hers, doing her favorite Double Crostic in a floppy hat and flowered shirt, with the remains of a small Cavaillon melon they'd had for lunch on a table nearby.

I don't know how the financial disparity between my parents affected their marriage. If my father's family had been wealthy, perhaps he'd have been brought up differently. Perhaps his parents would have had different expectations of him. He might have had more worldly ambition—or, since too much money sometimes saps the urge to succeed, perhaps he'd have had less. He seemed content with his occasional work of designing houses and making renderings of them with his friend and partner, the architect Auguste Noel. His own painting was a lifelong source of happiness. As I saw it, my mother made the decisions. It was she whose permission I sought, whose love I most needed. She won all arguments. It was she who determined that we should move from Aiken to New York when World War 2 began; where we would go to school; whether we would go to France or Canada in the summer. She certainly decided smaller matters: whether she and my father should play Canasta or go for a buggy ride, what time to

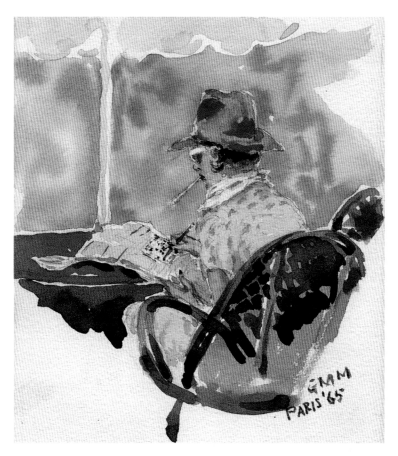

My father's watercolor of my mother in Paris, 1965

have dinner, when to travel to New York to see her mother. I suspect that my father didn't mind—no matter how they might disagree, his love for my mother was absolutely certain. If he wanted to be in charge, it wasn't evident—or, at least, only after many martinis, when arguments sometimes became loud and angry.

Surely, there was more going on than I knew. Alcohol fueled harsh words and feelings along with the flirting and secret affairs. But mostly there was laughter.

*

I wish I could ask my mother and father the questions I can only now formulate. I feel remorse that I never broke down the barriers, never responded to my mother's tentative overtures. She started, once, a tale of thunder and lightning, Daddy rushing to her bed, and a pregnancy they hadn't expected. But I put her off, laughing merrily. She probed the possibility of intimacy—relations with my husband, and female concerns, from menstruation to contraception to face creams—but I always resisted. I regret it now.

PART II: CHILDHOOD

CHAPTER 4

At Joye Cottage

When my great-grandfather, William C. Whitney died in 1904, he left Joye Cottage to his son, Gertrude's husband, Harry Payne Whitney. When Harry died in 1930, at only fifty-eight, Gertrude inherited Joye Cottage, and soon gave it to her daughter and oldest child, my mother Flora. Although my parents kept a house on Long Island and an apartment in New York, they began to live most of the year in Aiken. I suspect that they based this decision on the problems my mother had seen in her own family: her father's moodiness and alcoholism; her mother's illnesses, perhaps because of the stress of balancing her career, family, and social responsibilities; and her parents' love affairs and deteriorating marriage. Did my parents ever wonder, despite the fundamental love and loyalty that kept her parents together, if too much money might have been one of the problems? Wealth—the luxury of being able to have or do anything they desired—was a daunting responsibility for those who were also raised with a certain standard of morality. Understandably, my parents desired the pleasures of friends, sports, games, and the warm winters of Aiken. Their children would thrive, oblivious of their heritage and its responsibilities. They would be safe, far away from the threat of kidnapping, with the Lindbergh case fresh in their minds, and my mother's

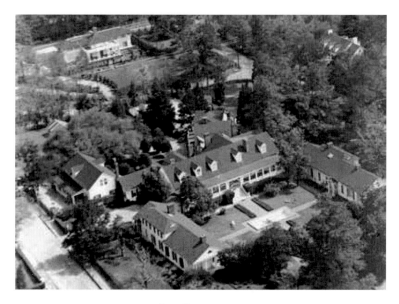

Joye Cottage, 1940

young cousin, Gloria Vanderbilt, living with her Aunt Gertrude, protected by armed guards.

Joye Cottage for the first time became a family home. With quite different personalities, my parents lived together in a harmony punctuated by frequent argument and acerbity, but leavened by ease and pleasure. As my half-sister Pam has written in the *Flora* book, published after our mother's death in 1986:

> I was very conscious of those 'vibes' between my mother and Cully. They were strong!!! He was just so devoted, patient, and supportive of her that it was a wonder. And, of course, she basked in the luxury of living with someone who gave so much.

Our mother dominated the relationship. Not because she was emotionally or physically stronger—she wasn't—and not because of her famous family and their money, but through her beauty, charm and winsome ways. People adored her. My father was also dearly loved by family, friends, and his stepchildren. Pam talks of him with stars in her eyes. *He never, ever interfered, but he was always there for us,* she remembers. *And he gave us mountains of laughs and fun.* He was more of a presence for her and for Whitty, she claims, than he was for his genetic offspring, Lev and me, perhaps because of our overriding fascination for our mother—distant as she often was, she was a goddess.

For nine months of the year Joye Cottage in Aiken, South Carolina, was my most dearly loved home. In the 1930s, when I lived there, Aiken was known as "The Newport of the South." As George McMillan wrote in *Gentlemen's Quarterly*:

> Aiken was different from other resorts for the wealthy: yes, a playground, but something else—an attempt to create a unique American utopia whose precepts would give meaning, even moral significance, and certainly style, to a life of total, not just seasonal or part-time, leisure.

Employment boomed at a time when much of the country was sunk in the Depression. Many skills were needed for the culture of the horse alone: trainers, grooms, jockeys, stableboys, blacksmiths, veterinarians. Farmers supplied feed stores. A tack shop sold saddles, bridles, whips, polo mallets, and specialized clothes. Workers were hired to build and maintain polo fields, racetracks, trails, and jumps. Aiken's winter colony required servants, hotels, clubs, and high quality suppliers of luxury items. Hahn and Company, for instance, was the finest grocery in the South. Chef Ernest Wiehl from Germany worked at the best hotel in Aiken, The Willcox. Privately owned Pullman cars lined the Aiken railroad track, awaiting their owners' springtime return to the North.

Here, in a nighttime view, is a description of Joye Cottage by its present owners:

> The house filled the moonlit horizon. From a dark stand of pines at one end, it emerged as from a cave: long, ghostly temple walls, a Doric portico, a glassed in colonnade, two high, massive gables, a balustrade in the air, a long, hipped roof, a glimpse of dormers, the curve of pagoda eaves; dozens of blacked out windows: in bays, in half-rounds and ovals, in arrays of tiny diamond panes and huge sheets, their old, flawed glass queering the light from our head-lamps. The façade stretched from darkness to darkness, the ends so far distant from the center they disappeared altogether. Sitting on a high, brick foundation, the whole seemed to float in shadow, like some grand architectural ghost come back from the other side of demolition to cold-kiss its old foundations and mock the wrecking ball.

The authors also quote the Sotheby's brochure in which they discovered Joye Cottage in 1990:

> Timeless appeal ... the very legacy of understated classic design ... the essence of American aristocratic style! 20,000 square feet of living space! Sixty rooms, 18 paneled bedrooms, 12 baths, 12 staff bedrooms, 4 staff baths... Main House: salon, billiard room, den, and 7 bedrooms, each with fireplace and full bath. The salon is paneled with three-quarter-height wainscoting, and an exposed beam ceiling, freestanding Ionic columns and pilasters ... elliptical arch framed by pilasters leads to a double-rung, open stringer staircase with newel posts topped with classical urns.

Of course, that's not how it appeared to me. I want to describe the way I saw it, many years ago.

Each September, William Scott, my parents' protective and kindly chauffeur, drove us in the big black town car from our Long Island home, winding along Grand Central Parkway and across the brand-new Triborough Bridge to Manhattan. Since I got horribly carsick, Scott stopped at least once by the side of the road, to the moans of my car-mates: my parents, my nurse, Pam, Whitty, and Leverett. In Pennsylvania Station, with an army of Redcaps carrying our gear, the throng of adults, children, dachshunds, and canaries spilled into the drawing rooms and compartments of Pullman car SR (Southern Railway) 40. The horses, their grooms and equipment had already boarded the horse cars common to trains in that era. The same porters greeted us each year with welcoming smiles, to stow luggage, and to make up berths with snowy sheets and tan blankets, nets stretched alongside for books and belongings. It was all an adventure: undressing while the train rolled in the tracks; brushing my teeth in the little basin; urinating in the toilet concealed under an upholstered seat; climbing the ladder to the upper bunk where the thick green webbing made a safe barricade. The train's motion soon lulled me to sleep, until the ringing of bells, and the boiler steamed and hissed with ear-splitting power. In Washington, there was a great hub-bub as we changed engines or tracks. Shade raised, I leaned from my berth to glimpse the strangers walking alongside the train. Soon, with a sharp whistle and whoosh, we'd be on our way again.

We awoke to a new world. The land stretched for miles, with black men, women and children bending low in the fields running alongside the tracks, putting white cotton bolls into cloth sacks strapped to their backs. Sandy roads, small cottages, mules, horses. Pine trees, skimpy and sparse compared to those in the Northern woods. Then, suddenly, we were there.

[73]

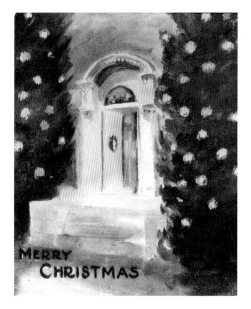

Front door, Joye Cottage, by my father

Down Whiskey Road, a right turn onto Easy Street, then left into the driveway. Two wings of Joye Cottage enfolded us as small yellow pebbles crunched under the wheels. We climbed the few stone steps to the front door, opened wide by the English butler, Herbert, who had organized the bevy of maids and strong young houseboys to carry our things. It was a tradition to pause to make sure that the Macculloch chronometer at the top of the hall steps was on time, and it always was.

The living room was big and square. In the middle, twin red and white blown glass lampstands, their white shades bordered with red, stood on my great-grandfather's wide, well-waxed partners' desk. In one corner, the piano; in another—and more often played—a slot machine, a gift from my father to my mother one Christmas, the proceeds given yearly to the local hospital. Doors opened all around to wide covered verandas. On warm days, we sat on the front veranda on pale corduroy-covered Aiken sofas, as wide and as long as beds, playing Old Maid or Slap Jack, and drinking Horses' Necks, fizzy concoctions of grape juice and ginger ale with necks of lemon twists, before diving into the small blue pool in the garden below.

On the far left wall of the living room, an oval gold-framed mirror soared over a high mantel where a brass clock struck the hours. Two wooden steps along the far wall led to a red-cushioned bench with a well-stocked bar in the middle; silver fox heads on the wall overhead surrounded my father's full-length portrait of J. D., a handsome black man who accompanied my father on dove shoots to hand him shotgun shells and collect his doves. The white woodwork gleamed. A white banister led up the red-carpeted stairs to the rooms, off limits to us, where Pam and Whitty lived with their governess, Sis. Whit's electric trains that Lev and I were forbidden to touch took up a room of their own.

In one corner of the living room was an L-shaped red window seat with a table where my parents played Canasta or, after cutting the white edges with a sharp paper cutter, pasted the black and white photographs my father took with his new Leica into red leather albums. The sound of the paper cutter still clashes in my ears: a violent schlunk-schlunk. Each stiff, creamy page of those albums is neatly captioned in my father's elegant script; each photo reveals his artful eye: Whitty, soaring in a gorgeous swan dive at one of the competitions he usually won, and Pam, her dark hair blowing, smiling as she steers the Johnson putt-putt around Forked Lake in the Adirondacks, towing her friend Jack Bergamini on an aquaplane. Lev, our nurse Miss Sligh, and me, having lunch on our grandparents' private railway car, Wanderer,

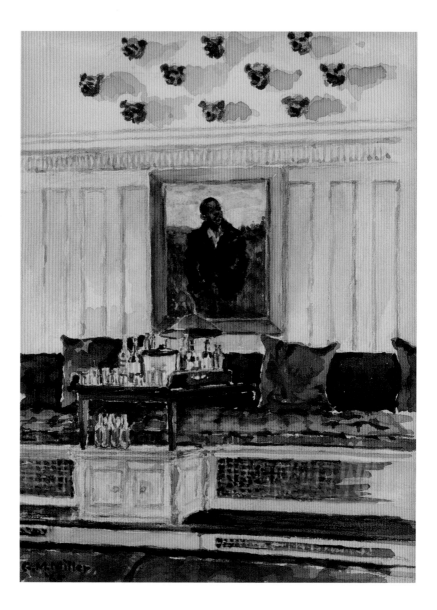

Living room, Joye Cottage, by Cully

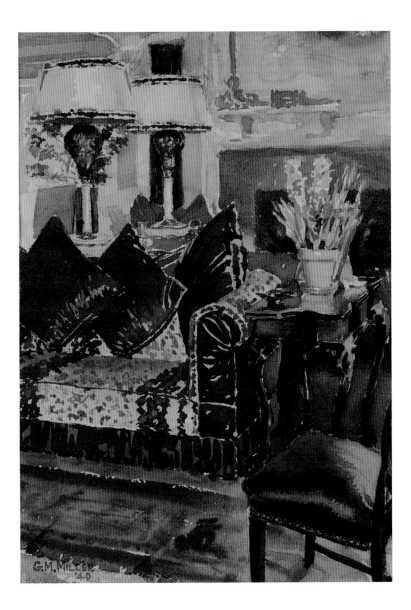

Living room, Joye Cottage, by my father

en route to Flin Flon, our family's copper mine in Canada. My mother, in Canada, in mosquito veil and thigh-high rubber waders, holding a thirty-pound salmon next to Dr. Weeks, her faithful admirer. My father, cooking hamburgers over an open fire next to the small log cabin, up the hill from Camp Togus, that he used as a studio. He's in a checked flannel shirt, and an old fishing hat, stuck 'round with flies. Lev again, holding a net with his first catch, a fine bass. I'm there, too, in blue shorts with a white stripe down the sides (black-and-white photos, but I remember), chubby and serious, reading in the back of the "Pickerel," a narrow mahogany launch, as we head down the lake to visit our uncle. And a photo of the only snowstorm in Aiken in my memory: Pam and Whitty ride in a makeshift sled they'd cobbled together from parts of an old buggy, behind our pony, Snowball.

*

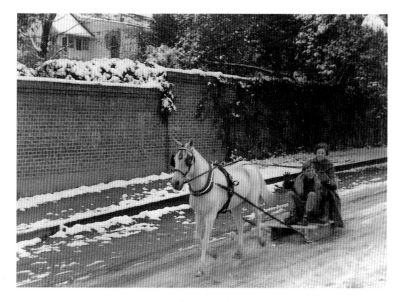

Pam and Whitty sleighing

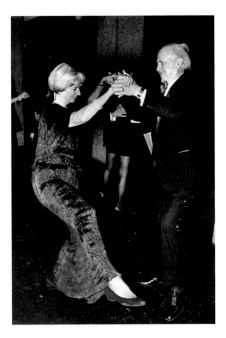

Dancing with Sydney, Whitney Museum, 1992

I, and now my children, have inherited the tradition of making photograph albums. As I leaf through mine, vivid memories arise: my second husband, Sydney Biddle, and I are in Morocco riding camels along the dunes at dawn; we're dancing at the Whitney Museum's fiftieth anniversary Ball; we're sitting on our portal in New Mexico with Agnes Martin. Snatches of conversation come to mind. Agnes: "Artists shouldn't be distracted. They shouldn't be married or even have a dog." Flora: "But Agnes, didn't you have horses you loved?" Agnes: "Yes, but I wasn't painting then." Sydney: "Oh, look, a double rainbow, over the mountain."

We're happy in the photographs, just as my parents seem to be in their albums. Artist-photographers—Nan Goldin, for example, or earlier, Walker Evans—testify to ugliness and pain as well as goodness and beauty. Since many of my memories are based on the rosy glow of family albums, perhaps I see the past unrealistically. Do I wish my father and I had been more probing with our cameras? I'm not sure. Recording happy times has its value. Turning the pages of these carefree times brings us much joy.

*

Back to Joye Cottage: a thick Turkish carpet was on the living room floor. The room was filled with flowers, chosen for their particular scent: delicate lilies of the valley from the bed of rich chocolate earth by the Spooky Wing; roses; winter's white narcissi, their fresh aroma promising spring; freesias, their heady perfume overcoming even the wood smoke that permeated the entire house; tuberoses (my mother's favorite) with their sensual, almost overpowering pungency. The flowers were in silver, glass, or china vases, with special wood and glass holders for the individual red, pink, white, or variegated camellias my mother grew in her greenhouse as well as outdoors, the camellias over which she spent hours consulting with handsome, charming Dr. Wilds.

My father painted many vivid watercolors of that room, preserving its freshness and joie de vivre. (On my wall today, on paper nine by twelve inches, I can see the chintz of the sofas, the texture of the rug, even the feeling of the portrait of J. D.—quite a trick to do in watercolor.)

Even then, I associated the room with constant flurry: the early morning maids with their carpet sweepers and dust cloths; family members and guests coming and going on their way to meals, riding, school, and the sporting activities that were intrinsic to life in Aiken; guests arriving for birthdays, lunch, dinner, New Year's Eve; friends playing cards, billiards, jigsaw puzzles and word games, or just dropping by for cocktails; the pull and jingle of the slot machine. Every afternoon at four o'clock, portly Herbert brought in the tea table, replete with silver kettle on its burner, green and white Meissen cups and saucers, and tiny plates for a variety of cakes and sweets. My favorite was a small egg-yellow layer cake, slathered with chocolate icing and encrusted with chopped nuts.

Past this room, which was the heart of the house, were my parents' two bedrooms. Among my parents' set, whether because their means enabled them to have so much space, or by choice, sleeping apart was commonplace. It was also in the aristocratic English style, which was much admired. The term master bedroom was coined during the late 19th century, but I don't remember ever hearing it called that. Just Mummy's room, or Daddy's room. No pecking order. This arrangement didn't seem to lead to any fewer children or more divorces than today, when—appropriately for smaller incomes and living spaces—couples share a queen-sized bed in one room, but I've often wondered whether sexual habits have changed as well. There must have been an erotic charge to moving around at night, opening doors, making one's way silently on soft carpets by shimmering moonlight.

My father usually went to bed first. My mother loved to stay up late, talking, playing games, reading, sipping chartreuse. Did he sometimes wait in her room? Or did she tiptoe to him? Certainly, I never saw them or even imagined them in bed together—it would never have occurred to me to enter either of their rooms uninvited. These adjoining rooms, each with a generous bathroom, were perfect examples of the period's masculine and feminine ideal. The colors, for instance: my father's room was in shades of brown and maroon, with dark varnished furniture and a twin-sized bed. In my parents' apartment in New York City, I sometimes was invited to visit Daddy as he had breakfast in his bedroom overlooking the East River. I recall the American Empire furniture that he had inherited—the room was more elegant than his bedroom in Joye Cottage, but there were the same neutral colors, with the same definite masculine aura. A sleigh-shaped bed, a settee with its original tapestry covering, two graceful armchairs, and a desk topped with a rounded cabinet.

The more lavish and alluring bedroom, of course, was my mother's: pink window seat, long, silvered glass dressing table with ivory brushes and mysterious pots of creams, and a French bed with pink tulle falling from its high crown. And of course my mother herself, sitting in a froth of linen, lace, and velvet. Her black curls cascaded over her shoulders as she trickled honey onto triangular bits of toast and sipped café au lait. Even at breakfast, the delicate porcelain cup was stained scarlet by her wide lips—all her life, no matter how early or how late, I never knew her to be without bright lipstick. She could retouch it perfectly, without a mirror.

Across the hall was the yellow dove room with the family shotguns arranged neatly in a case on the wall, the desk my father used for his business papers, and a passenger pigeon stuffed and mounted under a glass bell. Mornings, in this cheerful place, Herbert propped the *Herald Tribune* on a stand and served my father his orange juice and boiled egg with thin slices of crustless toast in a silver holder. My father sat in his yellow-rose-spattered spoon-backed chair,

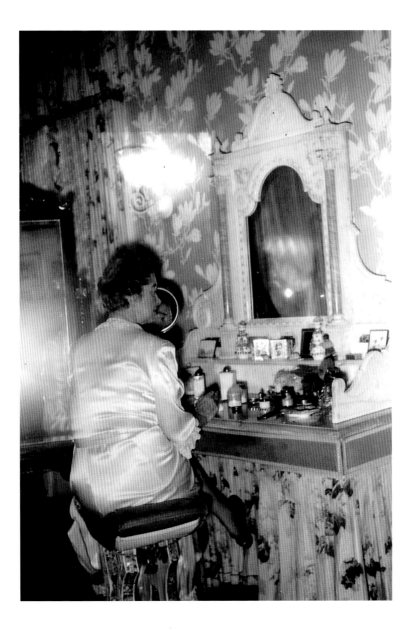

My mother at her dressing table, Aiken

atop a saffron rug with a birds-and-shotguns border that he had designed.

In the children's wing of the house were three bedrooms and three bathrooms. Lev's was at the end, on the left, with his crib, a white bureau, and some toys—cars, trucks, a ball. Miss Church lived across from Lev—her room was crowded with a big wooden four-poster bed, knitted afghans draped over two armchairs, and a dresser with lots of little china animals she'd brought with her from England. (When Miss Sligh replaced Miss Church, the room looked much the same. It always seemed overstuffed.) My room—the biggest—was off the hall on the right. In front of the two diamond-paned windows, overlooking a lawn and several big pine trees, sat my comfy brass bed. On the many shelves surrounding my desk, my beloved books awaited. My doll, Carrots, lived in the bottom drawer of the painted armoire. Dolls representing the Dionne quintuplets lived in that drawer, too. Born in Canada in 1934, their survival was considered a medical miracle, and they were removed from their parents and placed under the guardianship of the Ontario government. Unfortunately for the quintuplets, they had become a lucrative commodity, and the dolls were much in demand, but as special as they were, I never loved them as much as dirty old Carrots. Also in that drawer was my favorite toy: a set of tin soldiers—fuzzy-wuzzies with bearskin hats—and eight white horses pulling the King and Queen of England in a fancy coach at King George's coronation.

My few clothes were in the closet above. Jodhpurs and jacket, low brown boots, hard black bowler. Mrs. Schulhofer in the village nearby made my school dresses, which were very plain and straight; just right for my chubby figure.

[84]

My earliest Aiken memories are from the age of four.

I fall asleep to the crackle of fatwood and jack pine, the reflection of the flames flickering on my ceiling. I wake to the haunting calls of mockingbirds, the wind swishing through the pines outside my windows. There are birds in nests on the skyblue wallpaper that my mother has allowed me to choose. Pink and blue curtains on big windows give onto a green lawn. Leroy, a young black man whose job it is to care for the many fires in the house, lights a blazing fire to warm the cold room. I dress for school, and Miss Church, a cor-seted woman with cropped hair whose mouth turns down at the corners, tugs at my straight black hair with her comb.

Miss Church, Lev, and I go down the long hall, creeping past our parents' rooms to the main part of the house where Pam and Whitty, metaphorically and actually, live at the center of the house, sharing in the life of the house more intimately than we do. In the billiard room, there is the smell of chalk. Pool cues line the walls. Down a step or two, past a glass case with souvenir glassware of King George's coronation, we are in the paneled, dark dining room. In the middle, there is a long, polished table for the grown-ups, with a Delft-tiled fireplace at the far end. Our little table is to the left, next to a window.

Three years younger than I am, Lev is adorable, although he is less healthy. Along with hay fever, he has asthma. All this doesn't make me love him more, but the contrary. My impatience neither helps nor hinders him. I am furious when I have to follow the diet prescribed for him by Dr. Saint Lawrence, a fashionable New York pediatrician, whose pudgy fingers poke my body in a way I now recognize as bordering on abuse. Apparently our cook has decided that preparing one children's meal is enough, so we both subsist on bananas and rice. Miss Church makes us eat every bite, a torture that has me vomiting after meals. For disobedience, she threatens spankings with my hairbrush. Insensitive though she is, she knows that my parents would never stand for it, so I am safe, at least from spanking. Still, terrified by her empty threats, we never tell on her. Sometimes Lev and I crawl into bed with her to snuggle against her soft, warm body. It's the only physical contact we have with anyone other than Louise, a gentle nursery presence. Dignified, tall, beautiful, an African American of pale caramel color, Louise takes orders from Miss Church. She's the first person to hug me and hold me close. I'm only four or five when, suddenly and forever, she vanishes. Heartbroken, I keep asking for her, but disapproving voices tell me, "Never mind," and then, when I persist, they say, "She's bad."

Perhaps Louise was pregnant. I will never know why she disappeared. It was devastating to lose her—although the psychological, if not actual, absence of my mother was my first loss. So far, I'd only known the brief discomfort of cuts, bruises, sore throats, and inoculations. With Louise's disappearance, I felt the new, chilling stab of injustice. Louise was my friend and protector—why did she leave me? Were my nurse and my parents right that she was bad? My first doubts of their infallibility were as distressing as Louise's departure. Something was wrong; something I couldn't understand.

When Pam told our mother that our nurse was unresponsive and unkind, pfft! Miss Church also disappeared.

Miss Sligh, more intelligent and nurturing, but still a traditional British disciplinarian, took over our care. She enforced strict rules—perfect manners, perfect cleanliness and grooming, absolute promptness and obedience. I quickly learned to repress any longings for freedom. In my frustration, I ran in circles in the tall grass at the end of our garden and threw stones at Lev, who was smaller, weaker, and without recourse. Eventually, at about eleven, I learned to shoot a shotgun and became expert at killing tiny doves, delicious at lunch for family and guests.

Like most children, I understood instinctively that there was little I could control in my life. Lev and I, with our nurse, ate at a set time, isolated at the children's table. Along the far wall of the dining room, a high sideboard held a collection of majolica that I own today: the cups, green striated with pink, are hot shiny pink inside. Some have shelves with holes in them to prevent coffee from staining a moustache. Pam and Whitty visited us just as we were served dessert, which they claimed theirs by seigneurial rights. Our yelps and squeals had no effect, and neither did our nurse's stern, "No more, please." Still, we were flattered to have anything they might desire. Since we were expected to have perfect manners and always to finish everything on our plates, it's amazing I am not enormously overweight today. I still find it extremely difficult to say no to any food, or to leave food uneaten.

After breakfast, we repaired to the bathroom, where a bowel movement was mandatory, along with tooth-brushing and hand-washing. Our bodies were as disciplined, cleansed, and exercised as our minds. There was little time for fantasy or silliness. It is no wonder that I became a bookworm so early, hiding books under my covers when I was supposed to be asleep, reveling in the *The Wizard of Oz, Robin Hood*, or the cowboy stories of Will James. The combination of constant supervision and solitude turned me into a serious child; solemn even. I see today in my parents' photograph albums that there is never a smile on my face. I was afraid to disobey, or to let loose. I was a goody-goody.

In addition to our three bedrooms and bathrooms, a small door opened off the long hall to a dark, scuffed stairway leading to the cramped space with undersized windows where my mother's tiny French maid, Josephine, washed, ironed, and slept. Peenabo, as Pam and Whitty called her, always seemed to be rushing, frizzy ginger hair standing on end as if electrified, her hands furrowed like old leather and spotted with old burns. Silk night-gowns and filmy underwear were hung to dry in her little bathroom; flowered blouses, pleated skirts, and the long embroidered teagowns that our mother changed into every evening were spread on a table ready for pressing; short, wide, bright-colored high-heeled shoes in my mother's size four were lined up for polishing. There was a smell in the steamy, soapy air of the ironing board's scorched cover, and my mother's cloying tuberose perfume. Josephine didn't welcome our visits, and we seldom invaded her territory. "*Mais va t'en, les enfants, je n'ai pas le temps pour tes blagues, je dois finir cette jupe tout de suite, Madame sera en retard. Axi, Axi, tais-toi!*" Hexi was Mum's long-haired, dark brown dachshund, the mate of the paler Bodo, mother of my beloved Gili-Gili and Lev's Mousie. Like furry sausages with short legs, the dogs trotted everywhere with us, except for bad-tempered Hexi, who snapped and yipped at everyone except Josephine and Mum.

[88]

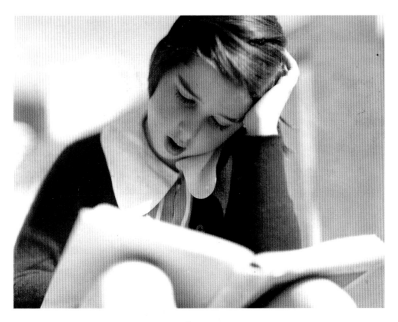

Reading, 1936

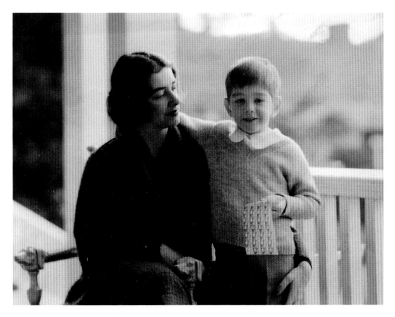

My mother and brother Lev, 1936

CHAPTER 5

Aiken Day School

My mother and two of her friends, Mrs. Katherine Von Stade and Mrs. Elsie Mead, founded the Aiken Day School in my great-grandfather's former squash court for their three oldest daughters, Pam, Dolly, and Katherine. My mother, who'd gone to Brearley, as had her mother, had persuaded the New York school to help them in setting up the school, and the curriculum was demanding. I realized how well I'd been prepared when, in ninth grade, I myself entered Brearley. The support and learning that took place within those Aiken walls formed my lifelong love for knowledge of all kinds.

*

Having left Barnard College to marry after only one semester, for many years I imagined that a college education would open windows to marvelous worlds of ideas, skills, and people. In my forties, with all our children in school, I enrolled in Manhattanville College. After seven years, I earned a BA, and was delighted by the publication of B. H. Friedman's biography of my grandmother, Gertrude Vanderbilt Whitney, for which I'd done research as part of my college credits. In that same year of 1978, I became president of the Whitney Museum's board of trustees, embarking at fifty on a new life.

As I reflect now on the 1970s and '80s, I see that Aiken

and my consciousness of our family's position there was a primary source of the inspiration, desires, and ambition that I developed in my middle years. As a child, growing up in a distinguished family, in the biggest house in Aiken, seemed natural. I didn't acknowledge the obligations attached to my advantage, but when I married and had children, I disregarded my connection to my renowned ancestors, wanting for my own family a simpler life.

Later still, I realized that some of the people with whom I was working at the Whitney Museum had higher expectations of me than I had for myself. When I took on my new job, I accepted responsibilities that pulled me away from my home in Connecticut. Mike's and my interests had diverged. Once a wife and mother, I became a working woman, plunging into the captivating and competitive cultural world of New York City. In order to lead the Whitney to fulfill its role as the primary museum of American art, as envisioned by my grandmother, I at last accepted my heritage, using my background to meet the powerful and wealthy people who could help. This seemed productive and good.

*

Lev's and my wing of the house had its own entrance, with a little porch from which steps descended to the back driveway. A clay tennis court was to the left, and beyond that a greenhouse by an enormous pecan tree with gray Spanish moss dripping from its branches like the beards of Chinese sages. Between the ages of four and thirteen, from mid-Sepember to mid-May, I walked down the painted blue-gray steps, turned right, my polished brown brogues rattling the small pale pebbles, and followed a short path past lawns

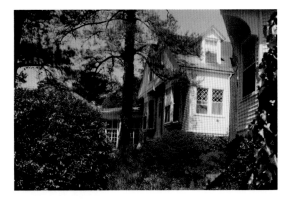

Joye Cottage: my bedroom

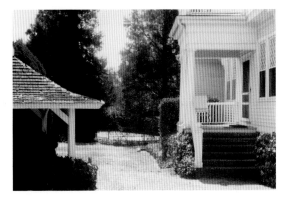

The children's entrance

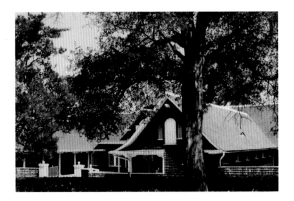

The stables

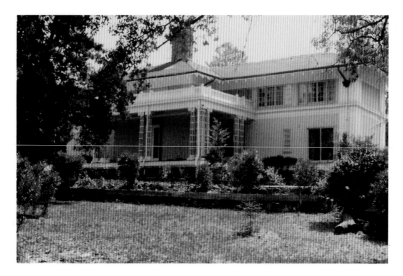

Aiken Day School, now a house, c 1970

shaded by green-black pines to a weathered gray wooden gate. Skipping across the red clay of Easy Street, I reached my school. With its wide porches and big windows, the cottage-style building, set in a grassy plot, was solid and inviting.

In a large square room with windows on two sides, ten to twenty boys and girls of different ages sat at wooden desks; their number changed from month to month and from year to year according to the length of time their northern parents had chosen to stay in Aiken. A few families, like ours, were the exception; the solid core. A big blackboard was at one end of the room, behind a desk for the teacher. In the one other room on that floor, we made maps, charts, wooden and clay artifacts, and sat on the floor to paint on big sheets of shelf paper. A central staircase led to the tiny room where we studied French.

Our teachers were an important part of our lives. First, always, there was Miss Lowe. Tall, beautiful, willowy, her long braided red-gold hair coiled around her head like a

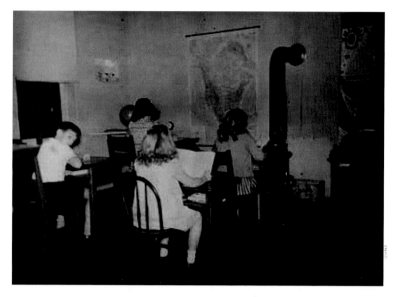

Schoolroom, Aiken Day School.
From left: Lev Miller, me, ?, Marianna Mead, c. 1938

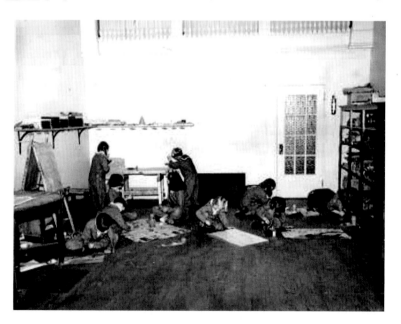

Workroom, Aiken Day School

crown. Her translucent skin smelled faintly of almonds; her fingernails were perfect rose-petal pink ovals. Her smile, her gentle touch, conveyed the love she gave, I was sure, to me alone. It was due to Miss Lowe's encouragement that I learned to read at four. Whatever she taught entered my head by magical osmosis. When nice Miss Prentice tried to teach me arithmetic, the magic wasn't there, and the numbers did not instantly fall into the right place as the letters had done. Finally, when someone took me for eye tests, they found I was nearsighted, which explained why I couldn't see the blackboard. Even with glasses, I never really conquered my difficulty with numbers.

After I outgrew Miss Lowe's classes, I visited her often. She always made me feel exceptional. That I could accomplish whatever I wanted if I did my best. How fortunate are children who receive that gift. Smoothly and capably, they emerge from childhood well rooted, and able to deal with life. I was lucky to find such kindness and wisdom in my teachers, because as much as we loved one another, my parents were often absent in body and spirit. With both the means and the imagination to enjoy their seemingly superficial lives in the ways they chose, they were busy shooting doves, quail, ducks; riding or driving on the soft clay roads; playing canasta (Mummy) and bridge (Daddy); watching or participating in lawn tennis, court tennis, horse shows, polo games, horse races, hunts; giving or attending lunches, teas, dinners; offering drinks to the many friends who dropped in before meals; reading and traveling.

The one thing that was *not* done was to talk about money. Earning one's living was rarely discussed. In *Old Money*, Nelson Aldrich illustrates the attitude of my parents' caste in this anecdote about Herbert Pell, a leading New Deal

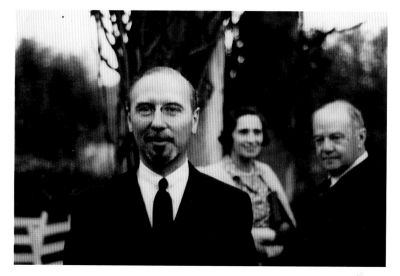

Schuyler Parsons, Elsie Mead, Yale Dolan

Democrat from an old and rich New England family:

> Herbert Pell's views of the hard hustle and hump of middle-class life may be judged from a story still told about him: that when a favorite niece of his one day joyfully announced that her new husband had at last found a job, Uncle Bertie replied, 'Oh, my dear, I'm so sorry.' The great gift of inherited wealth, in Pell's view, was freedom, and freedom ought to be put to better use—public service, for example—than holding down a 'job.'

Very few of my parents' friends actually worked; at least not when they were in Aiken. There were exceptions, of course. Schuyler Parsons ran a chic, popular shop for knick-knacks, wedding gifts, and furnishings. He was a popular bachelor, a natty figure with a Van Dyke beard and a sharp wit. Schuyler's sister Betty, originally an artist, opened a gallery in New York City remarkable for the early recognition of Jackson Pollock, Louise Nevelson, Richard Tuttle, Agnes Martin, and many others. Later, she became my friend. I learned much from Betty, whose strength belied her tiny, waif-like appearance. I admired her generous, wholehearted approach to *her* artists and their art, hardly aware that she herself was a talented artist. My mother's close friend Chi Bohlen, whose brother Chip later became United States Ambassador to France and Russia, worked hard, too—she was the manager of Schuyler Parsons' elegant shop, and during World War II served in the Office of Secret Services, the precursor of today's CIA. The OSS was more of a club then, with a certain cachet, where spying, dangerous as it was, was also glamorous.

The rather unnatural formality between myself and my parents made me care all the more passionately for my teachers and friends. Marianna Mead, a small rosy-cheeked girl, is still vivid in my mind's eye. Everything about her is smooth, silky, and tawny: the chestnut ringlets framing her round, freckled face; her caramel pony, Queenie; her cocker spaniel, Taffy; her brown jodhpurs, honey yellow sweater, and tan hair ribbon. She had gold-flecked eyes, a merry smile and bouncy gait—it was no wonder her boarding school nickname was Muffin.

She was my best friend throughout our childhood; really my only friend. When school let out in mid-May, I endured the loneliness of our four-month separation while I imagined her with cousins and friends enjoying a lively summer on Cape Cod. She was the youngest of six children in a gregarious, successful family from Dayton, Ohio. The Mead Paper Company, owned by her father, George, provided material security, while her mother nurtured and organized the children, who grew up to become successful adults in their various pursuits. Marianna and her husband became teachers and school administrators, and after retiring they

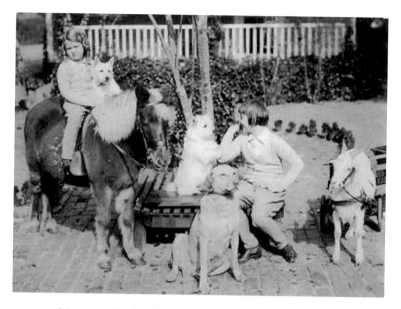

Marianna Mead on Queenie, with her sister and pets, c. 1937

founded a flourishing business advising parents on school and college choices. Even as a child, I recognized the difference between Elsie Mead and my own mother. Occasionally, Mrs. Mead's drive to galvanize us into activity intimidated me, and I retreated into the comfortable lassitude—reading for hours, taking long baths—that was acceptable at home, but not at the Meads' house. Their pulsing energy also attracted me, and I wished my parents were like Mr. and Mrs. Mead, rushing about with their children like a flock of chickadees, inviting friends for meals and weekends, playing tennis, riding, even eating dinner together. It created a dichotomy that has been with me ever since those days: a desire for activity, for a social life, and a countering need for solitude and reflection. There was no ambiguity, however, in my wish that my strict English nanny be more like Marianna's nurse, Alice; vivacious young Alice, endlessly kind, who played with Marianna. She even laughed. I'd grown to hate the plain dresses the local dressmaker produced every fall for my plump self, envying my friend's store-bought dresses in pretty prints with waists and swinging skirts. Marianna's world was much more eventful than mine, and far more fun. Even Marianna's school lunch was more exciting than mine, which always contained the same ham and cheese sandwich and dried figs, while hers was likely to have fried chicken, corn cakes, and delicious cookies and brownies. Although I was a year older than she and a grade ahead, we shared classrooms and teachers in our small schoolhouse.

One of the other students, Philip von Stade, was one of eight children. Marianna and I were equally smitten by Philip's blond curls, his teasing, his dimples. We chased him at recess, tagging him "it" over and over, not yet aware of our subconscious wish to touch him. Our schoolmates Seymour and Norty Knox, wiry and quick, were destined for great athletic success, becoming high-goal polo players whose teams consistently won international competitions. My brother, Lev, and his friends Jimmy and Timmy Laughlin, were too young to be of interest, but old enough to be nuisances. I doubt we were sorry when they transferred to the new boys' school, Aiken Prep. It meant more attention for us from our beloved teachers.

Kitty and Nanny von Stade were the sisters of our hero Philip and of my older sister Pam's best friend Dolly, but so much younger than Marianna and me that they didn't really count. Claudia Wilds, the doctor's daughter, was the only real Southerner in the little school; she spoke with more of an accent than our teachers. Her parents had less money than ours, and even her clothes were different—cut so they'd

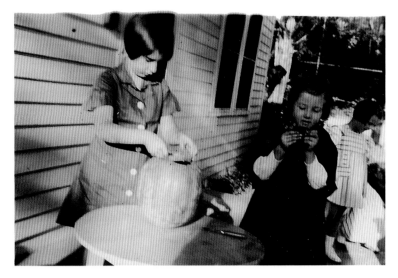

With Claudia Wilds, carving a pumpkin

last. We couldn't understand why she didn't have her own horse, like the rest of us. Why she wasn't a good rider. In the photograph I still have of Marianna, Claudia, and myself carving a Halloween pumpkin, Claudia looks sad and lost. And doubtless she was. As children can be, before learning the more subtle ways of adults, we were sometimes cruel. Prejudiced, before even knowing the word.

Eithne Tabor, a tiny fiery redhead, was the daughter of the headmaster of the boys' school. Thinking her a crybaby in the games we played at recess, we tried to exclude her, which, of course, only made things worse. "What have you been doing to poor Eithne to make her so unhappy?" our parents asked. "You should make a special effort to include her. She's new, you know, and she's younger than you are." So we knew that Mr. and Mrs. Tabor complained to them, and we resented Eithne all the more.

Marianna, above all, was my constant companion.

Unlike my children and grandchildren, we didn't have play dates or sleepovers. In our small community, we necessarily followed the same routine. Marianna and I shared secrets, played games, teased Lev and his friends. We had our dogs: her golden cocker spaniel, Taffy, and my long-haired dachshund, Gili-Gili. We took tennis lessons, and we even performed tap-dances with local girls in the local school gymnasium. (We weren't real Southerners, like our dancing partners, as a group of them made very clear one day, shouting at us from the steps of the post office, "Go home, damn Yankees!" Once out of their sight, I shed tears of shame, sorrow, and incomprehension.) We took piano lessons. We hated to practice, playing duets like "Sur La Glace A Sweetbriar" under the baleful eye of Miss Stoddard, whose one long hair, growing from a mole on her cheek, both fascinated and repelled us.

Above all, though, there was riding. We rode every day but Sunday; two or three times a week with our teacher, the other days with the grooms. Snowball, white, calm and gentle, was my first pony, followed by others more suitable for the jumping to which we all looked forward. Queenie was Marianna's pony, a furry butterscotch with a vanilla mane and tail. On this small beauty, she galloped over soft piney trails and vaulted over big jumps.

"Legs, body, reins—Whoa!" called our teacher Gaylard in a deep, commanding voice. Squeeze the thighs. Lean the body back. Only then, a slight pressure on the bit. These were religious precepts. Leaning back, down we'd go—my pony seemed to slide on his tail as I squeezed my knees against the saddle, hoping not to plunge over his head to be trampled. Up the bank—hup! I leaned forward, sure I wouldn't be able to grip hard enough, sure I would slide

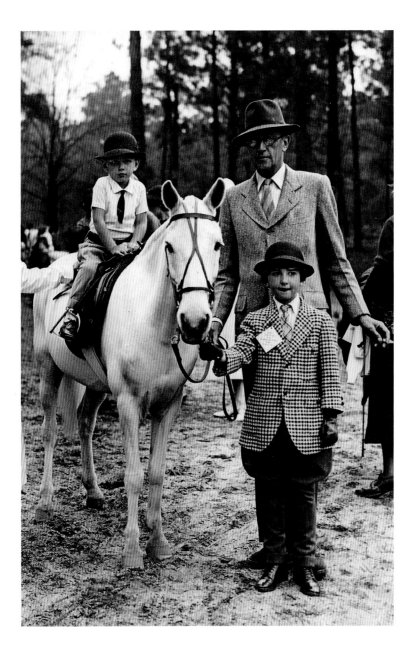

Horseshow, Aiken: With Lev on Snowball and my father, c. 1937

right down his tail.

Going home, we crossed Sand River. An old legend told of an Indian chief of the Creek Nation whose daughter had been very ill. Guided by a dream, he had her carried to a land of whispering pines through which flowed a river of sand. Here, the Indians built a village, and in the healthy climate of Aiken the princess recovered. In that same river, Snowball kicked up the fine white sand, tickling his belly. When he bucked, I was thrown into the surprisingly unyielding, cold drybed. "Whoa there!" I heard my teacher call as he chased my excited pony, catching him, and bringing him back to me, salted white, dazed. "Now, Flora, what have I told you a dozen times?"

"Hold onto the reins when I fall off, Gaylard."

"That's right, Flora. The next time, you'll walk home, leading your horse. Now mount him and let's go."

He ignored my hot tears of shame. I mounted my pony and followed at the end of the line of riding pupils. The next time, two or three weeks later, I did walk the long trail home, leading Snowball. And the time after that, I held onto the reins.

Captain William Gaylard was in many ways the most important adult in our lives. He was not a tall man, but to us, his pupils, he was a warrior of Herculean proportions. We knew that he'd been a British cavalry officer in the Boer War. His erect posture, neatly clipped moustache, immaculate jodhpurs and tweed jacket, polished boots, silver spurs and checked cap identified him from afar, even to my near-sighted eyes. I didn't wear my glasses when riding, afraid of breaking them when, as often happened, I fell from my pony.

Throughout those childhood years, our physical and emotional worlds revolved around horses. My budding sense of myself waxed and waned through my

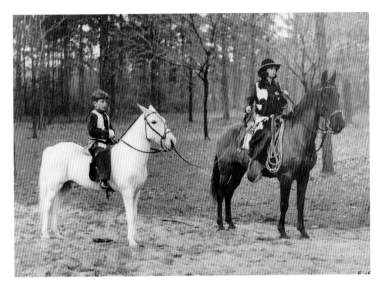

On Jackie, Lev on Snowball, c. 1937

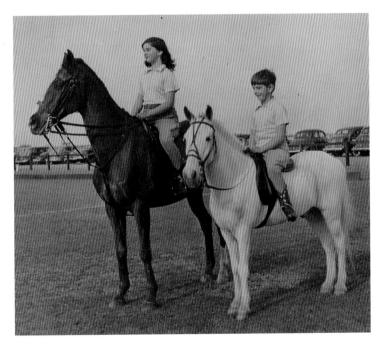

On Redbank, Lev on Snowball, c. 1938

proficiency—or lack of it—in controlling a powerful quadruped whom I both loved and feared. My character was shaped by this, filtered through the discipline of our mentor and coach. The idea of control was the key to maturity. I recognize it as a motif running through my life. It is still with me today—the conviction, as I was taught, that I can dominate events or people. Thinking it possible, when it so clearly isn't. Believing that if a thing is right, it will happen.

*

Much later, as president and then chair of the board of the Whitney Museum of American Art, I discovered the fallacy of my illusion. As we were raising money for a major building expansion, many trustees were losing confidence in the director with whom I'd been working closely. I continued to support this director, although the most powerful men on the board, those with the money to enable the expansion, wanted him out. In the end, the board voted to fire him. I was devastated. With a split board, the expansion was cancelled. Many artists shunned the Museum that had long been their home. After much negative publicity, attendance decreased; and the director's career was irretrievably damaged. If I'd been wiser, some of these effects would have been lessened. By admitting that I couldn't have my way, a compromise might have been possible. Instead, I stuck to my position, and lost. I foolishly took for granted my fantasy of entitlement, and I hurt the institution I loved.

CHAPTER 6

The Household

I don't want to exaggerate my parents' neglect. They did spend some time with their children. Through carefully chosen surrogates, they made sure we were learning what they thought we needed to know in order to have someday the same sheltered lives that they themselves were leading. Riding, shooting, tennis, piano, dancing, speaking French, and of course, the pleasures of alcohol—they taught us, by example, the cult of the martini; the importance of good wines. They were kind to their servants, maybe even generous. I'm unaware of the salaries they paid, but do know that most of the servants stayed with us for years and professed great affection for their bosses. (It's fashionable now, I realize, to ascribe this to the necessity of keeping a job when work was not easy to obtain. Still, I wonder.) My father was fond of the black men who cleaned his guns and retrieved his doves, ducks, or quail, especially J. D., of whom he made the portrait that hung in the living room.

A small army of servants, as we called them, made us very comfortable. Without them, our lives would have been entirely different. The top echelon was white; the lower, black. Walter, the formal and polite Scottish groom, in his brown tweed jacket and jodhpurs, tipped his cap as he brought the buggy around to the front door for my mother, covering her knees properly with a checked lap robe once she was seated. Walter helped me mount my pony in the stable yard, carefully adjusting my stirrups and reins before getting onto his bigger horse and following me to the Hitchcock Woods for our ride. Respectfully, he told me to use my legs to control my pony better, and not to pull too hard on the reins, hurting the pony's tender mouth. When we returned, he soaped my pony and rinsed him, then swooshed off the water with a leather-handled metal scraper, hissing all the while, "Sssss now, easy, boy, sssss, ssssssss."

The stables were warm and friendly: the clean golden hay, the thick smell of oily saddle soap on the dark old leather saddles and bridles, the clink of the bits as Walter polished them. The horses had a rich funky odor. There was the smell of their oatsy, sweet bran mash, and the sound of their hooves stamping in their stalls. I could hear their piercing neighs from my bedroom across the lane; I thought the horses were the most beautiful creatures on earth, and I loved them passionately. Being a bit afraid of them made them even more alluring. Despite my fear of being kicked or bitten, I learned to clean the pebbles and dirt from their hooves, and to brush their manes, their forelocks, and even their tails. But Walter was always there to supervise, help, and protect.

Walter taught me to drive my sister's high-stepping hackneys, giving emphatic and specific instructions that I followed fastidiously. He taught me to hold the reins in both hands, using my wrists for both sensitivity and strength; to wield the whip that sat in the carriage's holder to the right, where I could reach it easily; and to control the spirited ponies without hurting their mouths. I learned to turn right and left; to go faster or slower. I longed to be good at it, and I knew that Walter had the secrets I needed. He was always

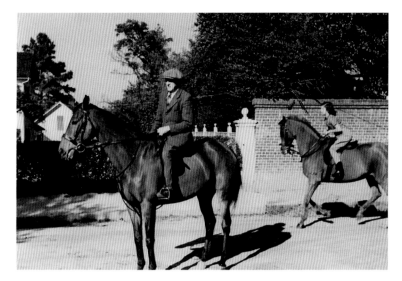

With Walter Douglas, c. 1938

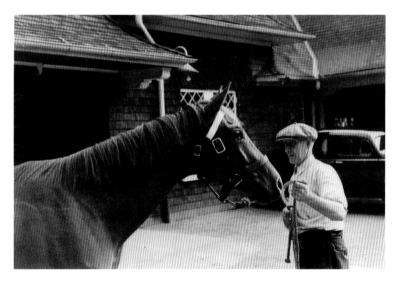

Walter in Aiken, c.1940

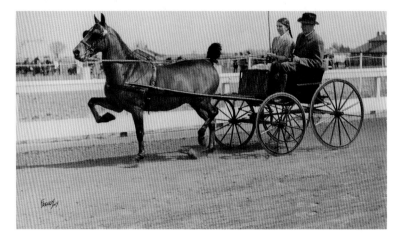

Blue ribbon! Fire Escape, c.1940

patient, but there was only one right way, and he knew it.

I never thought of Walter's home life. I couldn't imagine that he had one. I looked up to him, even though I didn't feel compelled to obey him as I did my parents, my nurse, or Gaylard. Still, I wanted to please him. How I wish, now, that I'd been more curious about his life away from the stables, and his childhood in Scotland. He'd come to the United States to work for my grandparents. And not only Walter—a burly Polish man did heavy work for my parents in Long Island—carrying suitcases and trunks, moving furniture and plants, scrubbing and rubbing all day long. We called him Pete, but that wasn't his real name. He once told me as he polished the banister in the front hall that when he'd first come to work in the house as a youth, my grandfather had spoken to him firmly: "We have too many Josephs on the place, your name will be Peter from now on." "But," I asked naively, "did you want to change your name?" Pete

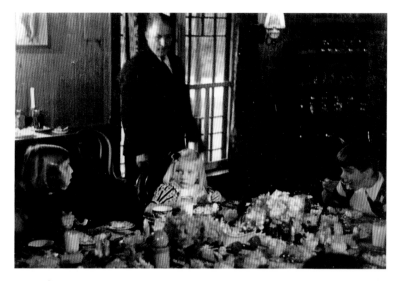

Herbert at Lev's and my birthday party, Togus, c. 1935

just laughed and went on rubbing the brass 'til it shone. If you wanted your job, you obeyed the boss. And, as a child, I took it all for granted.

Herbert was the head honcho of the staff. With his large, pink, balding head melting into a pear-shaped body, his tiny black shoes peeking from sturdy legs, he looked a bit like Tweedledee. Through torment and stress, he maintained his cool, and was smoothly effective in his management of the varied workers under his rule. I can picture him now, sitting at the table in the pantry in his dark blue apron over a snowy white shirt and black trousers, using his thumbs to put the final touch on the ornate silver cups our grandparents had won with their race horses. Was he sipping brandy as he rubbed? Maybe, but I could never tell. Impossible to imagine Herbert with a family—he lived with *us*. It was his responsibility to keep us organized and happy. What more could he possibly want?

My memories of our black servants are full of affection and sensuality. Tiny Myra was the housemaid, with a frilly white cap on her small round head. She pushed an ancient carpet-sweeper in the early mornings—shteeck, schtack—up and down the halls and carpets. "Good morning, Miss Flora," she'd whisper with a smile and a bob of her neat head. Although I never knew her well, never found out, for instance, if she had children, her familiar presence was comforting. Our central heating system was antiquated and ineffective. It was Leroy who piled logs in the many fire-places and kept the fires burning all day long. If I were not yet awake, or in bed when I was sick, he was careful not to look my way, even when I said good morning to him. My beloved nursery maid, Louise, and I would follow a well-worn dirt path to visit Maria (pronounced Mar-eye-a). Comfortably round, blue-black, with a warm, toothless smile and beads of sweat on her broad forehead, she presided over several younger women in the cabin behind the stables. They washed endless sheets and towels in huge tubs, squeezing rivers of water from enormous wringers, hanging linens from vast baskets to dry on lines stretching high over the red clay earth. The sheets billowed like clouds against the blue sky. There were different smells: hot, starchy, steamy, with a bit of pungent scorch. As I leaned down to sniff a delicious pile of clean laundry, Maria welcomed me warmly, making me feel that my visit was very special. She showed me how she heated her irons over the wood stove. Maria finished one of my father's blue shirts, placed the iron with several others to heat, then moved away from the cloth-covered ironing table to talk to me. Her mother was born a slave, and Maria told me that she herself felt blessed to be free. This was a new idea for me, something that was

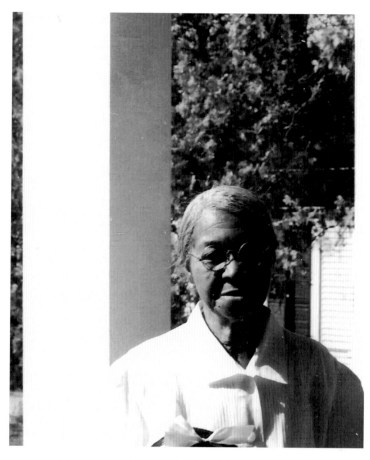

Myra, 1955, visiting our family with her granddaughter

important, and it stayed with me even though I didn't really understand Maria's words. I accepted her hug and hugged her back. She seemed to enjoy her work in the company of friends and to a child that felt comforting and safe.

Only a bit later did a question begin to form around the idea of being free. Although I'd have liked to rebel against rules and regulations, I never doubted that freedom was my right, particularly when I was grown. I thought of the signs I saw in the village at the two entrances to the movie house, at the twin water fountains, and other places, too. One said "White" and the other "Colored." I knew which one to drink from, and it never occurred to me to consider drinking from the other. Why would it? It was the society in which I grew up, and I didn't wonder at it.

In the April 3rd, 2008 *New York Review of Books*, Russell Baker reviewed several books about Condoleeza Rice, Secretary of State under George W. Bush. Her parents, he writes, were remarkable. Talented professionals who attended college, they lived in an upscale black section of Birmingham, Alabama. Despite their success, in the 1960s, when Condoleeza was growing up, parents like hers still "tried hard to shelter the children from contact with the ugly realities of segregation . . . when they wanted a drink of water or to use a toilet, they were taught to wait until they got home."

It wasn't until I was a little older that I began to think about the consequences of segregation. A friend of my father's once said he wouldn't have his hair cut by a Negro—one of the labels we used then. Our black servants ate separately from the white servants. On my walks, the small cottages without lawns and the tumbledown cabins were the places where blacks lived. I slowly became aware of discrimination and segregation, and I didn't like them. In the South of my childhood, darkies (another word we used in those days) and white folk were woven together, like the cotton growing in the fields around Aiken. Within the hard bolls, dark seeds were embedded deep inside, the fluffy white fibers clutching them with tenacity (a remote ancestor of mine had invented a machine, the cotton gin, to separate them). Cotton lay at the heart of the South's former prosperity, just as the African-Americans I knew as a child were the nurturing force enabling us to live as we did in comfortable ease. Just as cotton and seed were tightly contained within their hard shell, so custom and law joined black and white in harsh embrace. Someday, I would see the covering split open, spilling freedom, leaving black and white facing each other in liberation and hope, but it was to take many more years.

Can I imagine, today, how our black servants felt? Those shadowy figures whose mission, we assumed, was to serve and obey? It is impossible. They were impenetrable, many of them constrained by generations of fear, dependency, toil—and surely, at some level, hate. At our house, they had secure jobs, and we children were taught to be as polite and considerate toward them as toward our elders. We were close, but apart. They knew a lot about us; we knew nothing about them. Carefully, quietly, they served our meals, cleaned our rooms, ran our baths, fed, warmed, and comforted us. When we were ill, they held, emptied, and washed the pans into which we were sick or urinated. They were shy, admiring, encouraging.

White servants were separate from us, too, but somehow we knew that they belonged to a different category. Their children could go to good schools, could rise in the world and become more like us. Sometimes we played with them. And, of course, Sis and our nurses enjoyed a high status, although still not that of real family.

To be cared for almost entirely by servants paid to do so was normal for families of wealth. What effect did it have on us? It produced feelings of security and comfort, as well as loneliness. It also gave us a feeling of entitlement. Although we were taught that having much, we owed much, there was the implicit belief that we were superior to those who were different from us in color, race, or class. I can hardly believe that I was ever in such a cocoon; that I grew up in such a golden cage. I know that later, as a busy wife and mother, I struggled guiltily against occasional desires for former luxuries: monogrammed linen sheets ironed smooth; a peaceful cocktail hour uninterrupted by little children, while others—paid to do so—prepared a Sunday dinner of roast beef and Yorkshire pudding with a chocolate soufflé and homemade ice cream, leaving mothers and adult daughters free to work their needlepoint, sip martinis, and gossip.

Only rarely did it occur to me as a child that we were extraordinarily privileged; that we lived an antiquated and aristocratic life. In my early teens, in church, and even more from the books I read voraciously, I began to gain a sense of other worlds. The horse and dog tales I read were so distressing that I shuddered for Spunky, the pony condemned to work in a dark mine all his life, or the painful trials of the sheepdog in *Bob, Son of Battle.* Crying over the poverty, cruelty, and prejudice I encountered in *David Copperfield* or *Uncle Tom's Cabin,* I felt angry. But did I really believe such conditions existed? I must have or I wouldn't have wept. But they didn't exist in the world that I knew.

My own tribulations, at that time, had more to do with feelings of loneliness, sadness, and boredom—in particular, the yearning for my mother. As mild as they might seem in comparison to the troubles of others less privileged, these kinds of emotions were definitely not acceptable. We had no reason not to be cheerful and busy all the time. Look at all that we had; look at how fortunate we were! I didn't realize for many years that it was all right to feel despondent. Holding in my feelings, not even acknowledging them to myself, was the way I was taught to be. For a while, I passed this trait on to my own children, until they themselves generously helped me to see things more clearly.

CHAPTER 7

Le Petit Boulay · Christmas

Although my parents expected us to learn manners and discipline from Miss Church and Miss Sligh, they also required me to take lessons from Pam and Whitty's governess, Sis. Every other summer, my parents spent two months in France, a few hours from the Paris studio where Gertrude Vanderbilt Whitney, my grandmother, worked as a sculptor. In 1933 and 1935, we children were taken to France with them.

First came the Atlantic crossing on the unimaginably huge ocean liner, the *Queen Mary*. In our cabins, we slept hours longer than usual, rocked by the ocean; we ate early meals in the formal dining room, served on starched white linen. At four and a half, I hadn't been eating well and I had grown alarmingly thin. On board the *Bremen*, my mother later told me, she fed me my meals herself. By the time I was five, later that same summer, I was healthy again. I don't remember this, although her feeding me would have been highly unusual. Dizzy, but never seasick—although our nurses were—we walked around and around the deck, whitecaps roiling the sea. We sipped mid-morning broth, covered with plaid blankets in our deck chairs by attentive stewards.

In France, we were driven to Le Petit Boulay. A small chateau near Tours that my grandmother had given to my parents as a wedding present; it had a garden, pond, and

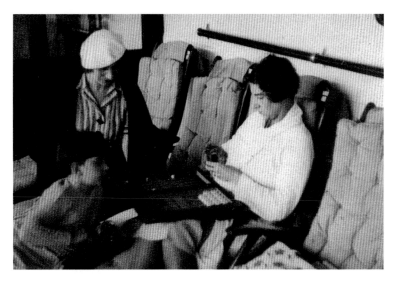

Backgammon on the Bremen: With Sis, and my mother

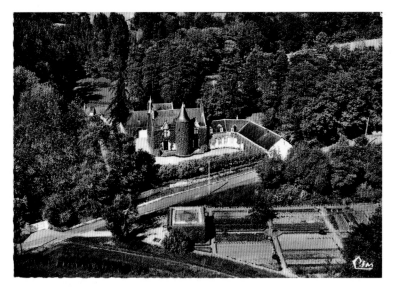

Le Petit Boulay

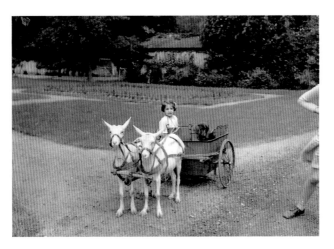

With goats Blanchette and Paquerette, dachshund Hexi, 1933

round tower. There were deep underground passages with wine stored in wooden casks where Pam and Whitty sometimes let Lev and me join them in playing Sardines. The hunt through cavernous spaces filled with the rich odors of fermenting grapes and chalky earth was terrifying, but exciting. We squeezed into small, dark spaces with other warm, wriggling bodies, and then experienced the joy of discovery as we were released into the light.

In hot sunlight we ran through fields of red poppies; one time, a seemingly tame fox by the river bit my hand when I reached to pat him. Two white goats, Blanchette and Paquerette, pulled us in a gaily-painted Sicilian cart. We wandered through the castles of Blois, Azay-le-Rideau, and Chinon, and our father photographed us standing on bridges over moats, and in the crenellations of old stone walls.

During those weeks, our nurse took her vacation in England and we were comparatively, blissfully free. Miss Hagerman, or Hagy, young and comforting, cared for me and for Lev, who was often ill. Although she was gentle, I look rather lost (thin with dark bangs shadowing big eyes) in one of my father's photographs. I remember those summers as happy. Joining the family at meals instead of eating earlier by ourselves as we did at home meant that we helped ourselves to whatever we wanted to eat. The only rules were those that the grownups also followed: no interrupting, and each English word required the speaker to place a sou in a bowl, to be given later to a worthy cause. All summer, we tried to catch out Sis, and finally succeeded when, in a discussion of current books, she named *Gone With The Wind*.

Our second summer, a dour Scottish artist arrived to paint a portrait of me. He was very serious, and wanted to work for much too long—he had no inkling of how a little girl might hate those silent hours of sitting still. My unhappiness shows in the finished painting. There's a doll in my lap, but the aloof way I'm holding her indicates a lack of care, and the little (and non-existent) dog near my chair looks lonely. My white linen dress with blue polka dots is uncreased, and my shoes seem better-suited for dancing school than a day in the country. My hair is combed straight, with neat bangs. I look stiff and bored. When my mother died, I didn't want the portrait. My elder daughter, Michelle, has it now, but I haven't visited her in California since she took the painting—I wonder if she has it on her wall. I fear that she may identify with some of the feelings in that painting.

*

The oldest of our four children, Michelle was born when I was twenty years old. She was a perfect baby: smiling happily, eating, and sleeping well. As the other babies came

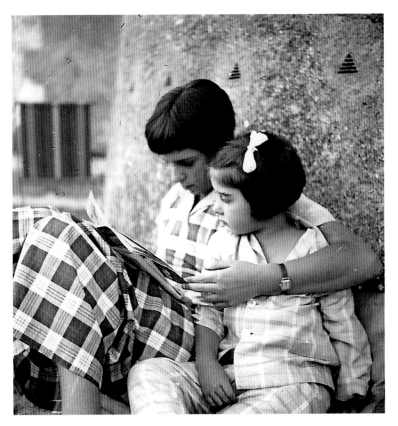

Pam reading Alice in Wonderland *to me in France, 1933*

along—I also had several miscarriages—as much as I loved her, the other children's needs drew my attention away from her. Young and immature, I wished for more time to be with my husband, to read, or to be with adult friends. I see now that my children, especially the older two, suffered through my growing pains as well as their own. Today, remembering my failings, I'm grateful to them for all they have taught me, and awed when I see them as spouses and parents in turn, who love wisely and well.

Once Hitler's shadow began to loom over Europe, my parents stopped going to Le Boulay. German officers were billeted in the chateau during the War, and the caretakers had a terrible time with them. In 1947, when Lev went to see if anything of value remained, he advised my parents not to return. My mother and father never stopped loving France, however, and always felt at home in Paris. From the late '40s to the late '60s, they stayed in my grandmother's studio every summer, sitting in the little garden, reading and writing. My father painted an orange-fleshed *cavaillon* melon, *porto* floating within, or rows of white asparagus with Hollandaise sauce, and a cluster of *fraises des bois* on St. Clement pottery, my grandmother's favorite, decorated with red roosters or bright flowers. Sometimes, he would arrange a breakfast on a little table: pitchers with coffee and hot milk, a wide cup, a croissant, a pat of yellow farm butter, a pot of raspberry jam. I treasure a watercolor he did of my mother, sitting in the sun with a big hat, reading the Herald-Tribune, needlepoint and Double-Crostic on a table at her side.

*

I was expected to speak French by the time that I was seven. We had prepared for this ahead of time in Aiken. That's when Sis became central to my life. I loved her from the start.

Babies, in their brand-new world, must make order from chaos. Slowly, a planetary system comes into being. Constellations appear brighter for a time, then, when their lustre dims, others take their place. My mother was the radiant sun of my childhood, brighter than any other star, but,

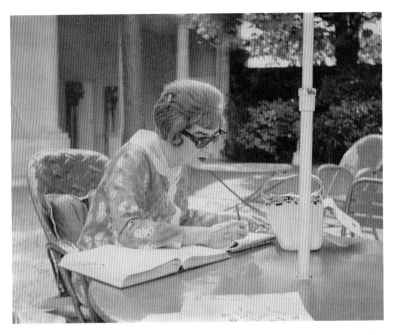

My mother in Gertrude's Paris studio, c.1965

like the sun, strictly a part-time presence. She and my father came and went to New York City, to distant places where they went shooting, or on trips around the country in their trailer, *Romany Rye*. They were out for the day, or the evening. Even when they were home, it was hard to get their attention. Sis, however, provided more constant ground. By her side, with her tacit permission, I grew up. She was a strong and steady guide. Her maladies and quirks only endeared her to me, never making me fearful or uneasy.

I never knew why Suzanne Bergès was known to our family and friends as Sis, or—in a teasing reference to her French accent—Sees. She was short and slender, with a mobile mouth in a small heart-shaped face. At night, she set her dark hair, as thin and airy as a dove's breast feathers, in curlers. Whether sitting or standing, she held herself rigidly, her back as straight as if constrained by a metal brace; I wondered if she slept in the same position. (I later discovered that she was held in, as were so many women at that time, by an inflexible whalebone corset.) This stiff posture seemed a metaphor for her unwavering principles, but it belied her great kindness and humor, and the emotional volatility she sometimes let slip with a sharp little cry, a sudden harsh word, or an expression of despair—mysteries for me to ponder later. Although I thought her long nose seemed that of an intellectual aristocrat, it was the subject of many jokes from Pam and Whitty, who teased her unmercifully, despite their adoration. Prone to waves of heat and faintness, which I later recognized as symptoms of menopause, she'd gasp, pull out a handkerchief and mop her forehead with a moan. Pam and Whitty would joke: "Oh, Sees, another *vague*! You're thinking of Jacques, admit it now!" To my amazement, they weren't struck by lightning; everyone, including Sis, would laugh. "Mais non, taisez-vous donc. You are terrible!" and she'd recover to continue a nonstop game of bezique with Pam, clicking the little ivory scoreboards I ached to manipulate—a ceremony that was still years in the future. *Ah, mais vous êtes impossibles!* she'd say, shaking her finger at the teenagers drinking Horses' Necks, which splashed and dripped on tables and sofas as they punched, tickled, and flew off together.

The day finally over, Sis retired thankfully to read. Claiming insomnia, she collapsed into what she called "the arms of Morpheus" the moment her head hit the pillow. It was Pam and Whitty's signal to escape. They galloped away with their gang, as swift as a herd of ponies, through moonlit streets and shadowy forest paths in cars taken from their parents' garages, frolicking and shrieking and kissing until

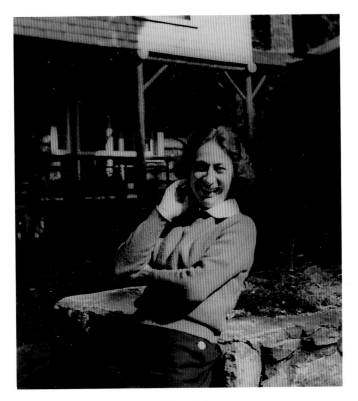

Sis in the Adirondacks, c. 1939

creeping back to the darkened house. Sis never understood how they could sleep so late.

Pam's friend, Nelson Mead, used to hide under her bed when Sis came into the room—not that there was a sexual relationship between them. It was pure deviltry. Even later, when the doctor came to see Pam when she was married, pregnant, and sick with chicken pox, Nelson, grown though he was, was hiding under her bed. "What in the world do you have to laugh about?" the doc asked in amazement, examining Pam's spotted, lumpy self.

In the beginning, Sis was a distant figure of authority who belonged to Pam and Whitty. My relationship with Sis was different than theirs; I dared not be disrespectful to any adult. Sis was warm and delightful, and I was always happy to leave our starchy English nurse at home with Lev to take a long walk with Sis on the red clay roads of Aiken to practice my French. Singing heartily, we trudged over wide log bridges, called corduroy bridges, and past gardeners raking and watering the smooth green lawns, all the way to the cabins on the edge of town where children played in the dirt yards.

> Il était un petit navire, il était un petit navire,
>> *Qui n'avait ja, ja, jamais naviguè, qui n'avait ja, ja, jamais naviguè,*
>> *Ohè, ohè!*
>
> Oh, poor little sailor, who drew the short straw!
>
> *On le mangea à sauce blanche . . .*

That image haunted me. Why did his shipmates devour the littlest sailor? What was the moral of the song? In the world that I knew, things weren't unpredictable; judgments were not arbitrary. To be right and fair was to be rewarded. Any display of unkindness or rudeness was punished. I wasn't, for years, able to enjoy food served with white sauce.

Sis took over certain recurring tasks, especially at Christmastime. "Mademoiselle," asked our mother, "do you have some paper? It's time to do some presents." Sis would scurry upstairs, returning with the box of carefully folded papers she'd saved from dozens of birthdays and Christmases. Using the minimum amount of tape, unrolling years of bright ribbon, she wrapped gift after gift exquisitely, neatly; new treasures in old covers. Like the tradition of Christmas itself, the wrapping was made new every year.

Christmas was a hub in the rhythm of our lives. Joye Cottage lent itself to celebration. My parents were attractive, bright, and sociable; their friends dropped by all the time, and the house was a center of festivity. My mother even made a room for parties in a wing of the rambling house. "The New Room" was decorated in brilliant purple and chartreuse, with streaming silk curtains at the French doors, pouffed sofas, fringed chairs, and a strange deeply-textured carpet. As in the other rooms, my father's paintings were on the walls. When the popular black musician, Lucky Roberts arrived, we knew a great time lay ahead. He played rollicking old songs on the piano, singing in his growly voice, smiling his wide smile. People talked, danced, ate, and drank, while I wished desperately to be old enough to join in the fun. Lucky played a fabulous instrument he'd invented: bells, gongs, and tin cans attached to an old washboard, with pedals and drums, too. My father loved to play Lucky's washboard with empty shotgun shells on his fingers. My mother shook her dark curls and leaned close to a handsome admirer, laughing and flirting. Everyone seemed happy. Being a grownup seemed infinitely desirable.

All the same, Christmas was for the children. First, we trimmed the tree. It had come by train from our family's Adirondack woodlands, a tall spruce or balsam, whose smell filled the living room. When I think of Christmas, I picture that room, with Sis playing her central role. The tree stood on one side, across from the fireplace, and near the piano. The workmen who set up the tree wound small colored lights through the branches, then tested them. If a bulb were out, Sis was there with a supply of fresh ones. Having stored the ornaments the year before, she now brought them from the dark closet where they'd lain undisturbed for eleven and a half months. In brown wool trousers and green sweater instead of her usual tweed skirt and silk blouse, she was ready to work; she polished a gilded fish, attached a wire to a painted bird, tied a ribbon to a snowflake. Oh, how happy we were to see once again those wood and glass treasures, red and silver bells, blue and gold trumpets and horses. "Now, darlings, work from the inside out, don't forget the back of the tree. Oh, look, under that branch, there's a bare place— Mademoiselle, can you reach back there?" my mother would ask, and Sis would crawl under the lowest boughs to hang bright baubles in the empty spaces. Heaven forbid one should see too much of the actual tree! At the end, we wove ropes of silvery tinsel through the branches, then tossed showers of soapflakes over the tree—there it was, the most beautiful Christmas tree in the world.

Each Christmas, our nurse saw to it that Lev and I learned a poem ("The Boy Stood on the Burning Deck" comes to mind) or made up a play based on the Christmas story, which we performed on Christmas Eve. I both loved and dreaded the moment when our father read "The Night Before Christmas," because when he reached the lines

> He had a red face and a little round belly,
> Which shook when he laughed like a bowl full of jelly,

Pam and Whitty would howl, pointing at my stomach. "Now stop that," my mother would say. "Don't tease poor Flora." Her scolding made me feel all the more humiliated. Later, we hung long beige cotton stockings on the high mantel. Milk and cookies for Santa, and we children were bundled off to bed, while the others busied themselves under the tree before midnight church service.

Christmas morning, our stockings lay heavy and lumpy across our beds. We carried them to our mother's bed, on the one day we were permitted to enter and awaken her. We tore open the packages in our stockings, excited about each little gift from Santa: puzzles, tiny stuffed bears, china dogs and horses; sometimes a silver dollar in the toe. Our parents opened their stockings, too, unwrapping the strange surprises they'd collected for each other all year, and exclaiming with delight—just as we did.

Creeping through the darkened living room, averting our eyes from the tree, we had a special breakfast of pancakes with melted butter, sausages, and maple syrup. We waited impatiently for everyone to assemble—then—presto! The tree lights were turned on, and we pounced on the mountain of presents.

In those days, we children didn't go shopping. Our allowances were tiny. Our presents for parents, nurses, teachers, and each other were handmade: painted bookmarks or oranges stuck with cloves to freshen closets (our thumbs were sore for days). When I was older, I'd laboriously cross-stitch pincushions or samplers with dates and names. Finding the Western saddle I'd prayed for under the tree was an astonishment. Or, when I was eleven, from my grandmother, the typewriter I'd dreamed of. There was always a box from Cousin Joan Payson in Long Island, owner of the store "Young Books," which yielded gifts for each of us.

Did Miss Sligh or Sis have a stocking? I was too enraptured by my own to wonder. And Sis, what was she doing during this rampage of tearing and shrieking? Was her thrifty French self offended by such profligacy? Perhaps she made the best of it by collecting ribbons and gathering each unspoiled sheet of paper to be used the following year. There she sat, in the midst of chaos, winding, rolling and folding, an eye of calm in the tumult.

Just in time, we gathered ourselves for the eleven o'clock service at St. Thaddeus's Episcopal church, where we sang the hymns and carols we knew and loved. Then home for a feast of glistening turkey with chestnut stuffing, cranberry sauce, rich brown gravy, Brussels sprouts, sweet potatoes topped with marshmallows. Finally, Herbert bore in the plum pudding, flaming on a silver platter, hot to the tongue against the cool, sweet hard sauce.

The servants, naturally, had been up since dawn on a day so special to us. They left their families to work even harder than usual, providing the wonders we expected and took for granted. Kitchen maids, stableboys, gardeners, cooks and chauffeurs, even proud, fat British Herbert worked on Christmas Day to make us comfortable and happy. After Christmas lunch, they were summoned to the living room where the family was gathered and shepherded by Herbert into a neat line. My parents went down the row, shaking hands, wishing *Merry Christmas*, handing each one an envelope and a present. The servants thanked us, they smiled, they wished us well (they seemed happy), and they left.

Without knowing exactly why, I felt embarrassed and ashamed. Something seemed wrong. I didn't understand it, but I must have sensed our condescension and patronage and felt humiliated on behalf of that formal row of smiling faces. Otherwise, my feelings about those Christmases were purely joyous. They signified a time of rare family closeness. Each of us had the same expectations, the same happiness, the same thankfulness and love.

*

Despite feeling ill at ease at times, I had no concept, then, of materialism as transgression. Even now, those Christmases remain pristine, enshrined in a bubble of joy. Trying

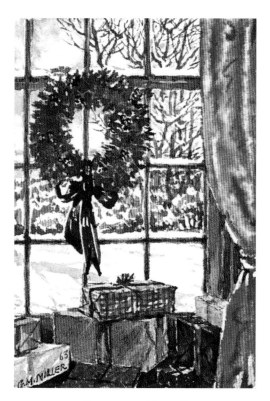

Christmas card by Cully

to reproduce them for my own children, I became aware of the excess, but that avalanche of gifts remains embedded in my concept of Christ's birthday. To separate the spiritual and material aspects of Christmas might have forced me to question the whole order of the class in which I lived. Later, I perpetuated these values in my own family, insisting on the same manners, dress codes, and propriety. Of course, that questioning is exactly what finally happened, thanks largely to my own children, who rebelled against customs they found antiquated. The closeness and respect we parents felt for our children eventually enabled us to hear them, and to modify our expectation that they'd be perfect little replicas of ourselves. We even came to realize that *we* weren't so perfect, after all.

In front of me today as I write is a card my father painted—a wreath with a red ribbon hanging in a window by a pile of gaily wrapped presents. Inside are words from Francie Train, a close friend and former sister-in-law, who found and sent me the card:

> I'll never forget those Christmases—so many beautifully wrapped presents that it was impossible to find a seat on any sofa or chair. Your Mum oohing over every piece of ribbon and taking forever to open things; and your father letting the wine breathe, and at lunch singing his famous H-u-huckle B-u- buckle Huckleberry Pie—and Cheffie's croquembouche or profiteroles and puree de marrons—and Hexie [the little dachshund] and Banco [the big brown poodle] in their red velvet bows. It was magic . . .

She's right. It was.

CHAPTER 8

Flin Flon · Old Westbury

In 1936, elections in Germany gave Hitler 99 percent of the vote. His troops occupied the Rhineland, and his Nazi Party passed the Nuremberg Laws against Jews. President Roosevelt was re-elected for a second term by a landslide, although not with my parents' vote—they were staunch Republicans. Nearly eight years old, I was more conscious of Alice Marble winning the women's singles at Forest Hills than I was of politics. I did notice grown-ups all around me reading *Gone with the Wind*. (Soon, with funding from cousins, including a little from my parents, it became the first Technicolor movie.) But I was not yet aware that the world was on the brink of war.

That summer, my parents took Pam, Whitty, Lev, and me to visit Flin Flon in the Canadian province of Manitoba, hoping to teach us a little about the copper mining business upon which we depended. We traveled on "Wanderer," my grandmother's (and her brothers' and sister's) private railroad car, owned by the family since the early days of the New York Central Railroad, which was also a family business. For a month or so, "Wanderer" became our home. I was thrilled to be traveling with my parents and my idolized older sister and brother, and to have them close to me all day. Lev and I were freer than we'd ever been. Instead of our daily baths,

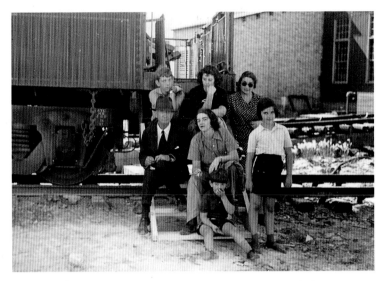

On steps of "Wanderer". BACK: *Whit, Pam, Miss Sligh.*
FRONT: *Mr Channing, head of Hudson Bay Mining and Smelting;*
my mother, Lev, and me, July 1937

we washed in the pull-down basin of our stateroom. Family-
style eating replaced segregated mealtimes. Once rigid time-
tables were now punctuated by unscheduled arrivals and
departures—our car was often shunted to a side track until
we hitched a ride on the next train headed northwest. We
shared a living room, dining room, and—best of all—a
raised deck on the back of the car from which we could
watch the towns and countryside rush past. Greasy, black
grains of coal smoke stuck to our skin, and we stayed happily grubby for days until we finally reached a bathtub in a
room rented for the day in a Flin Flon hotel. The black porters joked with us, and the meals, cooked by a chef with a
white hat in the tiny kitchen, were different from our fare
at home: fried chicken, mashed potatoes, sweet desserts.
There were Art Deco lamps and comfortable sofas and
chairs in the wood-paneled cars, monogrammed linens

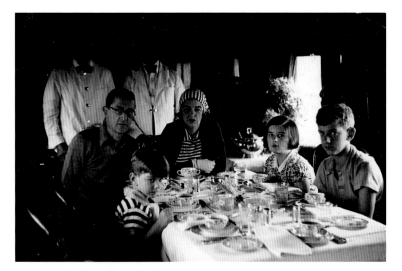

Lunch on "Wanderer;" Back: Randolph, Ike;
Around table: Lev, Cully, Flora, me, and Whit.

and silver, and a table for the games we often played. After brushing my teeth in the tiny basin, I'd climb the ladder to the upper bunk-bed with its little light, and green net for my clothes and my precious book. The porters would hand us down to earth when we pulled into a station to stretch our legs and run around until the whistle summoned us back—all this was a thrilling contrast to our regulated lives in Aiken.

At first, I saw horses and cattle grazing in fields, but the farther north we sped, the more lakes there were, ringed by dark evergreens, flashing in the sunlight. Winnipeg, the capital of Manitoba, was the first real city we saw—it didn't look big compared to New York. The engineer explained that we'd head northwest from Winnipeg for 740 kilometers to the border of Saskatchewan. I liked to roll the unfamiliar names on my tongue.

In Flin Flon, a Precambrian volcanic belt, formed 1.9 billion years earlier, was the source of vast mineral deposits, primarily zinc, copper, silver, and gold. Hudson Bay Mining and Smelting had developed Flin Flon into a thriving community, with mining the heart of the local economy. We were introduced to the head of Hudson Bay, Mr. Channing, who gave us a tour. Going in an open elevator into the mine was frightening. Surrounded by big gruff men who always seemed to be shouting, we left the bright sunshine for profound darkness. I felt dizzy and queasy until the miners lent us some helmets with lights. Walking through damp

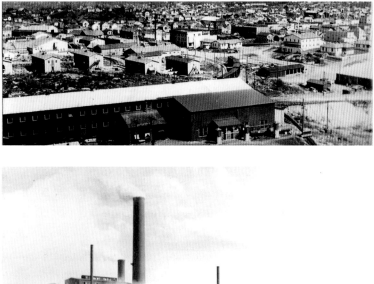

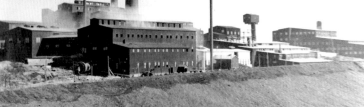

Smelter, Flin Flon

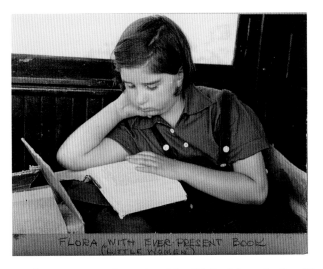

FLORA WITH EVER-PRESENT BOOK (LITTLE WOMEN)

Reading Little Women *on a boat trip to Island Falls, eighty miles from Flin Flon*

tunnels where men chipped at the dark walls, we passed the cars on narrow tracks that carried the copper ore to the smelter up top. Although glad for the experience, it was a relief to be once again in bright daylight. I knew about poor mine ponies from the books I'd read, and it made me feel even sadder for the men.

One day, we traveled across a lake to the miners' recreation camp to have a picnic and to fish. On the long boat ride, I was once again the only one with a book: *Little Women*. Mum and Pam wished loudly and often that I'd hurry up and finish it so that they could read it. It was rare for me to have something they wanted—I felt newly important.

On the return trip to New York, after steaming our way through Saskatoon, we stopped at a huge hotel in Banff, Alberta. First love struck hard in the person of Bill Matthews, a cowboy who took us around the lake and into the mountains, surprised to find that we actually knew how to ride. His flashing smile, his English accent, his leather chaps with silver trimmings, the way he sat his palomino horse when it bucked, his kindness—all enchanted me, and I urged my piebald pony to greater speed and liveliness in the hope of impressing Bill with my skill and daring. Pam, a vivacious fifteen-year-old, was extremely popular, enthralling a horde of young men who clustered around her. When we left, a number of cowboys and scarlet-coated Mounties came to see her off, galloping after Wanderer, yodeling, singing, and firing their guns into the air.

My parents liked to tell the story of coming that evening to kiss me goodnight, when I wailed, inconsolable, "Oh, dear, when I wake up, he won't be here any more!" For years I kept Bill's photo by my bed, determined to become a cowboy like him, eating up romantic books about horses and cowboys.

*

When we returned, we spent a few days at our house in Long Island. My great-grandfather, William C. Whitney, had bought a large tract of land in Old Westbury, where the architect Stanford White had designed a house for him and his family on a hill overlooking the fields where his horses grazed. White also designed a tower to provide water for the buildings on the property and stables for a hundred horses—polo ponies, thoroughbreds, and trotters for racing; horses trained for driving; hunters; ponies for children; and huge work horses to plough and harrow fields. Their roomy box stalls were carpeted with thick straw, and an engraved nameplate of shiny brass was fastened over each stall. Carriages of all shapes and sizes, cleaned and polished, stood ready for a summons from a family member or guest. The tack rooms had mahogany boxes filled with blankets,

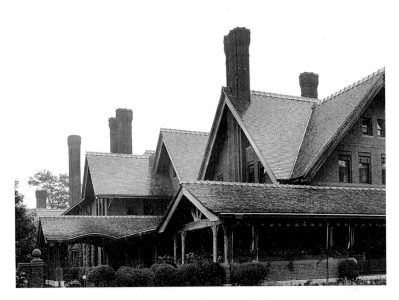

William C. Whitney's house in Old Westbury

and their walls were hung with dozens of bridles, saddles, harnesses, halters, and crops; there was a sink with running water, and shelves holding chamois for polishing, as well as scrapers, brushes, and currycombs. An indoor exercise ring encircled the whole space, and on the second floor were the bedrooms for the grooms and stable boys. As always, there were the enticing smells of horses, hay, bran mash, saddle soap, and wax for the tack, as well as the captivating sounds of horses nickering as they were rubbed down, blowing through their noses and stamping their feet impatiently.

Down the hill there was a blacksmith's shop, equipped with anvil and forge, where the burly Patrick stood over a blazing coal fire, heating iron for horseshoes. Since the hoof is constantly growing and changing its form, all shod feet were overgrown in four to five weeks. The blacksmith had to reduce the hoof to proper proportions by paring away the outer horn before shaping and hammering on new shoes. Our dogs liked to chew those hard bony scraps of old hoof—the tasty parings were rich in calcium.

Well-trained farriers were in great demand. Patrick was a member of an ancient guild, the Worshipful Company of Farriers. He was good-humored, allowing us to collect the extra nails and the shoes tossed to the ground that brought good luck. We kept the shoes upside down to retain their magic. Sometimes when he had a moment, Patrick talked with us. Few people, he said, were aware of the terrible results of neglecting the horse. Napoleon, for example, retreating with his army from Moscow, had horses that weren't properly shod. The horses could no longer drag the heavy guns and wagons, and artillery was abandoned. Horses and soldiers suffered terribly.

When William's son, Harry Payne Whitney, inherited the Old Westbury estate, he built lawn tennis courts and a big swimming pool near the house, a building for offices and a bowling alley, as well as a winter sports structure with an indoor tennis court, swimming pool, changing rooms with showers, and a large room with comfortable sofas and chairs for eating, drinking, or watching a tennis match. This complex was run by an officious man (also named Harry) who scared us when we tried to swim, or play tennis, or just hang out in his immaculate spaces. He either hated children or was himself terrified of his boss—my grandfather's moods were unpredictable, and sometimes violent, depending in part on how much he'd had to drink.

A ten-minute walk in the opposite direction from the main house, Harry's wife, my grandmother Gertrude Vanderbilt, had a beautiful marble studio designed by

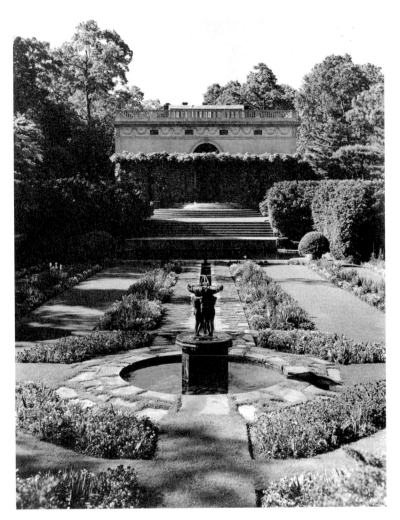

My grandmother's studio, Old Westbury, c. 1913

William Adams Delano (my sister Pam lives there now). Gertrude's friend, Rawlins Cottenet, had designed an Italian garden with a pebbled pool, and water channels running through the brilliant flower beds. Arthur Lee, an artist, described his visit there just after it was finished in a 1914 letter to Gertrude:

O what a god-like place or should I say goddess? The studio as splendid as a temple and the garden O glorious . . . As soon as I saw the strangely dull blue pool I ran back to the enchanted house and stript and I dove in . . . I danced around your lawn like a faun in a fine frenzy and frightened your queer gray blue silk colored birds who fled awkwardly out of my way . . .

When their children grew up and married, Harry and Gertrude gave their house to their son, Cornelius, and built a somewhat smaller house for themselves nearby, along with two houses for their daughters. My mother's house, known as the French House, was also designed by Delano. It was very pretty, with a round tower, a cobblestone driveway, and old chestnut trees. I never felt settled in Old Westbury, perhaps because we didn't spend enough time there to make friends. Later, during World War II, when we did live there, we could not drive because of gas rationing and so were restricted to our own enclave.

CHAPTER 9

The Adirondacks &
Louis Duane

Although Long Island never felt like home, it was different in the Adirondack Mountains of northern New York. As children, and then as adults with our own children, the mountains gave us the great gift of time and space. And the mountains gave us the luxury of freedom. In the summer peace and beauty of the mountains, in pouring rain (it sometimes rained for a solid week) and brilliant sunshine, generations of my family took solace in the dark lakes and forests.

William C. Whitney, my great-grandfather and the designer of Joye Cottage, had also built the compound in the Adirondacks. By the late nineteenth-century, this man with an infallible eye for beauty—whether for land, architecture, art, horses, or women—acquired one hundred thousand acres of forests and lakes adjoining New York State's Adirondack Park. Created in 1892, with six million mountainous acres and thousands of lakes, the Adirondack Park was bigger than the state of New Hampshire. The logging that would pay for Whitney Park's upkeep and taxes was regulated under guidelines written by Gifford Pinchot, newly appointed by Theodore Roosevelt to be the first Chief of the Bureau of Forestry of the United States Department of Agriculture. Pinchot, who was also Governor of Pennsylvania from 1923–1927 and 1931–1935, was the author of the Bureau's visionary policies, aimed at saving the magnificent forests from the unregulated development that already threatened their survival. He coined the term "conservation ethic" as applied to natural resources, and supervised Whitney's project himself, using principles of good forestry that were followed for many years, until the spread of corporate policies such as the clear-cutting of forests. I still remember the manager of the Whitney Realty Company, as my uncle Sonny called his logging business, explaining some of the rules to me: the largest trees in a given area were marked and cut, after which that section was left untouched for thirty years. Only then would big trees again be cut. Around the lakes, Whitney ordered stands of majestic white pines to be preserved, the wind hissing through their long needles.

For his family, William C. Whitney built modest but spacious camps on the shores of Big and Little Forked Lakes, Little Tupper Lake, and Salmon Lake. These simple but elegant houses were made of logs or boards cut in the sawmill on the property. Designed for summer living, they had wide porches and big stone fireplaces. Few bathrooms were needed—the lake sufficed for bathing, and the plumbing was primitive. Several small cabins and big white tents on platforms were for family and the many guests who came to visit. Three-sided lean-tos made of fat logs, with soft balsam boughs over earth floors, were erected at more distant lakes for picnics, fishing, and overnight camping. White floats and sailboats were moored near boathouses filled with slim varnished guide boats and their fitted oars; green canoes with a variety of paddles for all ages; and the putt-putts in which my older siblings, cousins, and their friends loved to make shavers. They would throttle the old Johnson or Evinrude engines to their utmost speed, whizzing alongside

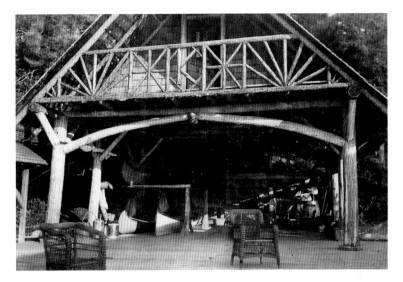

The boathouse at Camp Killoquah, c. 1935

terrified swimmers, and nearly swamping rowers or canoers as they zoomed perilously around the lake. Camps and land were available free to those of us who came every summer, until, with my generation, we had to sell our share of the property to pay taxes on my mother's estate, and my uncle Sonny and his wife began to charge rent.

Togus, a sprawling complex of mustard-brown buildings placed high above Forked Lake, included a boathouse, a tent, and two log cabins close to the lake with small structures behind the main house for ice, laundry, a primitive generator, and several servants. The butler had his own cabin, where he nightly took the table silver and hid it under his bed. He wore formal clothes in contrast to the rugged look his employers adopted in the Ads. There was also a clay tennis court, and a tiny cabin up the hill where my father retired to paint. The main house was horseshoe-shaped with screened porches at each end where on fine

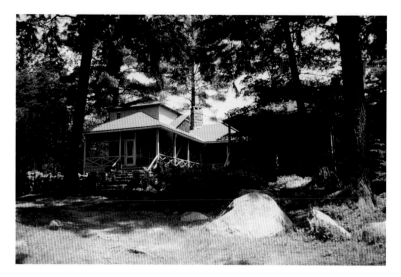

Camp Togus, c. 1990

evenings fierce games of bezique, canasta, or checkers were played. On the outside porch, ping-pong paddles clacked, accompanied by howls and shrieks. Adirondack chairs sat on the grass between the two wings. Facing the lake, one could watch the sunset behind Niggerhead Mountain, as it was then shockingly called. (I've tried to discover its current name, but apparently it's not enough of a mountain to have an official designation, and any remaining family there have become estranged from us.) There's an evocative painting of that scene by my cousin Macauley Conner in Camp Deerlands on Little Forked Lake where Uncle Sonny lived, and where his widow and her husband live today.

Inside the Togus main house were the big dining room and living room, a pantry and kitchen that we rarely visited, and three bedrooms where Lev and I lived with our nurse. The big bathroom had been painted by one of the Straights— our cousins from England—and depicted members of their

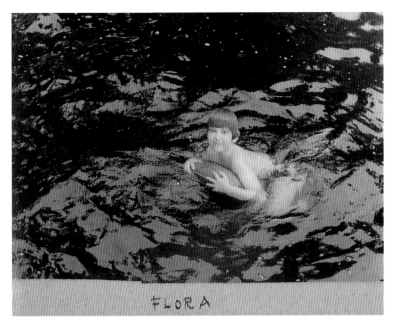

FLORA

Swimming in Forked Lake, c 1934

family: Leonard Elmhirst, in an upside-down L, bending over the water with his fishing rod; his wife Auntie Dorothy, my grandfather Harry's sister, in a blue-and-white-striped dress with a bucket of blueberries; Ruth and Bill, their two young children, in their English sunbonnets and bathing suits; and Beatrice Straight, Dorothy's daughter with her first husband Willard, who died in the influenza epidemic of 1919. Beatrice was already an accomplished actress, with glowing pink cheeks and a cloud of auburn hair, reclining in her chaise-longue in a mauve silk dressing gown. Orange and purple fish swam through seaweed under the blue waves. As the big tub in that bathroom was the only one in camp, it was in great demand, although the children's great delight was to bathe in the lake. We even washed our hair

[147]

in the lake, ducking far below the surface to find water cold enough to rinse the suds.

The bedrooms were painted blue, yellow, and green. Each had twin beds and dressers, and a pair of wooden chairs. The rooms were very plain. The living room, 20 feet by 60, was packed with sofas and armchairs. There were tables for games, fly-tying, and reel and line mending—one table was always dedicated to a wooden jigsaw puzzle. A coat-tree by the door to the porch was overcrowded with jackets, fishing equipment, rain gear, and all manner of hats. A stuffed black bear stood in a corner, and near the huge stone fireplace sat a wooden platform with a quilt-covered mattress where we would play Monopoly, or talk, or sleep during a particularly violent storm. With no heating system but the fires, it could get cold in the tents or even in the rooms with smaller fireplaces, and a storm could be frightening in the Ads—the woods might be set on fire, or a camp struck by lightning. I saw this happen once, and it was terrifying—a huge pine tree exploded near a window as we were playing charades after dinner. There was a wild crashing and a scream of wind as razor-sharp pieces of wood hurtled through the living room. The electric sockets melted. By great good luck, no one was hurt. The next day, I saw large shards of the tree impaled in stronger trees a quarter of a mile away, and thrust into the earth to a depth of several feet.

Louis Duane stands out from the other men that I cared for as a child. My fists could have fitted into the hollows under his cheekbones, my fingertip into the dimple in his chin. A brown fedora hat sat atop his high forehead, shadowing the deep sockets of his dark eyes. Smile lines radiated from his eyes and bracketed his mouth. Although his expression was watchful and serious, he had the kindest

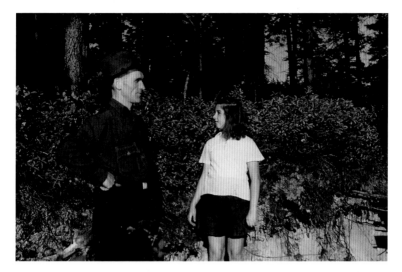

With Louis Duane, 1939

face I knew. From afar, I could recognize his muscular lean body in the familiar dark green plaid shirt and khaki pants. He wasn't tall or short, but just right. Striding through the woods, his pace was just right, too—neither fast nor slow. He melded into the Adirondack woods, flowing through them lightly, observing everything and altering nothing.

Lou, as I called him, was wise, laconic, funny. I wanted to be with him every minute. He worked as a guide. It was an honorable profession in that sparsely inhabited land, requiring expert knowledge of lakes and forests. The Adirondack Guides Association was formed in 1892 to ensure the competence of the woodsmen and to guarantee the guides a minimum wage. I understand now that my parents gave Louis the responsibility of teaching Lev and me, far from our normal comforts and routines, to know and respect the mountainous, watery land, and to understand its ecological fragility.

Lou worked for my uncle, Cornelius, walking the forests and scaling (the woodsman name for measuring) the trees to determine which were big enough to be cut and transported to our sawmill, and marking them carefully. We learned the difference between softwoods (mostly evergreen conifers with needles, like hemlock, spruce, and pine) and hardwoods (broadleaved, dormant in winter, like oak, maple, birch, and beech.) We learned to recognize which tree had good sap we could slice off the bark with our fishing knives and chew (spruce), and which had the best smelling and softest branches to cut for a bed (balsam).

When I was about eight, I went with my parents to visit the lumbering operation. I remember being held up to the lumberjacks' enormous Clydesdale and Percheron horses, stroking their velvet noses as they softly nickered. The men felled great trees with two-handed saws, and I was amazed when, crashing through the undergrowth, flinging twigs

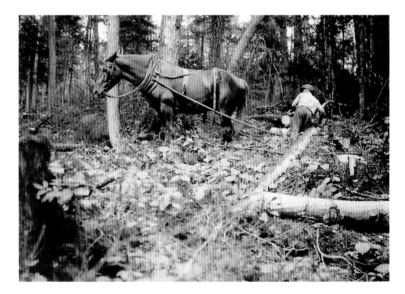

Logging in Whitney Park, c. 1936

and leaves explosively, the trees landed exactly where the men intended them to fall. The men shouted at their teams, "Haw, Gee," as the powerful beasts strained to move the massive timbers. Man and horse were intimately connected through words, gestures, and unspoken urgency.

At the sawmill, there was a clinging, acrid smell, and the piercing whine of logs as they slid under the spinning blades to emerge as boards. Sweet-smelling sawdust was piled as high as a roof. The manager showed us little wooden spoons made by the Ovalwood Dish Company in neighboring Tupper Lake, made with wood unsuitable for building. His thick-furred huskies were like wolves, straining at their leashes as he described sledding with them in winter.

The summer guides sawed great blocks of ice from the frozen lakes each winter and stored them, layering them with sawdust from the mill, in the icehouses at each of the ten or so summer camps. Twelve-inch-thick rectangles, at least two by four feet, they must have weighed one hundred pounds. The chore-boy, who cut kindling, carried wood, built fires, and scrubbed pots would go to the ice-house to chop big hunks of ice, lugging them in a canvas sling the hundred yards to the house. He'd fit them into coolers, as we called the iceboxes, in the kitchen and pantry. With a sharp metal ice pick, the butler and maids slivered smaller chunks for the silver ice bucket they brought to the living room before meals. That ice was colder and harder than any other; little pieces of it were delicious treats on a boiling hot day. Evenings, my father would chop the ice into even smaller pieces, and drop them into his silver cocktail shaker to make the perfect martini for my mother and their guests.

The ice kept all summer. If I raised the heavy iron latch of the ice house to swing open the massive door, a pungent cold tickled my nose, not unlike the smoke from pine logs burning in the big stone fireplaces, clinging to my clothes and body until I ran back into the hot sun to grow warm again.

Louis and the others maintained the dozens of trails, repaired damage to the camps and boathouses from the fierce winter storms, and cleaned, painted, and varnished our canoes, guideboats, motorboats, and small sailboats. They replaced the shingles clawed from the walls by bears seeking food (especially sugar) in early spring. They checked the plumbing, lamps, and, after World War II, generators and electric wiring. (Until then, camps had been lit by kerosene lamps, and some remained so even after the War.) Their wives opened and closed the camps, cleaning and polishing, but we rarely saw these women. If by chance they were still working when we arrived, we didn't learn their names, or thank them for all of their hard work. We took it for granted that the camps would be spic and span, our beds made, everything in place. Of these women, I don't remember a single individual. This kind of work was of no interest to us, unlike that of the guides and woodsmen we loved. I'm not sure this shameful attitude has entirely changed.

Starting when I was seven, Lou took me fishing in Plumley Pond, a fifteen-minute walk from our camp, Togus. He maneuvered the golden guideboat from its rudimentary housing and pushed it along the ground into the lake. These special boats, designed in the 1880s, are noted for their maximum flexibility and ease of motion. Like many things designed primarily for utility, they are also works of art. Elegant, fast, and graceful, they're double-ended, with cedar planking, and ribs of spruce. Shiny copper nailheads bejewel exterior and interior. There was just enough

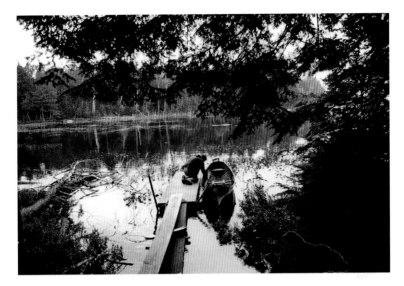

Plumley Pond

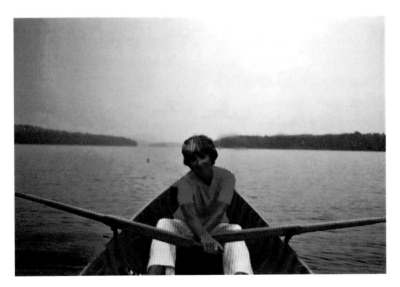

Rowing a guideboat, 1976

room for the guide, his sport (as his client was called), their camping and hunting equipment, and a dog, with space left for a deer. *A Stradivarius of a boat*, said an anonymous nineteenth-century writer, *that soothes the soul and delights the spirit.* Henry Van Dyke describes one of the boats:

> A Saranac boat is one of the finest things that the skill of man has ever produced under the inspiration of the wilderness. It is a frail shell, so light that a guide can carry it on his shoulders with ease, but so dexterously fashioned that it rides the heaviest waves like a duck, and slips through the water as if by magic. You can travel in it along the shallowest rivers and across the broadest lakes, and make forty or fifty miles a day, if you have a good guide.

To me, though, it was just a means to fish with my hero. Slowly, carefully, I stepped into the precarious boat and sat on the cane seat in the bow. Lou sat in the middle, facing me, and fit the oars into the brass oarlocks. He rowed backwards up the lake, steadily, rhythmically, his workboots pressed against the curved ribs of the slender, varnished boat, alternating strokes of the oars hand over hand. Removing a squeaky oar, he dipped it in the lake. He was the first to speak. "Be ready, now, Flora," he said quietly. "Here's a good place—come on, come on, fish-ee," and, sure enough, my rod bent double. I set the hook, as he had taught me, jerking it hard against the pull of the fish. "Raise the tip now, keep it up—don't give him any slack—that's right, Flora, just reel in slowly when he lets you. Don't try and hold him if he wants to run. Give him a bit of line now, that's right—he's a keeper—look at him jump! Keep the tip up—whoops, there he goes. Well, he'll be bigger next year. Come on now, we'll catch another just around that point. Hard to hold them when they jump that way."

[154] ·

Tears of disappointment and shame spilled over my cheeks. I'd already savored the excitement of landing the fish and bearing it proudly home to the praise of Whitty, Pam, Mummy, and Daddy, to whom catching a sizeable fish was an achievement to celebrate, a measure of skill and maturity like riding over high fences or shooting well. After all, it was one of the few ways I could become like my models and heroes. I felt it was my fault the big fish got away. Louis, however, refused to acknowledge my distress. After checking my line for knots, and my lure for bits of fish that might spoil the realistic look of the translucent plastic minnow, he rowed calmly onward. Pursing his lips, he whistled a rather mournful melody.

"We'll whistle one up. Come on, Flora—"

"I can't seem to whistle, Louis."

"Well, let's wet your whistle. See what that does for it."

He dipped water out of the lake in a tin cup, handing it the length of the boat to me. After drinking thirstily, I managed a feeble rendition of "Whistle While You Work" from *Snow White and the Seven Dwarves*, the new Walt Disney movie my little brother and I were not allowed to see because of the presence of germs in the movie theatres. There was a fear that polio could be contracted in public places. We didn't believe in the germ theory. It was just plain meanness. Louis would have let us go to the movies.

The wind began to blow, and Lou put on his green and black checked lumber shirt.

"What's it like here in the winter?" I asked.

"Real cold. The ice gets so thick, you can drive to camp in a truck."

"I'd like to see that," I said. "I've never seen snow. Does anyone fall through the ice?"

"Once in a while. A few years ago, Don and I were checking our beaver traps up in Charley Pond stream—it was a warm day for March—and as we came near the head of the lake we heard a crack, then saw the black of the water. Our truck was starting to sink, and all we could do was get out the doors."

I shuddered, horrified, but excited.

"We managed to haul ourselves onto stronger ice. There we were, five miles from the nearest house, the water freezing right on us."

"But how did you get back? Why didn't you freeze to death?"

"Well now, Flora, we were lucky. We walked fast to keep the blood moving through us, just like Doc says—remember? We hadn't forgotten our matches, but they'd gotten wet so we couldn't light a fire. We walked and walked. After an hour or so, we got to Headquarters. We were sure glad to be where it was warm. Folks there were mighty surprised to see us."

Louis put more effort into rowing, grunting as he pulled hard against the rising wind. Clouds were threatening rain, so we headed for the nearby dock which always smelled of fish. "Let's try some garden hackle on the way home," he said, reaching under his seat for the old Maxwell House coffee can of worms. Although we never admitted to using such cheaters, they were sure-fire if we wanted fish for dinner. Just as we reached the first lilypads, shallow water indicating that it was time to reel in, my rod jerked again, and I struck the fish with all my might. Reeling in carefully, keeping the tip up, giving the fish line when he wanted to run, I finally brought him close enough to glimpse him as he struggled to swim under the boat. A beauty, a pound and a half at least, iridescent scales gleaming. His mouth was full of sharp teeth. Lou scooped him into his long-handled net and hit the head of the fish smartly with his headache stick, tossing him under his seat. We clambered out at the dock, pulled the boat onto the bank, and lifted it into the shed. Louis knelt by the lake, slitting the soft underbelly of the bass, showing me how to cut between the head and the gills and then pull the innards out all at once. If I wanted to catch fish, I had to learn the hateful process of cleaning them. Louis opened the stomach to see what the fish had been eating. He found several tiny minnows.

"Cannibals," he said with a smile.

"That's disgusting."

"They have to eat. Anyway, Flora, your 'he' is a 'she.'"

A mass of orange eggs spilled from the cavity. I looked away, anxious, alarmed by the glistening flow. I wasn't sure why I couldn't look at it.

"Only about one in a thousand eggs survives," Louis said. He rinsed the fish in the pale caramel-colored lake water, cut a branch from a sapling, hooked the fish's mouth over it, and handed me my prize. I followed his long steady strides along the mossy trail and before long the brown wooden outbuildings of Camp Togus were in sight.

"Mummy, Daddy, look what I caught!"

The group in the screened-in porch looked up at us. My parents stopped their game of canasta and exclaimed at the size and beauty of my bass. Even Pam, playing checkers with her latest beau while "Frankie and Johnnie" blasted on the Victrola, and Whitty, in a wild game of ping-pong with the doctor's sons from across the lake, had to admit that it was a fine catch.

That night, voices and the roar of a motorboat woke me briefly. In the morning, I asked to go fishing again with

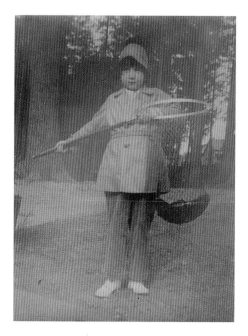

My first bass, c 1934

Louis, and my mother told me that he'd become sick in the night. He'd been taken to the hospital across the lake, forty miles away.

"I'm sure he didn't want to tell you, darling," my mother said, "but he had a pain in his tummy while you were fishing."

Louis turned out to have acute appendicitis. The doctor had caught it just before his appendix ruptured. He'd said nothing all that afternoon, as the wind rose and my rod bent. Louis was the person I dreamed of all winter in South Carolina when I thought of the Adirondacks. Miss Sligh was leaving for her annual vacation in England that day, to be replaced by Jeanne, a delightful young woman who loved to laugh and play with us, but Louis was my hero. He was all that I loved about the summer.

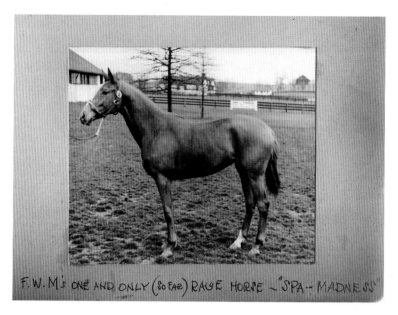

F. W. M.'s ONE AND ONLY (SO FAR) RACE HORSE – "SPA – MADNESS"

Spa Madness

"When will Louis come back?"

"Two weeks, maybe three," my mother replied. "Your father and I will see him on our way to Saratoga. We'll tell you about him when we return."

"Oh. Do you have to go to Saratoga?"

"Yes, darling. Uncle Sonny thinks his horse will win the Travers, and my lovely Spa Madness is running the same day. We can't miss that! Next year we'll take you; maybe by then you won't get carsick."

I knew how much Mum loved Spa Madness. Her only race horse, she was a beautiful chestnut mare. So we waved them goodbye at the dock, watching old Charlie Avery back the gleaming mahogany Pickerel out of the boathouse. Turning it slowly, he headed into the wind, throttling down its powerful engine so as not to splash his passengers who had left their khakis and faded cotton shirts in camp. Adorned in bright silk and linen, their finery instantly lifted them from our midst and removed them to some unimaginable gaiety where they mingled and chatted with the snappy racetrack crowd, raising their German binoculars in unison to watch their horses gallop across the finish line. I felt even more forlorn than I usually did when my mother went away.

"What's the matter, Flora, I've never seen you lose your appetite before." Whitty held his stomach, making fun of me for being fat. Hand to mouth, I ran from the table, barely making it to the bathroom. I threw up violently. Lying in bed, sick and miserable, I remembered the afternoon's planned visit to our grandmother at Killoquah, the neighboring camp. She was writing a play and hardly ever invited us to the houseboat anchored in the lake where she worked every day. But that day we were to dive from its high white prow, and feast on delicious iced cocoa and buttery cookies with her. There might even be time for the special game she played with me in which we folded papers to invent stories and fabulous creatures. I was determined to recover, but instead I was repeatedly nauseated, developing a violent pain in my abdomen. Doctor Bergamini across the lake was summoned by Whitty in his putt-putt, the primitive phone in the pantry having failed. Doc poked and prodded, and his face grew serious.

"We must take a little ride, Flora. Let's get you dressed."

The pain had taken over, and I didn't care about anything. I was bundled into a boat, then into the ancient taxi belonging to Okie Helms, a man fascinating to us because of the hook that replaced a hand blown off in World War I. He used the hook with delicate and wondrous skill to fill our gas tanks, and to drive. Even the prospect of a night drive

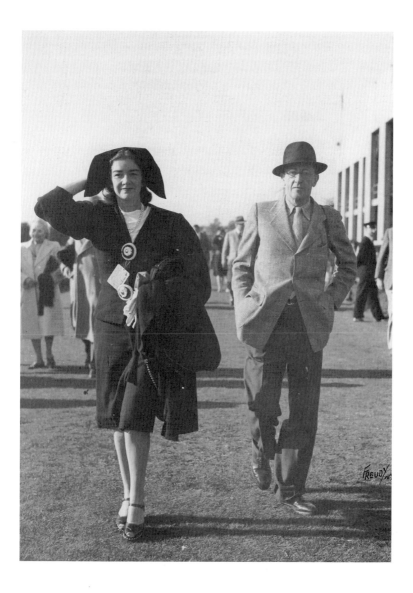

My parents at the races in Saratoga, 1937

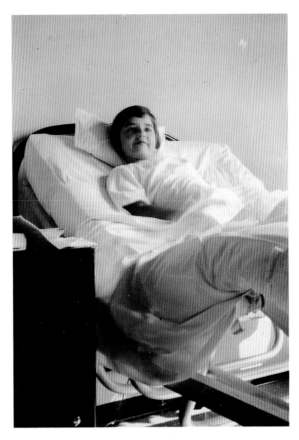

In the hospital, 1936

with Okie couldn't alleviate the pain. We bumped along the dirt road and slid around endless curves. Finally, at Mercy General Hospital in Tupper Lake, I was handed over to gentle, capable nuns. I awoke the next morning, adhesive tape tightly strapping my belly, an agonizing laceration beneath it. I felt even sicker than the day before. Only after a few days did I feel well enough to notice the airy plant-filled room and the heavenly singing. I'd been put in the conservatory, next to the chapel where the nuns held their services, as there'd been no other empty room. It seems that

I'd almost died of a ruptured appendix. Doc saved it in a jar for me, a horrid wormy-looking object, assuring me that I could charge at least twenty-five cents a look. My family was astonished that I'd managed to join Louis in the hospital the day after his own emergency operation, and with the very same ailment. As soon as it was permissable, my greatest joy was to visit or be visited by my hero. We talked about the next fishing trip to Plumley. We talked about our scars, and compared our journeys in the middle of the night to the hospital. I gave him a free view of the jar with my appendix. Something special had happened to us, linking us forever.

*

Although I wouldn't have put it this way at the time, Louis epitomized goodness to me. I see now that he'd worked out for himself how to be in the world. He had infinite patience with adults as well as children. Never a cross word, never a spiteful comment about anyone; only kindness and good cheer. He was never boring, his sense of humor always bubbling below the surface. He shared all he had. In his generosity, he passed on knowledge and decency to those he touched. His life of simplicity contrasted profoundly with the life of my family. Ever since those days, my own ideal of how to be in the world harks back to Lou. Not that I've lived up to it—but Lou's influence has seeped into me. He created the standard by which I will always measure myself.

I recognize that although Louis cared for me, I existed in only a tiny part of his life. When he invited me to his little house in the village of Long Lake, his wife welcomed me warmly with a chiffon cake with coconut icing that she'd baked. I can hardly bring her into focus, so intent was I on

Lou. I felt shy and uncomfortable. How seldom had I visited a modest home, and how far it was from the world I knew, a world where Lou seemed equally at ease. Guilt and teenage awkwardness made me wish to cut short my visit. They had no children, but I recall meeting Mrs. Duane's brother and his wife. For a few years, until she died, I corresponded as an adult with their nephew's wife, Clara Otis, who lived near the Canadian border. We exchanged news of our grandchildren and the weather, and she described her memories of her visits to Whitney Park, and of Louis. She sent me a photograph of him. Still, Lou's life away from our summers in the woods, on the lakes and streams, remains pale and unreal. It was only when August came that he sprang into being for me, filling me with happiness.

The last time that I saw him, it was icy winter in Long Lake and he was lying in church in a simple coffin. He looked at peace. I knew he had been treated badly by my Uncle Sonny, who owned the largest share of Whitney Industries, as it was then called. Louis hadn't been properly rewarded for his years of service to the company, and my family hadn't been able to change my uncle's decisions about Louis and the others who'd worked for us. I still regret my powerlessness and my lack of bravery in confronting injustice. I'm reminded of other times when I haven't spoken up strongly enough for what I believed to be right.

Louis would have done it.

For example: In the nineteen fifties and sixties, my family and I lived in New Canaan, Connecticut, a small town with many commuters, many of them politically conservative. Policy decisions were made at town meetings. I could have been a part of these, could have spoken up on issues with the small group of liberals whose views I shared. We were opposed to building nuclear shelters, because their very existence implied that nuclear war was a possibility; for the same reason and also because of the pollution of grazing lands from its by-product, Strontium 90, we were against testing nuclear weapons; we were against racial segregation and the Vietnam war; and we were in favor of building more low-income housing in our town. I convinced myself that I needed to stay home with the children; that I was shy and inarticulate—in effect, powerless. I see now that I could have taken more responsibility as a citizen, and as a woman representing a once-prominent family. It took me too long to accept that responsibility.

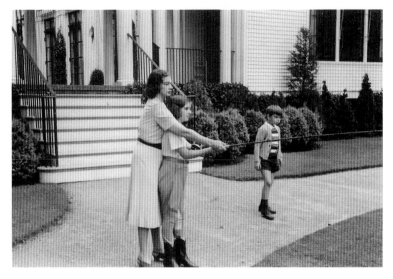

My mother teaching Lev and me to fly cast, at Gertrude's house in Newport, 1938

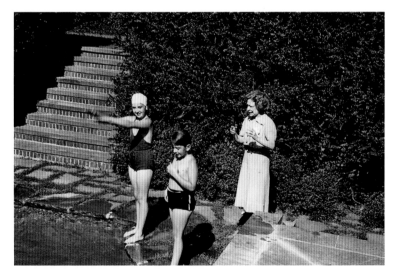

Juliana Force teaching us to dive, Gertrude's studio, Old Westbury, c. 1938

CHAPTER 10

Newport

Of long-gone family luxury, I keep many memories. Traveling in one's own railroad car was more than the equivalent of having a private plane today—more space, more comfort. Trains are slower, but the gift of time is the height of opulence. The tranquil pace of our lives seemed normal to me then.

Another memory of opulence is The Breakers. In 1938, our family spent part of the summer in Newport, at my grandmother Gertrude Vanderbilt Whitney's white clapboard house, a distance from her sister's grand cottage, while Whitty took summer classes at St. George's Preparatory School. Gamoo, as we called our grandmother, was only present in her sculpture. Her studio, perched by the ocean at the foot of the lawn, intrigued us with its wire armatures and the oily, earthy smell of the plasticene she used. I sometimes visited Gamoo in her Long Island studio, an elegant classical building with exotic birds wandering through the Italian gardens. One hot summer's day, Juliana Force, director of the Whitney Museum of American Art, taught us to dive in the blue pool. I remember enormous clay jars along a gravel path, like those in *A Thousand and One Nights*, where djinns crouched in hiding. I remember, too, the game Gamoo played with me, a Surrealist game where you drew part of a figure on a folded piece of paper, then passed the paper on to the next player, who continued the drawing and passed it on in turn. Later, she taught me to do this in writing: where and when they met, what he said, what she said, what they did, and, not least of all, what the moon said—it was a spine-tingling game. I was enchanted by my grandmother with her beautiful clothes, alluring scent, and husky voice.

In Newport, that summer of 1938, I was included in a formal lunch at The Breakers. The house, built by my great-grandparents, now belonged to Gamoo's sister, my great-aunt Gladys Vanderbilt Szechenyi. I was very shy. In the gloomy dining room, swallowed by a huge tapestried armchair, I was mystified by the many utensils and glasses at my place. The monogrammed linen napkin was as big as a pillowcase, and the fingerbowls had little blossoms floating in them like tropical fish. A liveried footman stood behind every chair, and, even though mine winked at me, their stiffness made me uneasy. I was awed by Auntie Gladys, dressed in immaculate white at the head of the table with an inscrutable, severe expression. I learned later that she thought it wrong to acknowledge weakness, and, despite her terrible eyesight, refused to wear glasses in public. She could hardly see me.

At the front door was a tall Chinese vase full of canes. When I lifted one to look at it, a footman took it from me and unscrewed the top, drawing out the long sharp sword hidden inside. My grandparents had bought it on their honeymoon in Japan, he said. I remember that more clearly than I do all the rooms and their furnishings.

The hurricane of 1938, still remembered for being the most destructive ever, marked a turning point in my childhood. Until that summer, I'd taken it for granted that my world was safe. On my tenth birthday, the 21st of September, I was sitting in the ballroom of that seaside house, posing

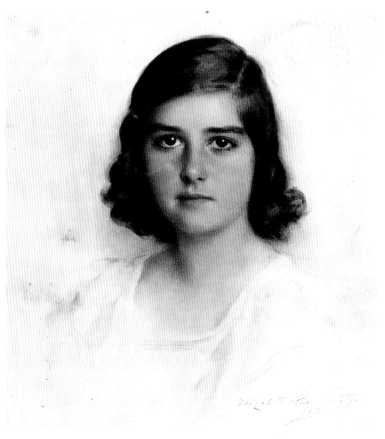

Me in a watercolor by Madame Shoumatoff, 1938

for a watercolor by Madame Shoumatoff, a Russian artist who would later be painting President Roosevelt at the time he died. The wind was rising fast and so was the sea, and a huge tree suddenly fell through the roof at the other end of the ballroom. I was frightened, but I was excited, too. Lev was upstairs, ordered away from the windows, but he sneaked over for a look, just in time to see Gamoo's studio lift from its rocky foundation and fly out to sea with all its contents. That *was* terrifying. (He lives now in the heart of hurricane country, in Florida, and still thinks of that long-ago storm as the worst he ever experienced.) Madame Shoumatoff and the maids were hysterical. My parents were extremely worried because Pam and Whitty were driving from Providence across the bridge to Newport, but we all survived—our only casualties, other than the roof and windows, were Gamoo's sculptures and the club building at Bailey's Beach that my father had designed. The fear and helplessness I sensed in the adults, though, were something new in my young life. My parents, whose omnipotence I'd always trusted, had been powerless when faced by this natural disaster. Perhaps the hurricane prepared me for the greater disaster that would begin the following year.

In Aiken, fifth grade was harder than the previous year, but I liked the challenge, especially reading. Across from my bed was a massive desk surrounded by shelves. There were my companions: the Oz series, Will James's cowboy tales, *The Bobbsey Twins, Robin Hood, King Arthur, The Deerslayer, Treasure Island, The White Company*, along with several Dickens novels. These books, many illustrated by Arthur Rackham, served to offset the goodness and mercy in the Collects and Psalms I learned from the Episcopalian Prayer Book. (I didn't learn about Job or Cain or other Old Testament cruelty and violence until later.) Put to bed before I was sleepy, I hid the books under the covers and read in the gloom—a forbidden delight. I began to understand that bad was just as real as good. The Wicked Witch of the West and Long John Silver were just as true as Jo and Beth and Maid Marion. Like most children, I was fascinated by the element of cruelty in my favorite stories. *David Copperfield,* for instance, and animal stories like *Bob, Son of Battle, Black Beauty*, or *Spunky,* which was about the mine pony. I was interested in the very things that

I feared. I wasn't unique—children want and need to know the depths as well as the heights. An awareness of limits is necessary to a child's understanding of the world. It was safe, at least then, to explore all the information available to me.

I did not question our family's values, perhaps because of the good manners we were taught as if they were moral imperatives. When I started to examine my family's way of life and its conviction that our way was the best way, I sensed it was a subject too dangerous, too frightening to pursue. Suppose I were to act on my discoveries—how would I do that? Would it mean rejecting my parents, family, friends? Would I find myself adrift in the *real* world? Perhaps some children are strong and mature enough to question their families' assumptions, but I surely wasn't. Instead, I enjoyed all that my idyllic childhood offered, and read, and read some more.

There were contradictions in the books that I read and what I was told or what I experienced for myself in the world around me. Protective adults often feed children sugar-coated pills. Happy endings. Whereas great books, even those for children, tell the truth about sickness, poverty, pain, betrayal, and death. These things were in the plays and books that I read, but they were not present in the paradise of Aiken—or, more accurately, they were not visible to me.

Father Smith, a priest who enjoyed life and really cared for his flock, once told me about pellagra as we rode through the Aiken woods. A disease caused by dietary insufficiencies, especially the lack of B vitamins in refined wheat and corn flour and polished rice, pellagra leads to physical and mental deterioration. Many families in a certain part of Aiken suffered from the illness. "Why don't we do something to help?" I asked my parents after my ride. They were upset, I

see now, that I'd heard about it at all. "Darling, we are help-
ing," they assured me. "We give to the hospital and to the
church. That's the best way to help." But I wanted them to
visit the sick with me, bringing them food and comfort. Or
did I really want that? Wouldn't I have been nervous and
ashamed? Wasn't I secretly glad that my parents protected
me from such inequities?

CHAPTER 11

Sis

As I grew older, Miss Sligh's influence was eclipsed by Sis's gentle personality. Still walking sedately together, still studying French outside her classroom, Sis and I bellowed out patriotic verses:

> *Allons, enfants de la Patrie*
> *Le jour de gloire est arrivé!*

Thanks to Sis's introduction to Victor Hugo, I could readily imagine the fighting, the guns, even the guillotine. I was Florence Nightingale in a red-lined cape, tending to the wounded. In Sis's little room at the top of the stairs—the only private space in the two-room schoolhouse—she and I spoke in French of King Clovis and the Emperor Charlemagne, of Queen Berengaria dragged to her death by wild horses, and of my particular heroine, Joan of Arc, smiling beatifically as she burned at the stake, all graphically illustrated in my French history book. Sis focused her energy and intelligence especially intensely on me. She brought to such vivid life her language and the literature she loved that years later I was still able to recite lines and even paragraphs from her favorites: La Fontaine, Jules Verne, Victor Hugo, Molière, Racine, Alfred de Musset.

Together, we giggled at Molière's *Le Malade Imaginaire.*

Draped with a towel, as Iphigenie at Aulis, I bared my breast so my royal father Agamemnon might sacrifice me to Artemis and the fleet could set off at last for Troy. Racine's stately couplets issued from my lips with the conviction of a serious eleven-year-old girl who had more books than friends. When Sis and I read *The Three Musketeers,* I was D'Artagnan for days at a time, striding through life with a new purpose.

I memorized Musset's poem to Victor Hugo:

> *Il faut, dans ce bas monde, aimer beaucoup de choses.*
> *Pour savoir, après tout, ce qu'on aime le mieux:*
> *Les bonbons, l'ocean, le jeu, l'azur des cieux,*
> *Les femmes, les chevaux, les lauriers et les roses.*

Later, the words would resonate differently—but in Sis's little classroom, I already loved Musset with the intensity of a child who was often alone.

Sis was a wise teacher to start her students with the best. I still have some of the novels, histories, and biographies that arrived regularly from France. Paperbacks, mostly: Andre Maurois's *Ariel, ou la Vie de Shelley*, with a romantic youth engraved on the cover, drooping lovelorn ladies behind him, as clouds swirl over an Italian cupola. Everything by Colette and, most especially, Marcel Proust. There were hardbacks, too, including my grandmother's copies of Madame de Segur's *Bibliotheque Rose*, its gold-lettered covers faded to a lush pale cherry, and *Les Malheurs de Sophie,* the delightful adventures of a naughty little girl. After a morning of teaching school, Sis shepherded us to our various lessons.

She tried to maintain control over the rowdy bunch of teenagers who were always in our house—an impossible task for anyone, especially Sis, high-strung and nervous as she was. "Mais, nom de Dieu, what do you do, you will drive me crazy— and think of your poor mother!" Her voice rose. Her hands fluttered. She attempted a severe look. But Pam, in gales of laughter, would hug Sis, who, in the end, couldn't help laughing with her.

Once a week, our family listened to the symphony. The big console radio and victrola had at its center a Cyclopian eye, obscured by a tightly woven tweed scrim behind which I imagined musicians playing exotic instruments that I could only imagine, since I was only familiar with our Steinway piano. I myself played elementary versions of the classics, eventually progressing to Schumann's "Traumerei." Sis's benign supervision was very different from that of our teacher, Miss Stoddard, who despaired of Lev and me, mopping her brow dramatically while she recounted methods employed upon other unfortunate pupils, involving strict metronomes, fingers slapped by rulers, and steel rods shoved down the backs of slouchers. Confident that our parents would protect us from such horrors, we weren't intimidated enough to practice faithfully, so we didn't progress far enough to produce the lovely sounds that might have induced us to work harder. I began to recognize how deeply Sis's feelings were aroused by music when I saw, from the corner of my eye, deepening creases between her eyes. Her ears were pained by my playing. I watched her more closely during the symphonic programs to which, under her influence, I, too, was beginning to respond. It was as if her heart had escaped from the cage of her ribs and soared, like Maeterlinck's *Oiseau Bleu,* far from the red and white living room where our family gathered on those Sunday afternoons. Tears filled her eyes. All the emotions of her noble, yearning soul were encapsulated in the rich chords of Cesar Franck, Faure, or Chopin. Her eyes closed. Rapture transfigured her anxious, weary expression. Sometimes, watching her, I was transported, too.

*

With time, the faces of my schoolmates and other friends have blurred. Sometimes I will remember a student at Aiken Prep—Mark Rudkin, for example, to whom I was drawn. He was asthmatic, interesting, possessed of a searching, probing mind. His mother, hoping for a cure for her sickly child, had invented Pepperidge Farm Bread for him, which may or may not have helped him, but surely benefited the whole family. Years later, we found that we'd spent much of our lives in different but related worlds, knowing many of the same artists, our admirations similar. Separated for some sixty years, we both wished we'd discovered those similar interests earlier.

Patsy, from Pittsburgh, appeared only briefly. She was just my age. We became great friends. Once, finding me withdrawn, she said, *I understand. We've lost a lot, too.* And then she disappeared forever. It was my first inkling of the Depression. Only later did I understand what had happened, since, although some in their social circle lost their fortunes, it didn't seem to touch my parents' daily lives.

When her family alighted in Aiken, Cintra Carter became a vibrant member of our group. Brilliant and volatile, she existed in a vortex of divorces, moves, changes. Her father was one of my favorites. Unlike most adults, he talked to me at the cocktail hour, when, although I was only eight or nine, I mixed martinis for my parents and the friends who always dropped by.

"Where did you ride today?" he would ask. "Did you

see Miss Mann riding with the good Father? What was she wearing this time?"

"A purple hat with a yellow jacket," I answered with a giggle, making him smile.

"Did you jump? How did it go?"

"We did the Loop Line. I managed all the jumps." I was shy, but proud. I asked him why they all teased Nancy—Mrs. Bourne—so often.

With a surprised look he answered, "Oh, you noticed that? Well, to tell you the truth, she likes to be teased. How about you?"

"No, Mr. Carter," I answered solemnly as he laughed and held out his glass for a refill.

Thin, with long black hair, a white face and huge dark eyes, his daughter Cintra was a dramatic presence at recess, turning us into horses, circling and jumping over sticks that she held higher and higher, shouting commands as she mimicked our riding teacher's English accent. Cintra drew and painted lifelike horses: galloping, jumping, or standing still. As fifth graders, she and I spent weeks making a book together. My story, which Cintra illustrated lavishly, told of a girl and her horse, and that girl's first big challenge. Delighted with our end result, we sent it to a publisher friend of my mother's, sure he'd be equally enthusiastic. When he returned it with polite thanks, we were crushed.

I wonder, now, how my mother could have let us in for such a disappointment. She surely knew we were sending it, as she must have seen it and given us her friend's address. Insensitivity? Or did she really believe that his lifelong respect, even love for her would make him publish a childish story? Either way, it was careless. By not recognizing our need for acceptance, our vulnerability, she allowed us to be hurt.

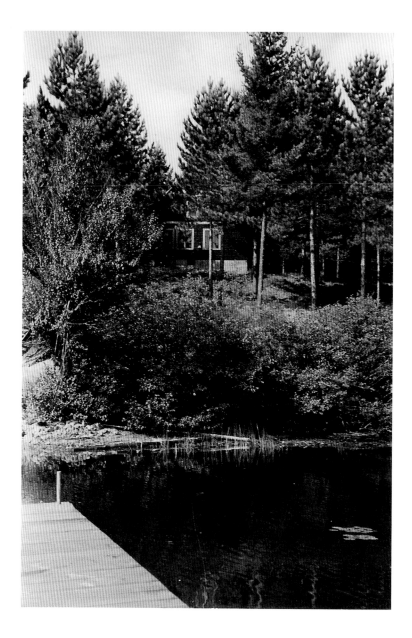

Camp Bliss, c. 1936

CHAPTER 12

Trout Fishing

In the summer of 1939, we went to the Adirondacks as usual. In England, conscription was underway. People sang "Hang Out the Washing on the Siegfried Line" and "Lili Marlene," while in America, "Over the Rainbow" and "God Bless America" were popular. After years of the Depression, orders from Europe for war equipment were pouring in. The economy was booming.

For the first time, my parents, in recognition of my eleventh summer, included me in their last trout-fishing expedition of the summer: an overnight stay at Camp Bliss, built for them in 1928, the year of my birth, at the end of nearby Little Tupper Lake. It was an idyllic spot. A log cabin sat on a hill in a grove of white pines, looking down eight miles of lake to the mountains beyond. As we arrived, the sun was setting in such a burst of orange, pink, yellow, and green that my father quickly unpacked his Leica with its glittering variety of filters, lenses, and light meters, loading it with his new Kodachrome film. With Louis doing the major share, we carried our food and drink up the path and collected wood for the fire. Pulling down the ladder that led precariously to the tinroom in the attic, we found the blankets, sheets, and towels stored there to protect them from mice, raccoons, and even hungry bears. Late summer chill

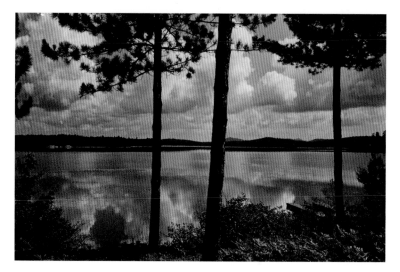

View from Bliss, 1939

made me hungry for the corned beef hash and tiny canned Lesueur peas my father began to prepare after the evening ritual of cocktails. Even in camp, martinis were ceremoniously prepared in a silver shaker and slowly sipped while Louis and I played a game of cribbage.

Finally we sat at the white enamel table in the tiny kitchen, wood stove blazing, and devoured the crisp hash, and the peas to which my father had added tiny onions, lettuce, bits of bacon, salt, pepper, and a little cream. Canned peaches and the chef's cookies for dessert. We did the dishes in two pans, one to wash and one to rinse, using water from the reservoir heated in the cast iron stove. I brushed my teeth, dipping water from the bucket I carried up from the lake, and was tucked into bed by both my parents. The murmur of their voices as I drifted to sleep was deeply comforting.

It seemed only a minute later when Louis knocked on our door in the dim light of dawn, and I left my warm

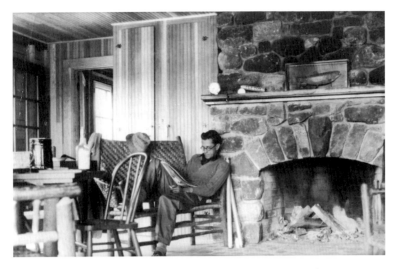

My father in the living room at Bliss, 1938

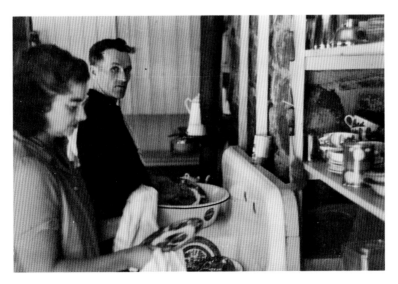

My mother and Louis, doing dishes at Bliss, 1938

cocoon of worn sheets and rough gray blankets. Down at the dock, my parents pushed off first in the canoe, then I stepped as lightly as I could into the guideboat. Louis rowed it through the thick white mist, past waterlilies with blazing yellow centers, to the sudden dark opening of Charley Pond Stream ahead. The sky turned pink behind Louis, bent to his oars. Once, not hearing the quiet drop of my parents' paddles, Lou stopped rowing. He gestured to his right. A black mound swam to shore and clambered clumsily from the water. I wanted to shout as the black bear shook sparkling drops of water from its coat and lumbered toward the forest, but silence was the rule if you wished to see wildlife in the woods. Sure enough, around the next bend a doe bounded away, flicking her white flag with a breathy snort, followed by her spotted fawn.

We reached the first springhole. It was called "Turtle" because my father had once hooked a sizeable snapping turtle in it that towed him up and down the river for a good half-hour before he realized with chagrin that it wasn't the record trout he'd taken it for, and cut his line. My mother tied the canoe to a pole placed strategically near a little feeder brook: a spot where trout often lay. A little beyond, Louis dropped a rock tied to the end of a rope to anchor us. Mummy and Daddy took sections of bamboo rods from aluminium tubes, removed them from their cotton sleeves and, rubbing them against the sides of their noses to oil them slightly, fit the pairs of metal ends together. Next, they unzipped two suede bags and attached two delicately engineered and artfully perforated Hardy reels to the long rods' cork handles, threading translucent line through the rod's five metal eyelets. The sun was still a red disk on the horizon as they attached fine nylon leaders to the lines,

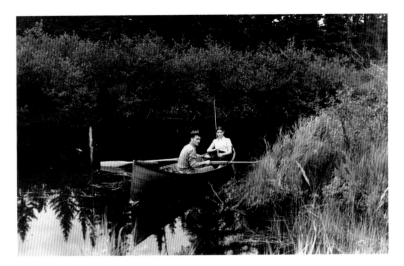

At Charlie Pond Stream, with Louis, 1939

then chose flies from small aluminum boxes—or from their hatbands—and tied them carefully to the leaders, testing them with sharp tugs. My father silently gestured "you first" and my mother cast her dry fly, a red and white Parmachene Belle, over the hole. Whipping it through the air in false casts, she floated it gracefully across the mouth of the little brook. As I held my breath in anticipation, a circular ripple broke the still surface of the water.

"There—a rise—right next to your fly," whispered my father. "You'll get him—a few inches to the left."

Sure enough, on the very next cast, the fragile looking rod bent double as my mother struck and hooked the fish, playing him skillfully, her tip raised as the fish leapt into the air in a twisting crescent, flashing green, blue, red, and yellow in the flame of the rising sun. The netting was an anticlimax, since the trout was small, even though Lou called it a keeper. My father hooked the next one in deeper water with a wet fly: a White Miller. Then it was my turn.

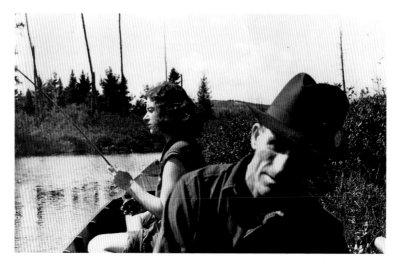

My mother trout fishing in Charlie Pond Stream with Louis, 1938

Although Louis had coached me well, I was conscious of my parents' watchful eyes, and caught the bushes on my second cast, and Lou had to clamber from the boat into the marsh to free the fly. All winter, taught by my parents' friend Dr. Weeks, I'd been tying flies, and Louis knew how precious my creations were to me. Again and again, he patiently released them from entangling bushes, trees, and even floating logs as we moved downstream in pursuit of the fish, who eluded me altogether.

There I was, though: Mummy and Daddy within sight and sound. What more could I want? And yet, and yet—success, which my small self sought and needed, seemed beyond my reach. By their example, and by the teachers and models they provided, our parents had set us up to win. I see now that they meant to train us to live as they did—good lives of pleasure, philanthropy, and service. We could succeed in specific things—patrician outdoor activities; a good

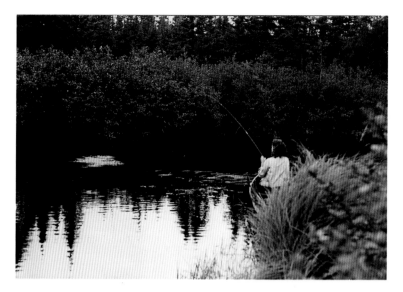

My mother hooks a trout, Charlie Pond Stream, 1938

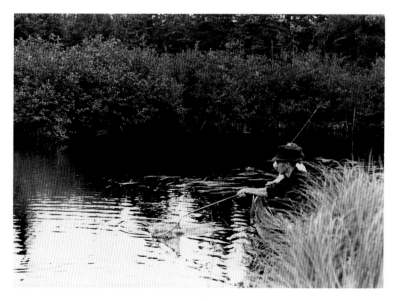

Lou nets the trout

education; good manners; and some awareness, although not too much, of other ways of life.

Back at Camp Bliss, it was time for breakfast. Louis heated the heavy black iron griddle until it smoked when he flicked drops of water on it. Beating his special mixture until he found the texture just right (he let me add two teaspoons of baking powder to it), he flipped fat pancakes onto our blue willow ware, pouring on melted butter and hot maple syrup. I ate at least two helpings, with rashers of crisp bacon, then curled up with Robin Hood while the grownups napped. After a swim in the lake, we headed back to the river. I was in the bow of the canoe. My mother was in the stern. Louis rowed my father in the honey-colored guideboat. My paddle flashed as I raised it high, then dipped it quietly into the water, using all my strength to pull my weight, trying not to splash as we followed the bends of the river.

"Look, look!" I whispered as a fat brown beaver swam across our bow, carrying a stick to the dam that bridged a brook to our left.

"We'll have to take care of him this fall," Louis said from the guideboat. "He and his family'll eat up half the trout in Charley Pond Stream."

"Oh, no," I murmured to Louis, "do you have to?"

"If you want to have any fishing next year—if not, we'll have a river full of beavers. What do you say, Mr. Miller?"

My parents laughed, but I could picture the buck-toothed beaver family swimming and playing up and down the stream. Suddenly my mother squealed "Hey, Flora, watch out!" I'd carelessly caught a crab—reversed my paddle—and I'd splashed her. I turned to look at her. She sat easily on the

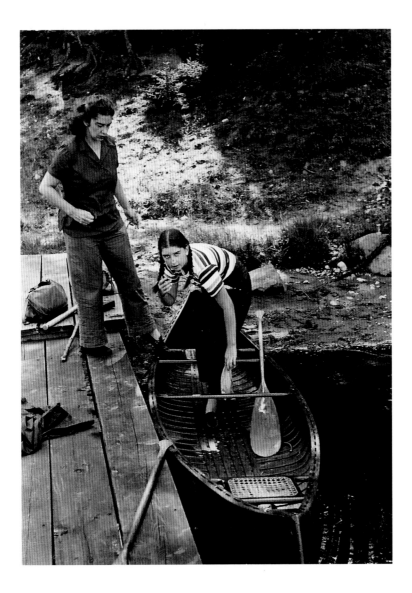

With my mother on a morning fishing trip to Charlie Pond Stream

cane seat, a dull green flotation cushion behind her back, the low sun glinting on the thick dark curls that tumbled to her shoulders. Her tan jacket and pants were meant for camouflage, replacing the bright colors she much preferred. Only her bright lipstick and long shiny scarlet nails were reminders of her customary colors. Her wide mouth and huge hazel eyes smiled at me as she wielded her paddle with the skill of lifetime practice, steering us on our curving course. I concentrated, paddling well and strongly.

"Look to the left," she said softly. A great blue heron stood motionless on one foot. At our approach, it took off with a splash. Flapping its wide wings loudly, its ungainliness disguised its aeronautic efficiency.

"A good sign," Louis said. "Trout should be hungry, too."

At the first springhole, we saw a hatch of tiny insects, with several trout feeding on them. We sat quietly for a few minutes, letting the water settle after our passage. A dance of dazzling grace and skill was about to begin, with Louis, Mummy, and Daddy as performers. Flexible nylon lines began to zing through the still air, inscribing parabolas and arcs against the luminous evening sky, vanishing only to re-form in yet more complex configurations. The tiny feathered flies seemed incidental to the complicated arabesques. Rods bent double; straightened. Hands wound rapidly, then released to the reel's scream as a trout raced for the safety of the depths, or leapt high over the water's silvery surface, a shower of drops flying like diamonds. The long-handled net scooped through the water, spilling sparkles of water; scooped again, and held a twisting speckled beauty. The dance continued until the sun was on the horizon when, suddenly, the world grew calm. The evening rise was over.

That night Louis cooked the trout, rolling them in corn-meal, salt and pepper, greasing the griddle with bacon fat saved from breakfast. My father stood next to him, round glasses glinting in the firelight, stirring canned tomatoes to which he'd added sugar and cream as he made sure the pota-toes didn't overcook. My mother cut a lemon into quarters. I dealt a hand of gin rummy, thrilled to have her all to myself.

Two perfect days. It was another milestone. The disap-pointment of not catching a fish was more than balanced by a new closeness to my parents. They accepted my pad-dling, my fishing, and my company. They had included me in their life, taking me to a place they preferred to go with-out their children.

On September 3rd, Lev and I celebrated our birthdays. Lev's was on August 31st, mine not until September 21st when we were already back in Aiken, but we always had our party in the Ads. Doctor Bergamini and his family came, and our cousins Gerta and Barklie Henry if they were at nearby Camp Killoquah, and Nancy and Harry Whitney, our cous-ins from Camp Deerlands on Little Forked Lake, if they were visiting their father and stepmother.

The doctor spent summers in Squirrel Point, across Big Forked Lake from Togus, with his wife and three sons. Hub, Eddie, and John were charter members of Pam and Whitty's gang. They zoomed around the lake in old putt-putts, aquaplaned behind the fastest Evinrude, competed in swimming races from camp to camp. They played ping-pong or Murder in the Dark, and explored the lakes and forests, trekking ten miles up Pilgrim Mountain, fishing in far-distant Mohegan Lake, or visiting our Webb cousins at their adjoining camp, *Ne-ha-sa-ne*. Whatever else they did, I was not privy to it, being too young, but I was thrilled when

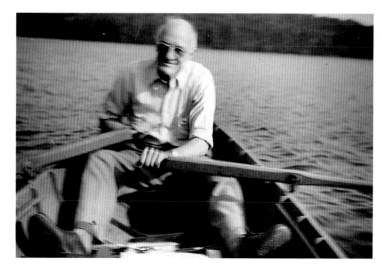

"Doc" Bergamini rowing on Forked Lake, c. 1940

our lives intersected, as they did on Sundays. Then, in our best white shorts and shirts, we crossed the lake for our emergency medical lessons, followed by cranking the ice cream machine, and the delectable licking of the dasher. The handle of the metal container nestled in a wooden bucket filled with chopped ice and coarse salt, moved more and more stiffly until only the older children could turn it—then, finally, the sweet, cold, creamy treat was ready.

But the high point of the whole summer was Lev's and my birthday party. The others worked on it for an entire day, while we were sent off to a distant lake. The day was always sunny and warm in my memory. All the younger kids were handed the end of a string and a stick to wind it on, according to our ages. For the older ones, the string led across the lake, or through the woods, or tangled around the barrels beneath the swimming float. Spider Webs, they were called, and we eagerly sought the prize at the end of the string, wrapped in gaily colored paper and carefully hidden in a

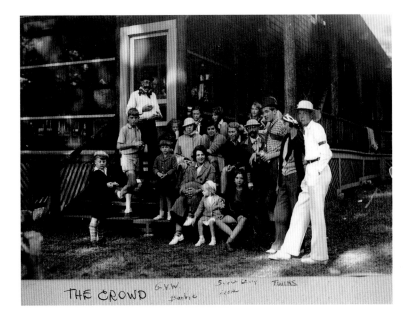

THE CROWD   G.V.W.   Sylvia Larry   TWINS
            Barbie   Rose

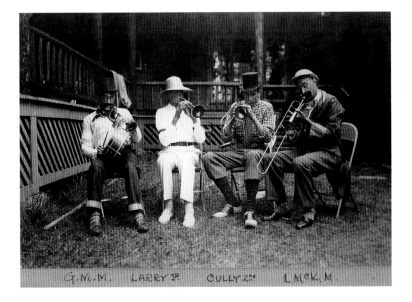

G.N.M.   LARRY Jr.   CULLY 2ND   L.McK.M.

tree trunk, or a boat, or under a tent. Then a glorious home-made cake with our names piped on its flowered top, and that velvety ice cream—raspberry was our favorite, made from the wild berries we'd picked the day before in a clearing down the trail to Plumley Pond while banished from the secret preparations back at Togus. Then came the presents—often things useful in the Ads—a pack-basket woven of thin birch strips, sized just right for Lev and me, or a stout fishing rod for trolling for bass, or—one year, wonder of wonders—a leather-sheathed knife to wear on my belt to clean fish or make a whistle or carve a little animal.

In addition to the precious knife, a small envelope lay before me. Wondering, I opened it and found, to my amazement, a note and a photograph. My gift was a bay gelding. All Satin was a throughbred retired from racing, but still young. My mother wrote, "You probably won't be able to ride him right away, but he'll be waiting in Aiken, and you can start getting used to him. He's a little excitable, still used to racing, but he'll be a lovely hunter for you soon." I couldn't believe it—a beautiful horse, hard to handle, perhaps, but a jumper, my very own. Tears were in my eyes as I thanked my parents.

In early evening, when Lev and I returned from trying out our new rods and knives, the camp seemed very quiet. In the living room, the fire had yet to be lit. Everyone, even the butler, was huddled around the radio.

"Shhhh," my father said, hushing us. Tears were running down our English nanny's cheeks, and I went to her. Through the static on short wave, a man was talking solemnly. Hitler had invaded Poland. England and France had declared war on Germany. We were shocked into silence. We knew that the world had changed forever.

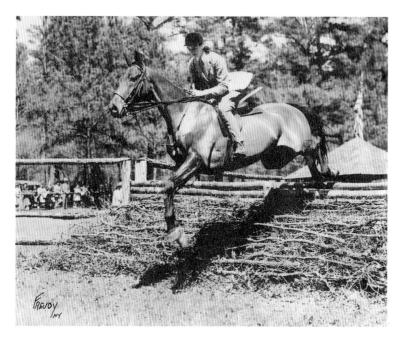

Jumping All Satin, Aiken Horse Show, c. 1940

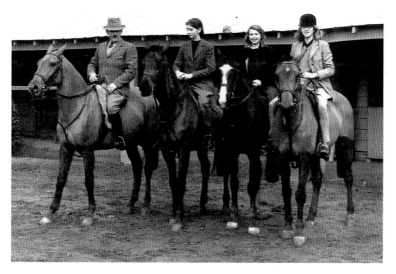

Riding class: William Gaylard, me, Marianna Mead, Claudia Wilds

CHAPTER 13

Gaylard · Duck Soup

Although the grown-ups spoke all the time about the war, it didn't seem especially distressing to us. Our nurse taught us to knit olive drab scarves for the British soldiers going to Europe to beat the Nazis, and a few boys we knew, sons of our parents' friends, were joining the Air Force in Canada. We understood that they might be wounded or even killed, but we didn't quite believe it—it was so far away. We went on with our lives.

I'd had ponies before, but they were old polo ponies, not fit for the big jumps I looked forward to taking. Now that I was eleven and had my own horse, riding became even more central to my life. My rides with Gaylard were more challenging. As I rode through the Hitchcock Woods toward the jumps, Gaylard recited Tennyson's poem:

> *Cannon to the right of them*
> *Cannon to the left of them*
> *Cannon in front of them*
> *Into the jaws of death*
> *Into the mouth of hell*
> *Rode the six hundred.*

Later, thundering:

Theirs not to make reply,
Theirs not to reason why,
Theirs but to do or die.

The Boer War was more real to me than the war in Europe, the six hundred British soldiers made vivid by Gaylard's stories. Their code of honor required that they avenge the murder of British women and children.

Three times a week I took Gaylard's class. Some of the other riders weren't fortunate enough to have their own horse and ride every day as I did. I didn't understand why he demanded so much of me. He often spoke harshly to me, but also praised me more on the rare occasions when, in his view, I performed well. I didn't make the connection with my nurse's insistence that we had to be especially thoughtful of others, emphasizing servants and tradespeople—those who were supposedly below us in class or status. Receiving much, we owed much. And we had to be better, too, to earn praise.

*

At a party about ten years ago, I enjoyed talking with a woman I had met that night. We have since become good friends. At dinner recently, she said "You know, if I'd known who you were, I'd never have talked with you so openly—I might not have talked to you at all." "Who am I?" I laughed, but I was taken aback. Despite the changes in our social structure, do the names Vanderbilt and Whitney still resonate and inspire awe? What expectations do people have of such once-eminent beings? That we are different, unapproachable, rich, haughty, powerful? I've assumed that people either don't know or don't care about my connection to American royalty. And yet I know that seasonal attendance at The Breakers, my great-grandparents' home in Newport, outstrips that of the Whitney Museum of American Art. We citizens of a democratic society are, clearly, intrigued by and attracted to aristocratic artifacts. Perhaps, in these terms, I am a relic. My friend's words impelled me to make sense of my heritage, more a responsibility than luck, perhaps because in my immediate family, today, few of the advantages of birth survive.

The privilege we enjoyed is wrong, I feel, and yet I'd like to think that we benefit from some of the good values we learned as children from teachers such as Sis and Gaylard.

*

I never wondered why I called him not Mister or Captain, but just plain Gaylard. Pam always called him Bill—I never dared go *that* far. Pam recently told me about the wild parties with Gaylard and her gang in our kitchen during the war, when our parents were in New York and there was no need to hide from the maids. Bill Gaylard was the leader; he loved games and he loved drinking. He taught them to play Cardinal Puff. You took a drink, said "Here's to Cardinal Puff," and bottoms up! I knew nothing about any of this. As a child, I wouldn't have been able to imagine such a shocking scene.

We drilled in close formation in the manège, the sandy oval carved from the Hitchcock Woods, in emulation of British troops, Gaylard commanding in a booming voice: "CIR-CLE, right!" Two lines of riders separated, circling flank to flank. As my horse met another head-on, I realized I'd made a mistake—I'd circled left—and blundered clumsily through the neat figure, scattering the other riders to either side until I was on the edge, facing Gaylard's angry scowl. I felt as if I'd jeopardized the lives of my fellow soldiers.

"Bite your thumb, *hard*, until it bleeds," Gaylard bellowed, his stern eye on my hand. "Harder! I don't ever, ever want you to forget which is your right hand again, do you hear? Now, get back in there. By the numbers, count!"

We numbered ourselves aloud: "One, two, three. . . ."

"Down the center, march! Even numbers, circle left. Odd numbers, circle right. Form pairs. That's right. Now up the hill to the Loop Line. Flora, take the lead. Follow along, the rest of you."

I could hardly believe it. The youngest of the group, I'd never been in the lead before. Why today? After my mistake?

That, though, was Gaylard's way. He disciplined us but never humiliated us. When he gave us responsibility, we gained a sense of our worth.

My parents arranged other ways besides riding to boost my confidence; the most important of them was shooting. I'd gone on dove shoots, of course, sitting with my mother in a cornstalk blind, reading aloud to her in the warm sunshine from *The Adventures of Tish* or the tales of Sherlock Holmes while we waited for doves to fly into the fields of benne. As the sun lowered and the birds came in to feed, she fired, and I ran to collect the dove from a sandy furrow, holding its soft gray body, still warm, in my hand. At twelve, it was time for me to learn this particularly Southern skill. My parents came along for my first lesson.

Doc Holley—weathered cheeks, a bit stooped, in dark corduroy trousers, scuffed brown boots, tan shirt, tweed jacket—was waiting for me. The brim of his cap was pulled down to shade his observant eyes from the low winter sun, a rusty cigarette dangling from his thin lips. With his loose,

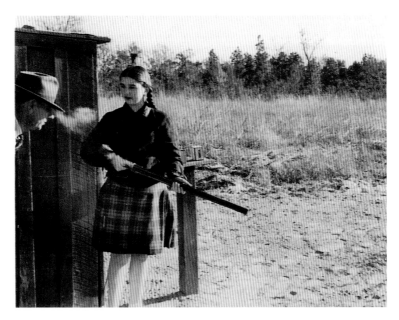

Shooting lesson with Doc Holley

ambling gait, he exemplified a patient man, untouched by the compromises of a toilsome life. He seemed rooted; grown from the hard clay earth on which we stood.

"C'mon over here, Floora," he drawled, leading me to a bare patch of ground near a squat wooden tower where Jed, a young black man, sat, his hand on a metal lever clamping an eight-inch wide black disc with a yellow center. The weather was raw, with a biting wind. My hands were cold against the steel of my 4-10 shotgun, correctly broken over my arm, as I followed Doc Holley to the shooting range.

At last, I thought, I'm entering the grown-up world where, until now, I've been only an observer. Soon, if I can prove my ability, I'll sit in my own blind, with my own dove boy to hand me two shells to replace those I've used, and to fetch the doves I've shot.

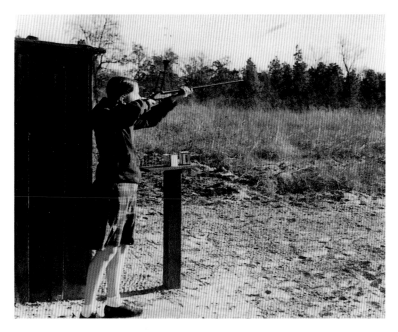

Aiming my 4-10 shotgun

"All right, load your gun. That's right, snap it closed," Doc Holley ordered. "Make sure it's pointed away. From me. From Jed there. From anyone. Now hold it into your shoulder hard, so you won't feel the kick too much. When you see the clay pigeon fly, look along the barrel and lead it by about two feet. Squeeze the trigger smoothly. You can try again with the second barrel, but don't wait too long and don't follow it low. You could shoot someone."

I understood. I'd watched many times—but this was different. I was nervous as I waited for Jed to spring the terracotta disc. I wanted so much to do it perfectly.

"Pull!" Doc shouted to Jed.

I squeezed the trigger jerkily, forgetting to hold the wooden butt firmly to my shoulder, hardly leading at all. Still whole, the clay pigeon fell to the ground. My shoulder was already sore, and my forefinger, along with my pride, felt bruised.

The next time, I barely felt the kick. I squeezed the trigger smoothly, but the shot flew far ahead of the target. Still, from a box of 25 shells, I managed to shatter several clay pigeons. I was quite pleased, especially when, as my parents approached, Doc said, "She'll be a right fine shot. Should be out there with you in a couple of months."

I practiced once a week. More and more clay discs ended in smithereens. I tried doubles, firing with each of my two barrels at two discs released in quick succession, and occasionally hit them both. Soon I felt ready for the real thing.

One cool, clear morning, my parents and I set out from Aiken on the hour's drive to Barnwell, our wooden-sided Chevy station wagon loaded with camp stools, ammunition, and guns. There, at the edge of a big field, about a dozen men and women were already gathered around a makeshift bar. Grady was there, a stocky white Southerner who'd organized the hunt and the picnic lunch. He was already bossing around a group of young black men.

Grady liked my mother and father. After greeting them heartily, he began to flip buckwheat pancakes on the griddle. Sausages sizzled in the huge black frying pan, drinks flowed, and so did conversation. Welcoming me to this club of likeminded old friends who played golf and tennis, gambled, hunted, and entertained each other at lunches and dinners all winter long, Bill Carter raised his glass. "We're glad you're joining us, Flora."

I noted my mother's face as she accepted a martini from an admirer, Huston Rawls: "Thank you, my dear, oooh, that's good on this cold day! You certainly drew the cards last night—but you know what they say—'lucky in cards....'"

Laughing, she tossed her head and turned toward my father, who was discussing yesterday's bridge game with his partner, Loretta. "Darling, you're beating a dead dog— let's have some lunch. The birds will come and go without any trouble from us if we don't get out there soon!"

My mother loved to flirt, but if my father seemed attracted to someone else, she was right there to stop it fast. Loretta, a bit miffed, moved over to Bill, who was whispering with russet-haired Nancy, bringing a blush to her pale cheeks. Tom Rutledge, the only true Southerner in this clique of mostly transplanted Northerners, brought me a plate of pancakes and sausages: "Here you go, Flora. Fuel for a long afternoon. How d'you feel—a bit anxious?" I admitted to a few butterflies.

"Absolutely normal," Tom reassured me. "Just remember not to follow your bird down low, and you'll be fine. I hear you've been doing great over at Doc's. Got your official permit? Sheriff's been coming over lately. Don't want him to drag you off to jail!" Tom smiled. "Your parents had better take you to Duck Soup soon—just wait'll you're paddling through those reeds. It's dark and quiet when the eastern sky starts to color up. You'll be cold as a bullhead. The wind in your face, huddling in the blind, and then the first duck whistling in. You'll know it's a canvasback. Pale feathers against the orange sky. You'll be thrilled, Flora. You'll be a real Southern hunter then."

My parents' hideaway near Charleston was called Duck Soup. A little pink house on the Inland Waterway, it was part of an old rice plantation. They went there to shoot ducks and do their own cooking. After hanging the ducks for two days, Daddy roasted them very rare, cut off the breasts and squeezed the carcasses in his silver duck press to make the

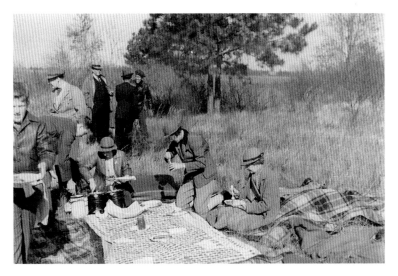

Picnic before shooting, Mrs Mead, my mother

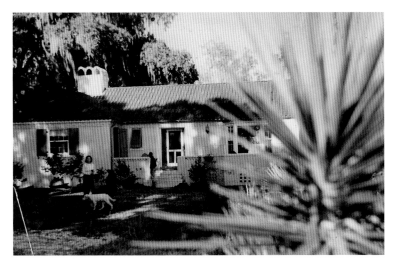

Duck Soup, just finished, 1939

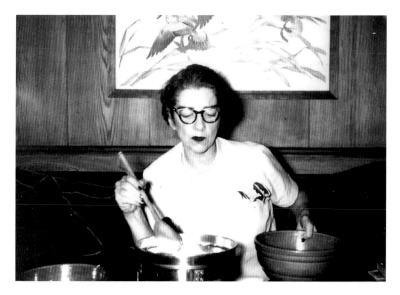

My mother making creamed turkey, Duck Soup, 1950

sauce in which he took such pride. Using all my strength, I turned the wheel as he added onions, red wine, and spices to the blood dripping into the bucket below. Meantime, my mother made her famous blue sauce for vanilla ice cream, using chartreuse with its startling turquoise color.

Later, when I stayed there in one of the two small bedrooms, we lived so intimately that I imagined we were just like regular people. No longer in our rarefied, luxurious world, I innocently wanted to know firsthand the toils, troubles and joys I'd read about in books like *Oliver Twist* or *The Little House on the Prairie.*

For my first day of dove shooting, my father loaned me J. D., the handsome man who'd modeled for my father's best portrait. J. D. picked up a few boxes of shotgun shells, and I carried my gun, broken, over my arm as we trudged across the powdery field to number six, a circle of tan cornstalks at the edge of a forest of scrub oak and jack pine.

1 plaque of chocolate — For 5 or 6
3 egg yolks in chocolate
3 whites beaten stiff —
Tablespoon of sugar —
Teaspoon of melted butter or Tablespoon
of cream —

sugar after chocolate is
melted
pinch of salt —
Then yolks —
Then the whites very stiff —

melt chocolate in coffee or sherry

Recipe "for chocolate pot de creme"

That afternoon, for what seemed like a long time, I watched, staying still and silent. J.D., sounding very like a dove, whistled softly. I'd known him for years, but we didn't say much—what could we talk about? I admired his good looks, his skill, his kindness. But how to bridge the immense gap in our lives? He couldn't eat with us, sit with us at the movies, or shoot with us. His children didn't go to school with us or play with us.

The sun lowered and the doves flew in to feed. Crack! Crack! Across the field, I saw birds fall to earth. "Raise your gun," said J.D., and I pressed it firmly to the leather patch sewn to my jacket shoulder. "There, to your left," he whispered, and I saw a dove. I fired, remembering to lead it, but perhaps not enough. It flew on untouched.

"There's another to your right," J.D. said. It was coming directly toward me. I hit it. Its wings folded as it fell. J.D. ran to retrieve it, stooping low near the ground to avoid shotgun pellets.

I took the dead dove into my hands. It was warm and soft. My triumph was mixed with something else. Grief? Guilt? But there was no time to think—another was coming, and another. Five doves were piled at our feet. The sun was setting. The shoot was over, and J.D. carried the birds to the back of Grady's open truck. The doves, after hanging outdoors for a few days to age and tenderize, would be our Sunday lunch.

I was proud that afternoon. I could shoot. I could kill, even if it made me feel uneasy. Fortified by the praise I received, I brushed away all doubts.

PART III: TEEN YEARS

CHAPTER 14

Beaux

As I grew older, I began to notice certain things. My mother's men friends, for instance. Beaux, as we then called male admirers.

Marianna and I fell madly in love, at the same time, with one of them. Ronnie Bodley was an Englishman in his forties, a beau first of my grandmother's, then of my mother's (although I wasn't yet aware of that). When he arrived at Joye Cottage for a long stay in our best guest room, we were instantly smitten. His little moustache! His British accent! Ronnie spent a great deal of time by the pool. We'd spy on him from a porch or a nearby window. We'd pick a bunch of my mother's favorite lilies of the valley for his breakfast tray, imagining that he knew who'd picked them. "Oh, they must be from Flora and Marianna, those angels! I hope they'll come and visit me soon." Our code name for him was "Blue Eyes." The mere saying of the words sent us into such helpless paroxysms of blushes and giggles that we could hardly speak.

I still have a book he inscribed to me in 1940, the year it was published by Macmillan, that he wrote about his friend, the explorer Gertrude Bell. When, much later, I did research for B. H. Friedman's book about my grandmother, Gertrude Vanderbilt Whitney, I found out more about Ronnie. Penniless, he'd stayed in Gertrude's house during the last months of her life, rewriting an impossible play she'd written, assuring her that it would be a big success. Making up to her, as he did later to my mother, making himself useful or at least decorative in their comfortable houses. Was he as charming as Marianna and I found him to be? Well, two other women in my family certainly thought so. I wonder, today, how my father felt about him. About other men, too, who spent days or weeks at our house, playing games, amusing Mum, charming her. Maybe it was a relief not to always have to play that role himself. I don't remember that he was ever impatient with any of them. Or with my mother.

Tim Coward, to whom I'd sent my story, was a publisher who'd been in love with my mother since they were children. I think of him as a friendly but growly bulldog, hefty, determined, with a voice that could turn in an instant from a contented rumble to a roar. With or without a wife, he stayed for a week or so in Aiken, or came for weekends on Long Island, reading the comics on Sunday mornings— the *Katzenjammer Kids* or, later, *Peanuts.* He excelled at all word games—if he missed a word or was beaten, we'd get a glimpse of his fierce temper when he turned purple and emitted staccato curses. Years later, when I married, Tim gave me the 1888 *Oxford English Dictionary* as a present. The faded volumes have followed me from home to home all these years.

There was Elia Tolstoy, related, he said, to the great Leo. Wiry, balding, with intense dark eyes, he described his adventures in a Russian-accented voice that promised dread calamity surmounted by great heroism, "When I in Gobi desert . . . escaping from Reds . . ." Pam and Whitty called him Elia Tallstory. He was working with our mother's brother and a cousin to found Marineland, the first theme

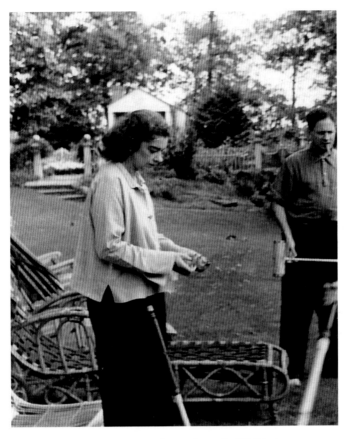

My mother playing croquet with Tim Coward, Old Westbury, c. 1946

park, in Florida. As a refugee, he needed to make a living, and Marineland was a fine way to do that. He raised money from our mother, and at some point the family traveled to see his creation. (Lev and I, considered too young, were left behind.) The others came back with glamorous photographs of Whitty diving into a pool and swimming with porpoises.

Pam's anger bubbles up when we speak of Dr. Weeks. (Once, he even made a pass at *her*.) Carnes Weeks and his wife, Maggie, went salmon fishing every year with my parents. Lots of fishing, lots of drinking. Lots of hanky-panky,

Pam thinks, in Canada, on the York River in the Gaspé. Carnes taught me to tie delicate artificial flies and brought me gorgeous materials for them from his travels: golden pheasant hackles from Africa, silver and gold thread from India, black and white panda hair from China, kangaroo fur from Australia—there was no end to the treasures he'd spill from an ancient leather bag dotted with exotic labels. This gave me status! No one else in my family could make the tiny, intricate lures. I could do so without using a vise—even experts needed one—since I could use scissors with either hand; as a child, I was ambidextrous.

I found Carnes handsome, funny, and warm. He didn't condescend to me. One of his daughters, Noni, and I became close friends. I was attracted to one of his sons, Bob, and Lev fell in love with his other daughter, Margo. Why my father didn't seem jealous is a mystery to me today. In New York, my mother stayed out late with Carnes at the Stork Club. They looked at each other with love and longing, and he visited her on leave from the Navy, looking particularly dashing in his uniform. He even removed her gall bladder! In those years, my father gave my mother a golden key to their apartment in New York, engraved, *So you won't have to worry about staying out late.* Carnes was a bit like Rhett Butler— charming, careless, irresponsible, and fun.

The flirtations and seductions were far beyond me in those days. Even as a small child, I remember our Aiken doctor, Harry Wilds, rushing to our house at the slightest sniffle. Especially if it were my mother's nose. She'd take to her bed happily with a Conrad novel or the latest mystery, while her maid would bear trays of scrambled eggs (soft), toast with honey, and ice cream. The fire blazing, she'd recline in a fur-trimmed satin negligee on her lacy pillows,

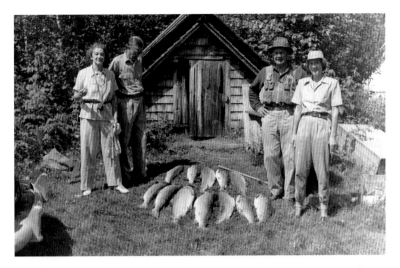

Salmon in the Gaspé, my parents with Maggie and Carnes Weeks, 1950s

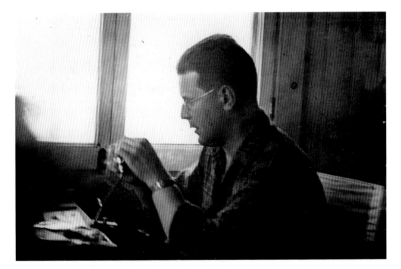

Carnes fly-tying, Camp Togus, c.1938

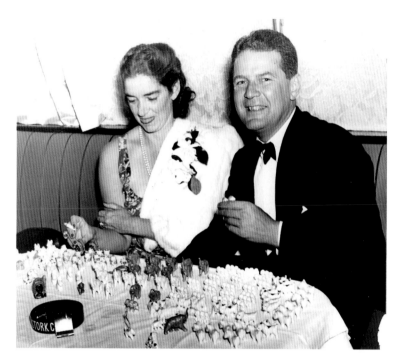

My mother and Carnes Weeks, at the Stork Club, c. 1942

sniffling mournfully while Dr. Wilds sympathized with her. When she recovered, she and the doctor spent hours in the camellia greenhouse, planning which new plants to buy, talking and laughing.

I wasn't aware of anything strange in any of this—it was, after all, the way that we lived. Reflecting now on my mother and her beaux, I see parallels with her own mother. They both found it natural to have relationships outside their marriages. They had grown up at a time when women had little power, and manipulating men gave them entrée to a larger world. Taught to be charming, they weren't warned of the dangers: men whose advances could turn to anger when unrequited, or the possibility of falling in love themselves. More idealistic and less cynical than

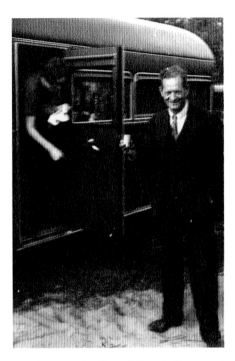

My mother, with Dr. Harry Wilds, in "Romany Rye"

many Europeans, Americans were more likely to get into emotional trouble. Perhaps my mother and grandmother absorbed the values of aristocratic French women. My grandmother had a studio in Paris, her favorite place to work, and also a house in the country near Tours. She and my mother spoke excellent French, and we children were taught early to speak and read it; I learned French history before American history. Gertrude even took an ambulance with doctors and nurses to France during World War I, and cared for the wounded herself. My parents continued this dedication to France, going abroad every summer until World War II and continuing after the war. Loving France was part of our family's culture. Gertrude, however, was very different from my mother; self-aware and self-critical, she was prone to depression, although she had a sense of humor. She worked hard to create and promote both her museum and her sculpture. Fully aware of her charm, she wrote in a 1904 diary about her power over men:

> I fear that it is the lowest kind of power. Howard Cushing said once I could have any man I wanted care for me. . . . Mabel Gerry said, 'I never saw a man yet that you could not make crazy about you if you wanted to.'

In her journals and letters, it's apparent that both she and her husband had affairs, although they stayed together and had, according to their letters, a loving relationship. Both my mother and grandmother emphasized discretion above all. Working with B. H. Friedman on Gertrude's biography, I was inclined to understand rather than judge Gertrude's desires and passions.

Harry Payne Whitney had died in 1930 when Gertrude was nearing sixty. Her own doctor was deeply in love with her. My mother's attraction to her doctors was strangely similar. She felt very close to her mother; it's likely that she patterned her own habits and morals on those of her mother. With no real commitment to work, my mother's ambition was partly, if not wholly, satisfied by her daily life, which included her family; decorating her houses; games; books; entertaining; fishing; shooting; and a number of male admirers. She had, like her mother, a kind of pride in being able to attract desirable men. She was captivating to all who knew her, enchanting even, and perhaps she felt that her mother had given her permission to conduct sexual adventures. My parents did not lead separate lives, as did my grandparents. Gertrude's beaux—an eclectic mix of businessmen, architects, artists, writers, a distinguished politician who wrote poems to her, even an Italian tenor—were stimulating colleagues, her peers in intellect and accomplishment. They seemed to have plenty of time to woo her with letters, flowers, dinners, and lunches; it was she who was often too busy for them. My parents had the same friends, the same interests; they lived with their family as a happily married couple.

With her mother's death in 1942, the Whitney Museum of American Art became the heart of my mother's life. Difficult as it was for her to assume a public role, she successfully led the Museum into a new phase. It too became a more public institution, with non-family trustees and two new buildings. My mother agonized over hard decisions, and experienced much stress, but for twenty-five years she exercised good judgment, courage and charm until in 1966 the building on 75th Street and Madison Avenue, designed by Marcel Breuer, was completed and opened. Then, she resumed the quiet life she preferred.

At almost eighty, macular degeneration made reading difficult for my mother, and I read aloud to her the manuscript of her mother's biography before its publication in 1978. I remember how intrigued she was by her mother's romantic liaisons, by the intimate letters and revealing journal entries. "Ooooh—I never knew that!" she'd exclaim with delight. She had no hesitation about publication. Women were entitled to have their own lives, including lovers, while keeping both their husbands and society's respect.

*

These women unconsciously passed their attitudes along to their descendants. Just as my mother was exposed to the sexual innuendos and desires of her parents and their friends, I too absorbed those of my own parents and their circle. Like most young people, I turned away from my parents' lifestyle, rejecting what I saw as excessive drinking, delegating much childcare to others, and the idea of relationships outside marriage. If attracted to another man, I usually fled. Sin was very real to me—but my grandmother and mother were even more important influences than my nurse and the church. Their characters and feelings were embedded in my psyche, but their actions were more risky in my world than in theirs, where play, whether cards, dice or love, had been a way of life.

*

My sister Pam is my only source, now, of stories about the goings-on in Aiken. Driving licenses were issued in South Carolina to twelve-year-olds. Hard to imagine now, but when Pam was fourteen and Whit thirteen, Whit's friend Nelson Mead had a Model T Ford, known as the Yellow Peril, in which they would all rush off to a fire when the sirens sounded. They'd sneak out of the house very late, borrowing my father's precious sapphire blue Lincoln Continental, to pick up the rest of the gang, and drive noisily around town, shrieking with laughter. One time, they drove to the Tea Cottage, a rustic cabin deep in the woods where the grown-ups had parties. There they found our mother and George Eustis, an attractive Southerner, parked in the moonlight! They shook their fingers at the pair, and went on their way. From then on, Pam says, Mum never dared confront Pam or Whitty about their escapades—a look, a raised eyebrow, from either of them would suffice to quiet any scolding.

Once a year, the Winter Colony, our group of transplanted

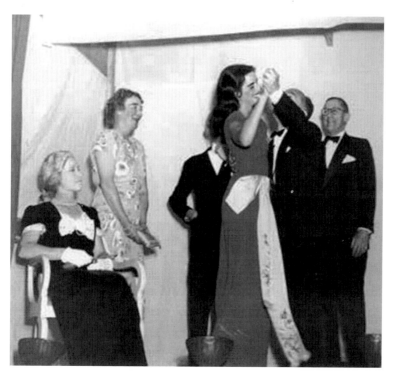

In "The Dinner Party", Pam as Flora Parks dancing with Seymour Knox; my father

Northerners, wrote and performed amusing episodes of life and times in our hermetic Aiken community. Too young to act in them, I went to the dress rehearsal, and sometimes to the play itself. When I was twelve, Fred Astaire, then married to our neighbors' niece, was in Aiken and came to the performance. I was excited and felt unusually important because Fred Astaire's baby was asleep in *my* old crib. Astaire even thanked me, saying the baby had slept especially well. Pam, acting as Flora Parks, a local beauty, danced with Seymour Knox who played the part of my parents' friend, the handsome and flirtatious Bobby McKim. Blushing as she cast a sultry look at the celebrity in the audience, Pam burbled, "Oh, sweetie, you dance just as wonderfully as Fred Astaire!"

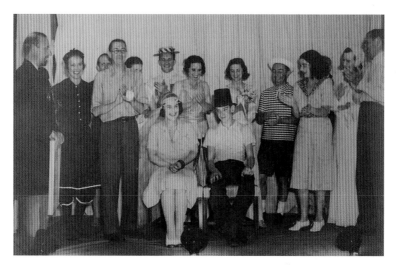

The cast: Schuyler Parsons, Nancy Bourne, my father, Charlie von Stade, "Chi" Bohlen, Elsie Mead, Whit Tower, unknown, Seymour Knox, my mother, Helen Clark, unknown

Being a strait-laced child, I began to notice the pervasive drinking that lubricated hosts and guests. A bit later, I realized that the fights occurring around cocktail time were at least partly due to those martinis my father taught me to mix. The sound of ice in a shaker—even the thought of that crisp tinkle—and the sight of frosty beads on polished silver bring back a vision of my parents and their friends, convivial at first, speaking louder with the second or third drink, their bright laughter sometimes sparked by cruel barbs and gossip. My mother might say, "Cully, how could you forget to tell Herbert that George and Elsie are staying for dinner?" and it would grow into a criticism of his general incompetence. Or, after a clever reference by my father to Mum's current obsession with Huston Rawls, sitting across the room with his wife, Francine ("Oh, darling, I thought you were going to tell Herbert, I didn't realize you and Huston would be in the woods so late"), my father would withdraw from the conversation, moving into a corner to talk quietly with another guest.

I didn't understand then that some of my parents' circle of friends were already addicted to alcohol, while others were well on the way. Like eating, drinking was an essential part of the day. While some people seemed able to manage the extended cocktail hours before both lunch and dinner, others, more susceptible, became alcoholics—a word that implies a medical condition that was not then recognized. My parents and most of their friends condemned as weakness the symptoms of the disease that we now know derives largely from one's chemical makeup. As alcoholics lost their spouses, jobs, and friends along with their balance and their health, words like "lush," "drunk," and "no good" divided the failures from the happy drinkers.

In that cloistered group of people who saw each other nearly every day, played together and drank together, relationships must have been complex—intimacies I was far too young to understand. Still, I observed, with fear in my stomach, the effects of alcohol and divorce. Heated arguments and ugly discussions have frightened me ever since. It is very difficult for me to face disagreement and unpleasantness. Early on, I learned to hide my feelings, pretending to like everyone and everything far more than I actually did. Did I realize this? Certainly not entirely. Much later, in my sixties, writing a book about my time at the Whitney Museum, I realized how deep-rooted this repression had been, and how destructive it was to my marriage and my work. Often, I hadn't been able to confront unpleasant truths. For instance, I hadn't faced my growing alienation from my first husband; hadn't really talked with him about it. Or, on behalf of the Whitney, I'd nominated trustees whose goals were opposed to those of the Museum; people whose egos required the kind of power and influence that can only hurt an institution. Unwilling to risk rejection, even from those I didn't respect or agree with, I hadn't trusted my basic instincts. The tendency persists—but now I'm more aware of it. I do my best to guard against it.

Watching these grownups over the years as they laughed, argued, and played, I wondered if my life would be like theirs, ostensibly so carefree and delightful. Approaching my teens, my days often seemed loaded with challenges: schoolwork, homework, riding lessons on my spirited, frequently uncontrollable horse. And, side by side, my growing doubts about God, and my even more frightening skepticism about the temporal authority personified by my British nanny. I felt a general emotional malaise, and a burgeoning sense that my body had a will of its own. In my daydreams, I yearned for friends my own age who might understand my deepest feelings.

Like a moth near a glowing candle, I was enchanted by the Mead family. Their friends, their lives were romantic and fascinating. One spring weekend in Aiken in 1941, when my family was at lunch, probably just finishing the traditional Sunday roast beef with Yorkshire pudding, Herbert, the butler, announced, "Mr. Kennedy on the phone for Miss Flora." For once, all eyes were on me. A call from a man? For you? asked their faces, as I went to answer, blushing with pleasure. Since Marianna had told him about our pool, and he liked to swim, Jack, who must have been about twenty-three, asked if he could come over to swim that afternoon. "But why did he call *you*?" asked Pam. Of our family, he'd only met me, when I was visiting Marianna Mead. That was the only introduction necessary, he'd thought—and he'd been right.

Of course, as soon as "Mr. Kennedy" arrived, Pam and Whitty took possession of him. I remember how good-looking he was; how he focused, thrillingly, if briefly, on me. He was already bright, assured, and charismatic. Mr. Mead said, as he watched him play tennis, "Some day, that young man will be President of the United States."

I see now that I was already caught up in the grown-up ways of my mother and my sister. Eager to be beguiled and bewitched by a man. Sexuality was all around me, although I didn't consciously recognize it. It had always been around my mother, but now, with the war in Europe soon coming to America, girls were more flirtatious, boys more bold. In Aiken, there was a rush to pair off and marry.

That summer, the Meads asked me to visit them on Great Island, near Hyannis. I was extremely excited. At almost thirteen, I'd never visited anyone before, much less someone in such a populated spot. Our family enclaves in Long Island and the Adirondacks were isolated by acreage, and the beginning of wartime gasoline rationing. Our summer social lives were limited to other family members and their guests. My nurse packed my few clothes, including navy blue shorts with white stripes down the sides and a halter top for swimming, and a few cotton shirts. Arriving in Cape Cod, I was astonished and overwhelmed by Marianna's cousins and friends. There were so many of them. They seemed so capable and sophisticated. They knew the same games, the same people. They could play tennis well, and they could sail; most of all, they could talk. Their fast chatter was full of jokes, secrets, short cuts. They even looked different: svelte afghans to my round puppy. Blond, with long wavy hair that they shook with nonchalance, I had childish straight hair worn in dark pigtails. They wore one-piece bathing suits, floaty skirts with skimpy tank tops, pedal-pushers, pastel sandals. I felt lost. Homesick. Marianna's nurse put me in a pretty bathing suit with a skirt, which helped a lot on the beach, but even though I was older and bigger than Marianna, I just couldn't keep up.

In not measuring up to the social scene, I thought I'd disappointed Marianna. I'd seen my best friend in a wider world, and hadn't been able to keep up with her. Without quite recognizing the source of my discomfort, I knew that our exclusive bond had loosened. We were friends, but no longer best friends.

During the war years, Marianna and I still returned to Aiken during our vacations from boarding school in Maryland. We rode our horses, we studied—and discussed in detail—the boys at Aiken Prep as they played bicycle polo, and we showed off our new figures in clinging silk dresses at races and polo games. We shared a secret infatuation for Pam's handsome and charming friend, Bill Preston. His dark good looks made our hearts beat like crazy; his smile ravished us. He occupied our dreams, and sometimes even our days. And then he went to war. On D-Day, he was wounded—if not for his dog-tags, he'd have been killed by the bullet that hit them before paralysing him on one side permanently. Pam and her best friend, Dolly von Stade, met the plane that brought him back to Long Island. They helped to carry his stretcher from the plane, and nursed him in the Mitchell Field hospital where they worked as nurses' aides, while Marianna and I, too young to help, wept and prayed. Miraculously, he survived to become a committed teacher, the first person I knew who repudiated the loyalty oath required in many universities during the McCarthy years, thereby sacrificing an excellent job.

CHAPTER 15

Bill Tuey

The summer of 1941 was to be our last in the Ads for a long time. Perhaps we sensed this, or maybe our prescient melancholy was only evident later, as if we'd been held in an iridescent bubble. The summers that followed were intensely colored by the war.

"Fifteen-two, fifteen-four, and a run of three make seven."

"Drop your voice, Nancy," Bill said when the count was done. "Okay, here's my hand: double run of four, fifteen-eight. Add it up, Flora."

His staccato sniff-sniff was triumphant.

"Wow, Bill, what a hand! Eighteen—that puts us over. The Grand Champions of 1941!"

I danced around, transported. Bill Tuey and I had just beaten my daring cousin and her best friend, both two years older than I, and, it seemed to me, in every way superior. I drew a crude picture of our game, including our names, and pinned it to the wall, where it joined about a hundred other memorials to championship cribbage games played atop Salmon Lake Mountain's fire tower.

"Time to go down, girls." Bill stuffed his thermos of water and the remains of his lunch into his wicker packbasket and disconnected the primitive two-way phone. Taking a final look across the hundred thousand acres of lakes and forest, he opened the trap door to the hole that dropped, like my stomach, to the rocks a hundred feet below. Bill told Nancy and her friend, who seemed oblivious to my terror, to go first. Then it was my turn. He had to go last to lock up. Climbing had been bad enough, but at least I could look up to see Bill encouraging me to persevere; going down was different. To be sure of my footing, I had to look down with each fearful step. Bill held my arm while I felt with my foot for the first rung of the ladder. My heart was pounding, but I'd rather have fallen than admit weakness. Bill's firm grasp, his pat on my back at the top of the eighty steps, made me suspect that somehow he knew my secret, and that helped me to put one shaking foot beneath the other. At last, I jumped happily down the last few rungs and hurried to catch the others.

My cousin Nancy was in the lead. For me, she was always in the lead. She was beautiful; she was brave. Her sky blue eyes, her golden curls, her smile that melted hearts—even her talent for telling stories—came straight from her father. In looks and eloquence, she resembled my undependable, seductive Uncle Sonny, who flew from Saratoga to the lake in his silver seaplane, told ghost tales of the terrifying *Windigo* around the campfire as stars blazed in the northern sky, and disappeared again into the sky with his latest wife. A sometime father, he was destructive to those who loved him.

Next to Pam, Nancy was my heroine. She helped me, at fourteen, to balance a canoe on a yoke on my shoulders: how proud I was to feel so strong! She showed me how she hid her Kotex in the clean socks she carried in her backpack. She never made me feel like a child, or excluded me. We often made the five-mile hike from the end of Forked Lake, where the bigger camps were, to Salmon, where there

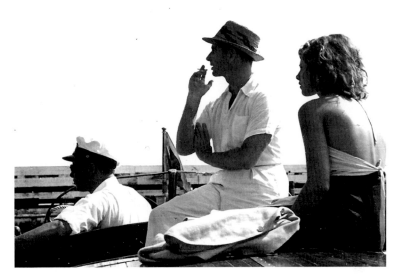

Nancy and her father, Sonny Whitney

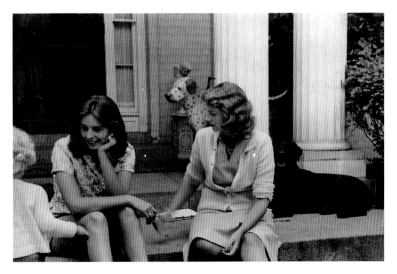

Pam and Nancy, Old Westbury, c. 1944

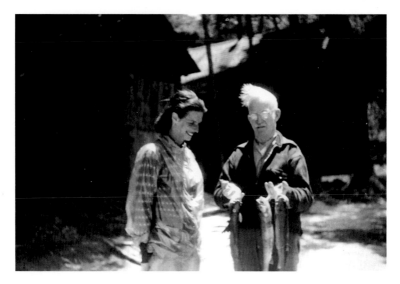

Bill and Pam, Salmon Lake, c. 1941

were no motorboats or electricity. Louis would light the fire under the grill, and we would eat ravenously, sitting on the porch steps as the sun fell beneath the indigo mountains. When the moon rose, we carried water from the lake to heat it and wash our tin plates and cups.

Bill Tuey, the "Mayor of Salmon Lake," sat by the stove, listening to the six o'clock news and then the ball game. The Yankees were his team, and his ear was pressed close to the scratchy plaid fabric that covered the speaker of his ancient radio. "G-g-go Joe," he stuttered softly. It was the year of DiMaggio's fifty-six game-hitting streak. Nothing distracted Bill as the static crackled across the hundreds of miles between the lake and New York City.

The amber reflection of the kerosene lamps in the kitchen lighted our way as we walked along the silvery boards to the outhouse (a two-holer). We squatted to brush our teeth on a massive log extending far into the lake, then

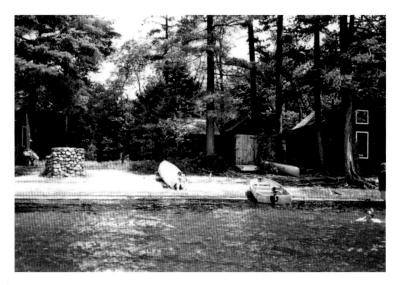

Salmon Lake Camp and beach

dragged our bedding down to the beach. The old gray blankets felt rough against our skin. We could feel the sand left by former campers too lazy to shake the heavy wool in teams, as we did, until every last grain returned to the beach. We looked for shooting stars, shivered at a coyote's eerie yapping, giggled as we mimicked Bill's sniff-sniff, and fell asleep.

I woke before dawn, a half-moon silver in the mist that hovered on the glassy lake. The guide house door opened and closed with a squeak of hinges. Bill stood for a minute on the beach, squinting in the dull light. With his bleached skin, colorless hair, and khaki clothes, he seemed part of the sand, sky, and water. Although I knew he had to duck his head when he came through the kitchen door, he looked small in the hazy landscape. I felt sad watching him. Peering at the gray mounds of sleepers, he caught my eye and winked, smiling. Good—he was once again champion and hero. He beckoned with one hand, one finger to his lips. I slithered silently from my warm cocoon, not wanting to share this moment with the others, and followed him across the spit of land that separated our beach from what was called the girls' beach, where the girls bathed naked in my mother's day. They would squeal in horror when they caught the boys spying on them, angry, but titillated.

Bill paused behind a large rock and pointed. A doe was drinking with her two fawns, their graceful necks curved over the dark water. When I drew a surprised breath, their heads lifted instantly, ears alert. The doe snorted a warning and splashed to shore, jumping high over the bushes, her fawns close behin. Looking at Bill ruefully, I apologized for spooking them.

"Last week I saw a bear with her cubs," he said. "You don't want to fool with them, though. A bear will do anything to protect her cubs."

On the long trail to Forked Lake, Nancy, her friend Minnie, and I talked about Bill. Once a month, he went out for supplies, taking the long way round; walking to Charley Pond, rowing two miles across it, then portaging his guide boat to the stream that ran into Little Tupper Lake. From the mouth of the river, he rowed seven miles to Whitney Realty Company Headquarters to pick up what he needed. He stayed the night. During the year, he saw the occasional group of children in the summer, and hunters in the fall. Only rarely did he see a forester, or a lumberjack with a team of horses. In contrast, we ourselves were hardly ever alone.

Nothing was more feared than a forest fire, in this land where everyone's economic survival depended on the lumber industry. If the weather were very dry, Bill delayed his trip to Headquarters until it rained, making do with the meager remains of the month's food. Bill's eyes were sharp. He had saved thousands of acres more than once by reporting a fire in time for the rangers to put it out. He was careful to smoke the cigarettes he loved only after work, in camp. Nancy had heard that in wintertime he lived in a small room upstairs at Headquarters, keeping to himself, emerging once in a while for a game of whist or cribbage.

"One day, he drove across the ice to the end of Little Tupper Lake," said Nancy in her throaty, alluring voice. "There'd been a report that a bear was clawing at the walls of Camp Bliss. Bill climbed the hill to the house, and there was the bear, standing on its hind legs pushing at the window to get some sugar that had been left inside. Bill raised his gun and that bear charged him. Almost got him, too—but Bill was faster. He shot the bear through the head."

I wondered if Bill were lonely. I knew what that felt like. My sister and her gang, lying on the float getting a tan, would suddenly leap up and dive into the lake, shrieking with laughter, to swim a quarter of a mile to flirt with the doctor's sons across the lake. Nancy, who lived five miles down the lake, would smoke a corncob pipe with her older brother and his friends. In a tall pine tree on the shore, they built big slingshots that could hit objects a hundred feet away. When unsuspecting visitors rounded the sharp corner from the rocky channel that divided Big Forked from Little Forked Lake, Harry and Nancy bombarded them with rotten eggs and tomatoes. And they got away with it.

In contrast, *my* gang consisted of Lev and our nurse. I was nearly thirteen and eager for life, but my biggest excitement was reading the next chapter of *The Deerslayer*. I stayed as close to Pam as I could. My sister, at seventeen, was the most beautiful person alive. She glowed. In her two-piece white sharkskin bathing suit she was slim, but voluptuous. Her dark, wavy hair vibrated with energy as she tossed it back with a burst of laughter, revealing perfect white teeth within the rosy curve of her lips. Her sea-green eyes were fringed with long lashes. Funny and smart, with dozens of admirers and girlfriends, she swam farther, ran faster, rode better, and danced more gracefully than anyone I knew. She was perfect. All I wished was to be just like her. When she rushed off to Plumley Pond for late afternoon fishing, I followed, offering to row the guideboat while she fished. My arms were falling off by the time she and her friends caught enough bass for a good chowder.

Oh, the boys that visited that summer, hovering like dragonflies around Pam! All mad for her. All headed for the Army, Navy, or Marines. The Armstrong brothers, John and Tobin, were big attractive Texans. I became thoroughly attached to John, who not only taught me to play checkers but took the time to actually play the game with me—he was unique in his sweetness. He didn't let me win, either. He showed his consideration for me by playing his best. Pam would marry another of these boys, Jay Secor, later that same year, but I don't remember him with the same affection.

I watched my friend John whispering in her ear when they played Hearts, or surfacing in the lake like a porpoise to blow on her neck, but even though John was my favorite, was anyone good enough for Pam? The days were filled with sexual energy, I now see. It was thrilling to be on the edge of it, to sense the force driving my sister and her friends through space and time. The war in Europe had much to do with it, and the suspicion that our country would soon be involved.

CHAPTER 16

Last Drag

At home in Aiken, riding was still the center of our lives. At thirteen, I was jumping lines of Aiken fences; always excited, often terrified. Each line contained a dozen or more jumps, widely spaced over several miles. These jumps were built of long branches piled high and wide, topped with sturdy poles we mustn't allow our mounts' hooves to tick. After drilling—a kind of warm-up to collect our horses and ourselves—we'd proceed to the Loop Line, the Travers Line, or the High Point Line, avoiding others—like the Bear Pit Line, still too difficult for us—that we knew about from older riders. Anxious lest All Satin take the bit in his teeth and run away, humiliating me in front of the older girls and incurring Gaylard's scorn, I prayed I wouldn't fall, knock the rails from a jump, or run to one side or the other, rather than soaring gracefully over the fence. In other words, I prayed for control of my horse and myself. Sometimes, all went well, and Gaylard praised me. "Dismount," he'd say sternly at other times, and he'd get up on All Satin himself to demonstrate his power to control. Loving Satan, as I sometimes called him, I dreaded Gaylard's rough treatment of my baby. He'd kick him with his spurred heels and squeeze him between his thighs while galloping in tight circles, first one way then the other, coming to an abrupt halt that drove the horse sharply back on his haunches. I'd remount a shivering, lathered, newly angelic All Satin. Patting his shiny bay neck, curling my fingers in his rough black mane, I'd apologize to him under my breath: "Never again. I'll never lose you again—I'll keep you collected."

Sometimes I kept my word, sometimes not.

In early October of that year, we were ready to take the Loop Line fences. My partner, Celeste, her beautiful face contorted, hissed at me, "For God's sake, hold onto him today, Flora." Looking enviously at her bright blonde hair tied elegantly under her velvet hard hat, her breasts swelling in a well-cut black jacket, I felt especially conscious of my juvenile pigtail, dull bowler hat, and flat chest. Contracting my thigh muscles, Satan's hind legs were properly collected under him. Celeste and I, side by side as we'd been taught, jumped and galloped in the fresh breeze, neck and neck. Suddenly, All Satin's neck stretched long as he took the bit in his teeth. Helpless, scared, I hung on, pulling the reins as hard as I could, squeezing my knees. He didn't stop until Gaylard rode alongside and grabbed the reins, turning and slowing him.

The next time, at the top of the hill, the line of brush fences looming, my prancing horse was ready to go, foam flying from the bit as he tossed his head.

"All right, Leila?" I glanced at my new partner, who was sixteen, blonde, lovely, and an excellent rider. Her chestnut mare was champing at the bit, and she nodded.

"Don't get ahead of me," she shouted. We paced our horses' strides so they took off just before the fence, collecting them so they didn't carelessly hit the top rail or refuse to jump. The last three jumps were topped with bright green freshly cut pine boughs set vertically into the brush, rather

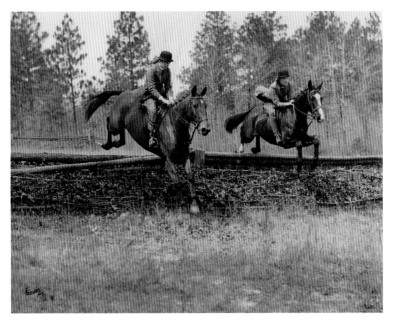

Pair jumping on All Satin

than the solid rails of the other fences, and we jumped them easily and fast, exchanging looks of triumph as we pulled up our horses.

"Well done, both of you; very good, all of you. Make much of your horses."

We did as Gaylard instructed, leaning forward, embracing the horses, murmuring lovingly in their ears as we patted their sweaty necks, smelling the rich odors of hot horse and oiled leather.

In those long ago days, I knew I was becoming a good rider. It was a way to escape adults, school, meals, sleep. While riding, I was in charge of a huge, powerful animal. *I was powerful. I* had control. I looked forward to those rides.

We spent as much time as we could with Gaylard. More than a teacher, he became a surrogate father to many of us.

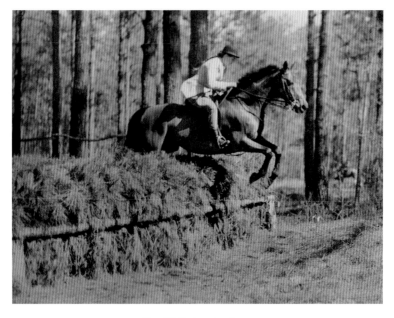

On All Satin, pine jump

My own father was kind and inspiring, but not a strong daily presence; not a teacher or disciplinarian. Always a bit of a mystery, he did teach me to make a perfect martini, giving me a certain status with my parents' friends, and he and my mother did take me shooting, when I was only twelve—that, too, was power! Still, my father was a distant figure. I admired his paintings, and I'd have liked to feel closer to him. My relationship with Gaylard, on the other hand, was absolutely clear: I obeyed him, I learned from him, I tried to earn his praise, I feared him, and I adored him.

All the same, I never saw Gaylard at home, or with his family. And never at a disadvantage. Gaylard, sleeping? Sick? In old clothes?—unimaginable.

"Name all the parts of the hoof, Anne."

"What is foundering, Flora? And what is the treatment?"

We learned to answer these questions. We picked stones from the soft insides of the hooves, an area known as the frog. We washed and brushed our horses. We soaped saddles and bridles; polished bits. We walked our horses to cool them down, and didn't allow them too much water. We never cantered on hard roads, although most of the roads in Aiken were made of soft red clay in deference to the horses. Nothing mattered to the Winter Colony as much as the culture of the horse. The ultimate test for a rider was the Hunt. These took place on Tuesdays, Thursdays, and Saturdays, fall and winter. Saturdays were devoted to young hunters.

Fox hunts had started in 1900 in Aiken, but unfortunately foxes had been extinct in that part of the country since the end of World War I. The original hunts had been replaced by drag hunts: a piece of bloody meat was dragged over a pre-set route (one or another of about ten trails through deep woods) with a dozen or more jumps per mile, each four-to-five feet high. Spotted foxhounds—purebred beagles—followed the scent. Immaculately dressed men and women followed the hounds in tailored black jackets with split tails, jodhpurs, boots, white shirts, and bowler hats with a hard crown, attached by a cord to the shirt. Around the neck, instead of a tie, a wide white stock held by a pin was neatly folded, which could serve, if needed, as a bandage or sling. The Master of the Hounds and his or her assistants, known as Whips—often women—wore black velvet hard hats and gorgeous red jackets, traditionally called pink coats. The pace was rapid, the fences high. Most participants were expert riders. The season started on Thanksgiving Day with Monsignor Smith's Blessing of the Hounds, administered to the riders and animals. The Monsignor was also expected to produce good weather on opening day—and, in fact, it was almost always balmy.

At thirteen, I'd only attended the preliminary meets where everyone gathered before the actual start. My mother and I drove in the buggy, a two-or-four-wheeled wooden cart pulled by our most dependable horse—one who would stand quietly in the crowd of horses, hounds, and other carriages, undisturbed by piercing whinnies, barking dogs, and the Whips cracking their long braided leather thongs as they called shrilly to the hounds. My mother's friends crowded around her as they made plans for lunches, dinners, card games, pigeon shoots, and picnics. Distracted and intent, I watched every move made by Gaylard and the younger riders.

Alongside Monsignor Smith on his spirited black stallion was the eccentric Jessie Mann, side-saddle on her gray mare in a black skirt, purple coat, yellow scarf and feathered red velvet cap from the nineties. A column of older students from Aiken Prep School in their uniform of gray jackets with navy blue piping clustered together, and nearby stood a group of girls in black coats from Fermata, the boarding school. In the middle of it all, Pam sat easily on her handsome bay stallion, Rare Charm, black hairs bristling from his neatly-braided mane and tail, not unlike the black curls tumbling from Pam's bowler hat. Animated, she talked and laughed, ringed by hunters eager to demonstrate to her their skill and daring. Also riding sidesaddle on a seasoned chestnut gelding was Mrs. Thomas Hitchcock. In her

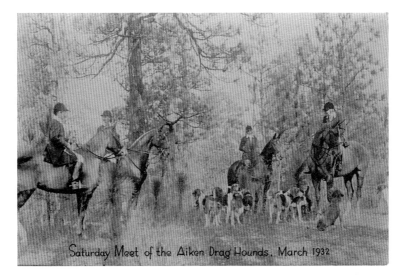

Saturday Meet of the Aiken Drag Hounds, March 1932

Mrs. Hitchcock and Whips, 1932

seventies, she took every fence, as she had for fifty years. She and her husband had been leaders of the drag hunts, and the early Winter Colony.

The horn sounded its compelling, mournful notes, and the milling crowd, mysteriously ordered, moved off in pairs to the first fence. My mother and I drove sedately along a sandy trail, the pleasure I felt in her company colliding with my intense desire to be one of those soaring over the huge obstacles.

Just after Thanksgiving that year, Gaylard announced to my parents that I was ready to ride in the next Saturday drag. I prepared by riding each day, giving Satan every chance to take the bit in his teeth and run as I tested my mastery of the beautiful, willful creature. Hissing to calm the horse as he worked, Walter, our Scottish groom, had polished him to perfection. Nevertheless, I brushed and brushed again his silky coat, combed his luxuriant black mane and tail, and checked his hooves repeatedly for the tiniest stone.

Friday morning, feeling sick, I forced down my breakfast of eggs and toast and dragged myself to school lest anyone notice my paleness and bundle me into bed. Coming home at noon, I had such cramps that I couldn't eat lunch. Our nurse walked to my room with me and asked what was wrong.

"I don't know. I'm bleeding—" I finally admitted.

"Oh, Flora, why didn't you say?" She sat me down to explain menstruation.

Why, I wonder today, hadn't my mother or my nurse told me sooner? Carelessness? Embarrassment? It seems a metaphor for the way in which I was raised. A quixotic combination of love and neglect. Love, when my parents remembered, coming in spurts, was always welcome. Neglect, when their own interests absorbed them, was less welcome.

I felt strange: sick and feeble, with painful cramps. My nurse tucked me into bed with a hot water bottle, and before long my mother appeared, glowing from a triumph at the Gun Club, where she, my father and their friends had competed that afternoon. "Oh, darling." she said, "What a thing. Poor you. Stay right there, I'll get you something to make you feel better." Off she flew, to return in a few minutes with an evil-smelling potion. "What my mother used to give me— hot lemonade and plenty of gin." I downed it all, and fell asleep. (Since that day, I have never been able to taste gin or even smell it without feeling sick. My mother thought it indispensable. She even sent me off to boarding school with a little bottle of it, which a teacher promptly discovered, and confiscated.)

I was not allowed to ride for several days. I'd been looking forward to riding in a drag ever since I could remember,

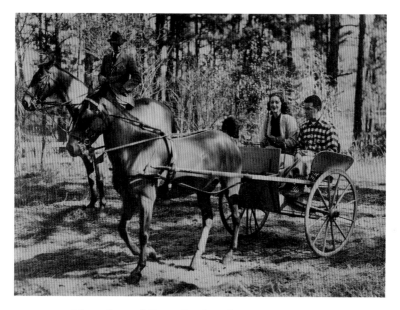

My mother and Carnes Weeks, in buggy at meet, c. 1940

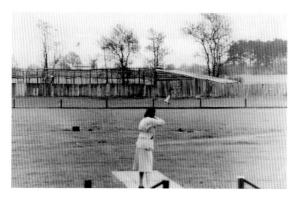

My mother competing at Gun Club, Aiken, c. 1940

and getting the Curse (as my mother called it) was very distressing. I cried like a child. Although my parents and my nurse treated me with new respect, nothing could make up for my disappointment. Apparently, my unwilling and unwitting accomplishment had brought me instant maturity, and I looked often in the mirror to see if I'd changed in some obvious way—but all I could see was a mournful face.

"How are you feeling today, darling?" my mother asked. "It's wonderful, what's happened to you. I've always been glad to be a girl. You'll be glad, too. The Curse means being able to have babies. That's the best thing. A nuisance, but worth it. You'll be over it in a day or two. Why don't you curl up here on my window seat with a book for the afternoon?"

With a hug and a kiss, her twelve-guage shotgun from the dove room next door slung over her arm, off she hurried, leaving me behind—my condition didn't quite warrant acceptance into the society of grownups. It was slowly becoming clear to me that the older I became, the more my mother would include me in her life.

Meanwhile, what about the Curse was so wonderful? I didn't see it that way. For me, it signified all that I couldn't do: ride, swim, play tennis. I couldn't even wear certain clothes—tight, light colored—in case my condition became apparent, especially to boys or men. Of course, my father steered clear of mentioning menstruation, although he was especially tender during those times of the month. (My mother, alerted by my nurse, must have told him.) The bloody sheets or clothes that shamed me were whisked away and washed by Maria, the laundress, far from sight. Later in life, when I scrubbed them myself, I felt the same embarrassment and humiliation I had felt as a privileged child—but with anger added to the mix. Anger at my mother for segregating me as

[242]

if I had a contagious illness. My discomfort and cramps had been exaggerated. She had been taught to romanticize menstruation, putting the burden of any messiness on maids, on laundresses, and on me.

The drag I missed was that year's last.

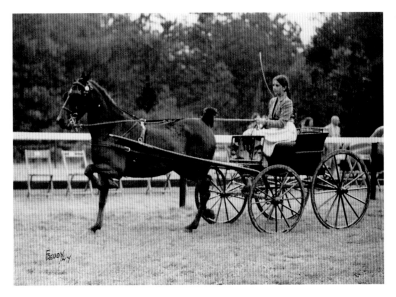

Driving Pam's hackney, Fire Escape, c 1942

CHAPTER 17

A Wedding

My parents had a friend in the army named Major Fargo, who was stationed in Augusta, Georgia, about forty-five minutes by car from Aiken. My brother, Whitty, already prone to falling desperately for one lovely girl after another, was extremely fond of Major Fargo's daughter, Pat. Although Whit was in Cambridge, a freshman at Harvard, the Major often brought his daughter when he came to visit. Whit's girlfriends were enchanted not only by Whit, but by his whole family; I can remember many of them appearing for a meal or a visit whether or not Whit was at home. Each of them longed to be the one and only, and for many years, one girl rapidly followed another in Whit's undoubtedly genuine affections. He charmed them with his rapt attention, sense of humor, and kindness. Being with him was great fun. Once the romance was over, Whit and his girls often remained friends.

After lunch one Sunday, I was delegated to take Major Fargo for a carriage ride. Pleased to demonstrate my skill at managing a pair of spirited horses, I took up the reins and we trotted around Aiken at a smart pace behind Pam's lively hackneys, Fire Escape and Fireboy. When we returned an hour later, my parents rushed out to meet us:

"Jimmy, you've been recalled to camp—the Japanese have bombed Pearl Harbor. We're at war."

Drag hunts were cancelled for the duration of the war. I was never to be anointed into that ceremony. Gaylard didn't mention my absence from the drag that year, and although our riding lessons continued, our lives were to change.

On December 20, 1941, Pam married Jay Secor. If not for the war, they might have waited, eventually discovering that they weren't suited to each other. My sister, despite having many close girlfriends, asked me to be her maid of honor. I floated on a cloud of happiness. To be chosen by my heroine for this honor, when I was only thirteen, gave me an exhilarating feeling of self-confidence and maturity. I stood as still as a statue while Mrs. Schulhofer measured and fit me for my long ruby-red velvet dress, and a snood of the same fabric to cover my head in church. I endlessly practiced the slow, measured walk I would take down the aisle of St. Thaddeus Church, book balanced on my head, holding in my stomach. I studied Pam and her friends intently, hoping to emulate their grace and poise.

In December, as the wedding approached, Joye Cottage grew crowded. Huge bouquets of flowers filled the house; there were guests at every meal. Jay's twelve ushers began to drift in, one by one; I'd find two or three in the evenings, lounging on sofas and armchairs, drinks in hand. When John Armstrong arrived, he and I continued our Adirondack games of checkers. Packages of every size and shape arrived daily—teatime was dedicated to opening the presents. Family and friends gathered to help cut paper and

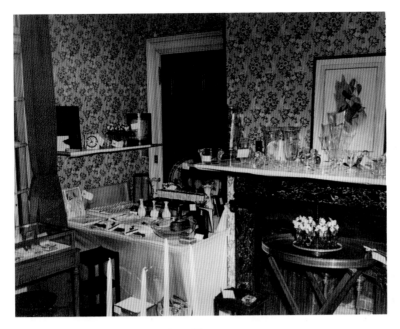

Pam's wedding presents

string as masses of presents, some of it furniture, emerged from the boxes. It was exciting to unwrap the many gifts.

My mother was practical about the presents: "You can return the bowl and get more of your silver pattern. And that teapot—you certainly don't need two."

It was almost like Christmas. The presents were carefully arranged in the New Room that my mother had made a few years earlier for parties. Plywood sawhorses covered with white cloths were crowded with glittering Steuben glass, flowered French linens, heirloom silver and porcelains. There was a special table just for clocks. Friends dropped in to look at the gifts as if they were visiting a museum, moving from one table to the next, approving, comparing, criticizing as they carefully scrutinized each engraved white

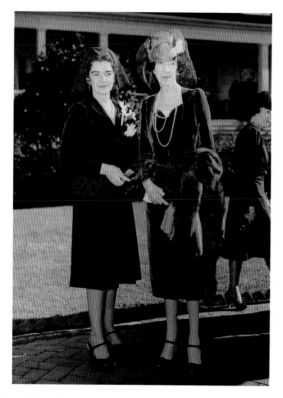

My mother and grandmother at Joye Cottage before the wedding

pasteboard card with the donors' name and message. Near the wedding day, a guard was posted in the New Room as jewels from older relatives arrived. Emeralds, diamonds, and sapphires in old fashioned settings; family treasures for this much-loved oldest granddaughter or grandniece.

December 20 was sunny and warm. My mother and Gamoo, as we called our grandmother, were the last to arrive in the church. Gamoo was elegant in a moss-green velvet dress with peplum, and a hat with a big plume. As always, my mother was chic in an embroidered black jacket and short black skirt by Hattie Carnegie, wearing black wedge pumps with open toes—not at all like Jay's mother, who wore a long

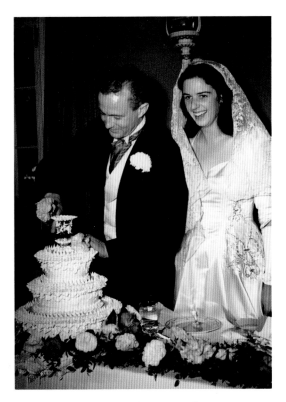

Cutting the cake—Pam and Jay

beige silk dress that somehow made her look both more formal and older than my grandmother. As ring-bearer, Lev, in
his first long pants and a dark jacket, carried the gold ring
on its cushion down the aisle.

Pam was dressed in white satin, her lace veil streaming
to the floor. Her expression was solemn as she held out her
hand for the ring. Her gaiety returned as she left the church
arm in arm with her husband, smiling at the rows of guests.

The wedding was over before I had time to savor
my starring role: accepting the white bouquet that Pam
handed me at the altar and, after the ceremony, holding
her long train so that she could turn to leave the church.

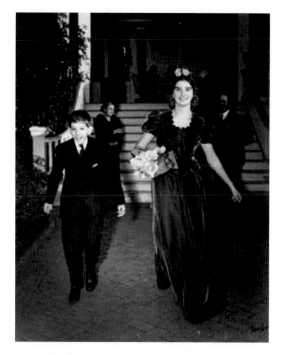

With Lev, Miss Sleigh, and Mr Grant behind at Pam's wedding reception,
Joye Cottage, December 20, 1941

I was concentrating too hard on my duties to fully absorb the Prayer Book's somber words, *Until death us do part.* It was more likely to happen in wartime than I realized.

The reception in Joye Cottage was a joyous blur; a long wedding breakfast with many toasts and much hilarity. The bride and groom left for a brief honeymoon before he would report for duty in the army. Right away, I missed my sister.

*

In 1942, Whit left Harvard to join the army. The summer before, he'd taken flying lessons in the Adirondacks with Herb Helms, hoping for a commission in the Air Force.

He loved to fly, but when it became apparent that he was color-blind, he knew that the Air Force wouldn't have him. He came home every weekend from Mitchell Field, in Long Island where we were living, and asked us to test him over and over, using the cardboard sheets of colored dots he'd somehow wrangled from the Army. He had to be able to see their hidden numbers in order to be accepted. I thought of it as a delightful game, little aware of the danger Whit would face if he couldn't recognize the lights of a landing field. Whit ate huge bunches of carrots as he memorized the numbers, only to find that the Air Force's final test used pages he'd never seen. He did eventually fly, but as a pilot working behind the front lines.

He and his friends couldn't wait to be sent overseas, and they joined the Service before being drafted. Their fathers and mothers, to whom World War I was still vivid, seemed nevertheless united in support of their sons, eager that they should be part of the fight against Hitler. Almost everyone felt that the war was just and necessary. A few differed, including Larry and Cully Miller, sons of my father's brother, Larry, who, as conscientious objectors, performed difficult and dangerous medical and physical alternative services during the war. Although each went on to lead an exemplary life as a Quaker, teaching at home or working in distant countries for the Society of Friends, they were left with painful memories of the hurtful attitudes of their friends and relatives during the war.

To Lev's and my amazement, our nurse, Miss Sligh, told us she was marrying Basil Grant, the Englishman who ran the tack shop near the polo fields. She'd always wanted to head that way on our walks; I finally knew why! I was delighted, having reached the romantic age—although I couldn't imagine anyone so old being in love—but Lev was crushed. "Oh, Miss Sligh," he wanted to say, "please, please don't marry Mr. Grant. Wait until I grow up . . ."

*

I gathered what fragments of information about the war that I could—the battles between the Allies and the Axis powers on many fronts, the capture by the FBI of eight German saboteurs who'd landed in Florida and New York.

At home in the US, Enrico Fermi split the atom; T. S. Eliot's *Four Quartets* was published; Irving Berlin wrote "White Christmas;" and Bing Crosby starred in "Holiday Inn."

I prayed for victory, and for the soldiers that I knew, even if death didn't seem real to me. Death applied to creatures furred, feathered, or scaled. No one close to me had died until my grandmother, Gertrude Vanderbilt Whitney, died in April of 1942, at the age of sixty-eight. The next day, my mother began to wear black. Her gloves, hats, stockings, even her jewelry were black. The brightly colored shoes, bags and scarves that she loved were dyed black. The men in the family had black armbands sewed to their sleeves, and replaced their colored hatbands with black ones—small gestures in comparison to those of the women. My mother missed my grandmother dreadfully. She refused to go to parties. She spent much of her time answering, on heavy black-bordered stationery, her name engraved in black at the top, each of the hundreds of condolence letters she'd received. (Exactly as I did, on lighter-weight but black-bordered paper just the same, after her own death many years later.) In Mum's clear, flowing handwriting, unchanged since her schooldays, she expressed gratitude to each correspondent for the sympathy

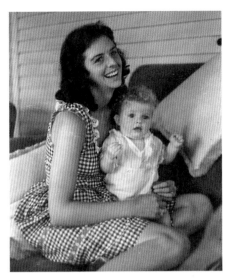

Pam holding Tim, 1943

given her, and said something, as well, about her enduring love and admiration for her mother.

Since I was only thirteen and at school in Aiken, I didn't go to New York City for the funeral. I was considered too young to wear black. During that hot summer, however, our mother expected my sister Pam, who was heavily pregnant with her first child, to wear black, and she did, although she was allowed to wear white at summer's end, when Pam, only twenty years old, feeling sick and already unhappy in her marriage, followed her husband to camp in the Midwest.

It was only late in their relationship that my grandmother, Gertrude, and her mother Alice became close, and it was the same with Gertrude and my mother. At eighteen, my mother wrote to a beau:

> ... I fell to wishing I were the daughter of different kind of people and in an entirely different environment. My life would probably have been so much more worthwhile. I have a horrid feeling that when I am old and look back on my life, there will

be no feeling of any satisfaction of having been of any use in the world. The powers that have been given to me, as well as to everyone else, will have been absolutely wasted, and I will die, having lived a useless, flippant and futile life. Pleasant prospect!

Here comes my only real sorrow. I can't talk perfectly frankly to Mama. I never feel that she understands or gives me the smallest bit of credit for any sense at all. She treats me as if I were about 12 and I don't ever feel that she makes any effort to give me a chance to say what I would like to. . . oh! It's awful. I admire and respect and of course adore Mama, but there is no companionship at all.

As my mother fell in love, married, and had children, her interest in books, writing, and art became akin to her mother's interests. Eventually, her relationship with her mother became very close, even if my mother always doubted her own accomplishments—her own use in the world. I wish she'd had a stronger sense of herself, and of her value to others.

Although my grandmother had been a tremendous figure in our family, I hadn't known her well. That she was famous—a sculptor of large monuments and the founder of the Whitney Museum of American Art—I knew. Moreover, that very Christmas, she'd given me a most prized possession, a typewriter. Painfully aware of the atmosphere of grief in our home, I wished that I, like my mother and Pam, could show my sorrow by dressing in the same, rather glamorous-looking black. But that was yet another ritual awaiting me.

For our family, the big event that fall was the birth of Pam's first child, Timothy Jay Secor. Since her husband was overseas and the family had no home of their own, she brought Tim to Joye Cottage and asked William Gaylard to be his godfather. Standing beside Gaylard for the baptism in the white church, I noticed his height for the first time. I was as tall as Gaylard.

CHAPTER 18

Clare Chanler

In 1942, when I was nearly fourteen, we moved from Aiken to New York. My mother became a Gray Lady, and Pam a nurses' aide, doing volunteer work in a hospital for wounded soldiers. Aiken was too remote, too isolated from the effects of the war, and they both wanted to be involved in the war effort.

I was enrolled at the Brearley School in New York City. Sis became my governess and companion. Every morning, she walked me the few blocks from our apartment on 86th Street, near the East River, to school on 83rd Street. I dreaded that little walk with the narcissism of a shy yet self-centered adolescent. I was sure all eyes were upon me. None of the other girls had chaperones. In school, with no friends and no real knowledge of the world, I was miserable. I could handle the class work, but the gym, the cafeteria, even the wide hallways were terrifying mazes I couldn't navigate. Among the other girls—accomplished, knowing, wearing glamorously shortened uniforms and costly belts—I was lost. Although I prayed I wouldn't meet any of my schoolmates when Sis walked me to school, my shame was tinged with secret pleasure. Sis provided a link to a world in which skills I'd learned in Aiken that were useless in New York—riding,

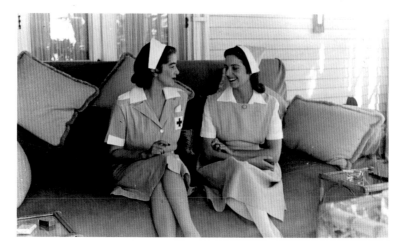

My mother and Pam in uniforms of Gray Lady and nurses' aide, c. 1943

shooting—held value. My classmates were smart and pretty. They played hockey and basketball. They could deal with girls their own age. I couldn't even climb the rope in gym class. Beginning his career, the now widely known and respected Dr. Spock was the school doctor. When he examined me for a routine physical and found my heart-beat erratic, he told my mother it was the result of anxiety.

Most daunting, the other girls knew boys. The pigtail down my back, and weekends with my parents in the country seemed childish compared to their permanent waves, mascara, and Saturday night parties. They rushed to share a special table in the cafeteria, claimed the back seats in class-rooms, talked in code. When I was at last invited to a co-ed roller-skating party, excited but terrified, I immediately fell, split my eyebrow and was carried to the doctor for stitches.

Removed from my home in Aiken, I was like a snail with-out a shell. I was too sensitive for my new, brutal environ-ment. At the small school in my grandfather's former squash court, I'd been top of the heap. Feeling helpless and hope-less in an unfamiliar, competitive world, I was frightened and depressed, even if that concept was not in my family's lexicon. I tried to hide my misery since I could never have told my parents how I felt. In front of those adored but distant figures I aimed to appear poised and happy. Now I see that they'd have encouraged my confidences, but my nurse and riding teacher had taught me to keep a stiff upper lip. There were some positive aspects to this misery, however. Learning to be self-sufficient was useful later, when I was somewhat isolated as a mother with small children and a busy husband. In school, I focused on academics, where I could reach some level of achievement. English. History. Latin. Not math. There, I was always lost.

Weekends, after tying a pillow over her tail, as Pam and Whitty called her sensitive sacroiliac, Sis took me ice skating at Rockefeller Center. Ice was new to us both. We circled the rink sedately, reciting Corneille's heroic verses or discussing the Count of Monte Cristo's latest adventure. We were an unlikely pair: Sis with her pillow and moth-eaten squirrel coat, and I, pigtail to my waist, ankles turning painfully on the slick surface, an awkward and shy teenager.

When, in my self-absorption, I was overcome with lone-liness, Sis's unfailing empathy cheered me. No matter how alien the territory, she remained my touchstone. I depended on her love. When we walked to Cushman's Bakery for a chocolate cake, I felt reassured. A sense of self returned, if only briefly, as we talked and laughed. Although I was much too old, she still tucked me in at night, lifting the edge of the mattress the better to tighten the covers, wrapping me in the cool white sheets as if to protect me from nightmares and the bad feelings of the day. *Bon soir, ma petite, dors bien.*

In the country, gas rationing made driving impossible. At my family's large enclave in Old Westbury, male company was limited to the Polish workers too old to be drafted. Lev and I were paid to work on my Uncle Sonny's farm, and we were extremely proud to line up with the farmers, stable hands, gardeners, and grooms each Friday afternoon to collect our small wages. Each morning, we bicycled the mile or so to the barns. We rode past my aunt's and uncle's houses, the French House where we lived before moving into my grandmother's house after her death in 1942, and finally the farm manager's house. Soybeans were planted where race horses and polo ponies had once grazed, and we were proud of our family's patriotic role in contributing protein to our meat-rationed country. My brother, only ten when we started to work that summer of 1942, picked strawberries and other fruits—the easiest job— while I was delegated to the chicken house after a short and unsuccessful stint milking cows. After chopping off the heads of chickens slated for one of our many family dinner tables, the men and I cleaned the chickens, dipping them into a tub of hot wax, stripping the feathers, and picking out the stubborn

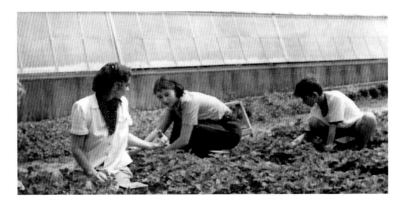

With my mother and Lev, picking strawberries on farm, c. 1943

pinfeathers. Another child might have been horrified, but I'd grown up shooting doves and ducks, and catching and cleaning fish. I'd learned to be quite realistic about the killing of animals. The cannibalistic Rhode Island Reds were made to wear red spectacles to prevent them from pecking each other to death—if everything looked like bloody flesh they wouldn't be able to distinguish their sisters' bare rear ends (the most accessible and thus vulnerable part of their bodies). They were vicious, those hens, even if they suffered from a calcium deficiency, perhaps due to a wartime scarcity. I was terrified of collecting their eggs and wore heavy gloves as protection from their angry beaks.

Thinking of those days now, I see that even though the men had no choice but to accept the boss's niece, they were genuinely kind. I surely wasn't much help; they could have done the job without me. Lev and I had been foisted upon them by our parents, who were no doubt trying to occupy our summers fruitfully at a difficult time. I thought of myself, however, as indispensable to the family's sustenance, working diligently as I taught myself not to mind the foul odor of innards. I listened to the men's tales, appreciating their efforts to make me feel at home in their world; wishing I could better understand their language and join in singing their songs. On the other hand, I couldn't wait for the day to be finished so I could return to our house where I'd find Pam and her fascinating friends. Spending time with them, listening to their talk—particuliarly that of my favorite cousin, Barklie Henry—was the only way I knew to learn about real life.

From the time he was fourteen, Barklie lived in our Long Island house. During the war, his mother, my mother's younger sister, Barbara, was ill, and his father, also named

Barklie, but known as Buz, was an officer in the Navy. Bark, only a year older than I but more mature in worldly experience, was my idol. He looked very much like our Vanderbilt ancestors, with strong features and a big, slightly hooked nose. Intelligent, outspoken, and funny, he planned to become a doctor. During the summer, home from Exeter, he worked as an orderly in the operating room at the Glen Cove Hospital. Arriving home in blood-spattered clothes, he'd head right for the old Victrola in our living room and play jazz records at top volume, much to my parents' dismay.

"But Auntie Flora, Uncle Cully, these songs are beautiful. Just listen for a few minutes." Bark was never able to convince them, despite his enthusiasm. His toeless, battered, bloodstained sneakers were another source of my parents' irritation, but my father's teasing would only elicit a hearty belly laugh as he begged Barklie to change his shoes for dinner. All I wanted was to be with him. I was convinced that he knew everything about life, especially sex. He was very attracted to Pam, who'd come home when her husband was sent overseas. Bark probably hoped to get the same from her as I did from him. Evenings, home from the farm, I would sit and listen to them talk. Sometimes Lev and I drove to the movies in the village as my aunt's electric car did not use rationed gas. Or, best of all, I'd ride behind Barklie on his powerful motorcycle.

An army platoon billeted in our extensive, now remodeled stables was of great interest to me. I had no idea where it had come from or how long it would stay. The soldiers were in the infantry. They climbed, as I did, the 120 steps of our Stanford White water tower, the highest spot on Long Island, where we kept watch for enemy planes and submarines. Those hours were the most thrilling of my adolescent

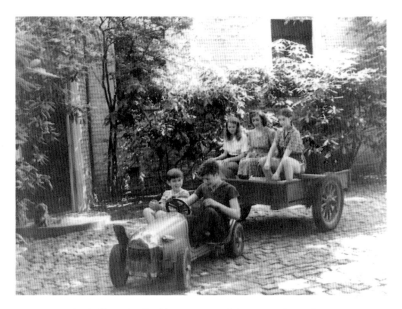

In Redbug, Lev, Barklie; in wagon, Marianna, Sis, and me

years. I now realize that those young soldiers must have been instructed to behave appropriately in my presence. Too bad for me; longing for experience! I managed to glean only a few new words, and a couple of salacious stories. The men were genial, and we played cribbage by the hour, the skies empty of even friendly aircraft. There was always the hope that we'd spot an unknown plane, when we'd be able to push the red button on the phone, but no swastika-painted Fokkers flew past the tower and no submarines poked their pernicious periscopes above the calm waters of Long Island Sound. I recently found my official instruction book, marked in big red letters, TOP SECRET. It was filled with the pictures and statistics of every known airplane and underwater craft. I also found the tests we'd taken in order to certify our capability. I'd felt very important when I passed.

*

Our summer activities may have occasionally been boring, but that first winter in New York was distinctly unpleasant. Only one person my age alleviated my distress. I met her on a day that began especially miserably. Dumping my books on a chair's broad arm, I settled next to a very popular classmate, who looked at me as if I had chicken pox. I suddenly realized that she was saving the seat for someone, but the bell was already ringing and it was too late to move.

Our math teacher, Miss Schuyler, like a hawk with a cruel beak hunting for its next meal, swept the rows of identically blue-clad girls with her fierce gaze, settling on the most helpless.

"Flora, come to the blackboard and write the first problem."

I hadn't understood the algebra homework, but I picked up the chalk and copied it on the blackboard. My x's and y's smudged the blackboard in a maze of errors. Symbols of orderly relationships, they remained beyond my understanding. The class was silent, cowed, while Miss Schuyler mocked my ineptitude.

"Well, Flora, this is a mess."

Slinking back to my desk, trying not to look at anyone, tears ran down my face. After class, I sat alone in the cafeteria. Soon, a girl I hardly knew came up to me.

"Can I sit with you? I hate Miss Schuyler, don't you?"

From then on, I had a friend. Clare Chanler. She was as good at math as she was at writing, music, art—all the things that really matter. Even boys. Why did she come over that day? There was no condescension—simply concern for someone who'd been hurt. Was it her kind and understanding self, or had she too been made to feel incompetent at some point in her own young life? Both, I believe now. She possessed extraordinary insight—she saw through my defenses, and found a kindred spirit.

In the self-deprecating way I've tried all my life to overcome, I said, "Well, it was really my fault. I don't know why I can't do algebra."

She sat down with a sandwich and a chocolate chip cookie. She loved sweets. I did, too. We compared classes. We both liked English and History. We didn't like Biology.

"Why aren't you taking French?" she asked.

"Oh, I've always spoken French. I have a French governess. They put me in a Greek class. It's really hard. Especially with the Latin I'm taking. I wish I could take a living language—Italian or Spanish. There are only three of us in Greek, though. That part's nice."

Clare spoke of her piano lessons, her chorus group, the art class she loved, and the play in rehearsal. My participation in the school's elective classes and extracurricular activities was nonexistent. Both my grandmother and mother had attended Brearley. Clare's mother had been in my mother's class. At school and later, when they came out and went to the same dances and house parties, they'd known each other well. My mother was godmother to Clare's older sister, Susan. But our mothers hadn't been close for years— they'd had some kind of falling out, so we had not been encouraged to become friends. Perhaps if we had, we might not have become friends so quickly. Other girls' parents had told their daughters to be nice to Flora, the new girl; but they had steered away from me, instead. At that first lunch, Clare and I discovered that we both liked Mrs. Macintosh, Brearley's headmistress. She taught only one class, our ninth grade English class. We were reading

Chaucer and Shakespeare. Clare and I practiced Macbeth with each other: "Double, double, toil and trouble," we chanted.

From then on, we had lunch together regularly. Although we were real friends, I don't remember visiting her family's house on 92nd Street or inviting her to our apartment on 86th Street. Perhaps there weren't many opportunities. I spent weekends in Long Island with my parents, and vacations in Aiken; the Chanlers went to their house on the Hudson River. During the school year, Clare's life was filled with projects, family, and, like me, plenty of homework. Maybe, too, such visits weren't welcomed by our estranged mothers.

Clare was all that I was not: creative, eager for experience, self-confident. With her, I felt released from solitary confinement. Oh, the joy of being accepted by such a girl, of talking and laughing with her! I expanded like a dry sponge in water. At fourteen, a red-gold frizz framed Clare's pale oval face. She was tall, with an upright stance and the graceful gait of a dancer. She sang often and well, breathing deeply; maybe that's why her ribs protruded. Her near-sighted blue eyes were tranquil. (Clear Forest, a friend later dubbed Clare Forster, which was her first husband's last name.) She was popular, chosen quickly for teams or as a partner for games and walks; the center of the group. The other stars in our homeroom had seen my social and athletic ineptitude and remained cool to me, but not Clare.

Clare and I left Brearley at the end of the year and went to Garrison Forest, a boarding school near Baltimore. I've never known why we weren't separated—but I suspect it was thanks to our headmistress. "Get that poor child away from New York," was Mrs. Macintosh's advice to my

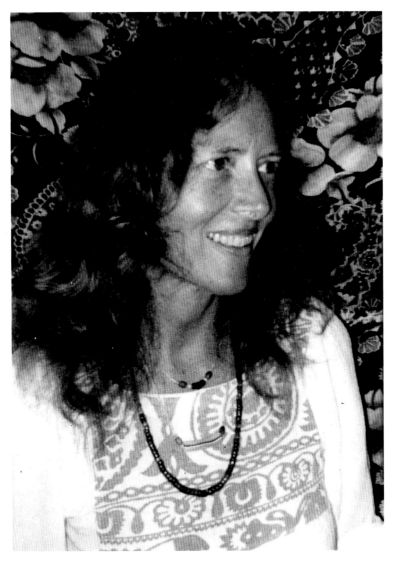

Clare Chanler, c. 1960

mother, so I escaped, unaware that one takes one's problems along. Why did Clare leave school when she was so successful and happy? I found out later that she and her mother weren't getting along—her mother's criticism hurt and undermined Clare at an age when one's self-esteem is often fragile. Maybe Clare's father thought that she would be happier away from home, and that his wife would also benefit. He'd have seen that Mrs. Chanler was jealous of Clare's intelligence and creativity, of her magnetism, and her inevitable emancipation. Perhaps even jealous of her looks.

By the time we left for boarding school, Clare at fifteen was nearly six feet tall, with robust, shapely legs, a tiny waist, and small breasts which she hoped to enlarge with special exercises. She set about improving her measurements on the train. Holding her elbows high, she would press her palms together, then relax them. I told her that our fellow passengers would take us for weirdos practicing some strange rite. She just laughed and squeezed harder. I laughed, too. It was impossible not to respond to her moods.

Clare's deep, reflective gaze was disconcerting to those harboring any thought they hoped to keep private, but fascinating to those she charmed. Her long hands with square-tipped fingers were those of an artist. Her vibrant alto was right on key, strong and tender. Although I, too, did well in school, I envied Clare's ability to write easily. She possessed—or was possessed by—a distinctive inner voice; an assurance that drew others to her like a lodestar.

I had to fend off classmates who wanted to be with Clare when we walked in the woods, talked, listened to records. We went to sleep early to avoid the hours of gossip, and the giggles of our classmates. One serious girl lured Clare with the poetry and music only she of all our schoolmates had discovered—Eliot, Auden, Hindemith. Clare accepted these offerings happily, but when the three of us went to the deli to devour Rocky Road ice cream with malted milk powder, the girl sulked. In her fury, she wrote a clever poem portraying my beautiful mother as a high-society witch with blood-red nails who scorned her ugly duckling daughter. With no idea how to get back at her, I kept my anger inside.

My nickname, Mouse, said a lot about me. My self-confidence was slowly strengthened by Clare's friendship. I'd lost my childhood tubbiness, but lacked the curves I envied in other girls. I couldn't think of a word to say to the few boys I met. Scorning my classmates' dirty jokes, probably because I didn't understand them, I studied hard and read a lot. I slept with rag curlers. I was ashamed of the thicket of black hairs that sprouted on my legs, which my mother arranged to have waxed on my visits home. Still terrible at team games, I was teased for too often using the only accepted excuse for cutting sports, which was having one's period. Clare, graceful in all things, played basketball, badminton, and field hockey.

"You'll never guess what happened," Clare said one day as she returned from choir practice. She told me about two friends who'd been caught smoking behind Manor House, and sent home. We were both distressed, but as we wondered if they'd be allowed to return after their disgrace, we found ourselves giggling, and finally howling, tears rolling down our cheeks. "Uncle Bronson laughter," Clare gasped. When their Uncle Bronson died, Clare and her sister Rosanna had rolled helplessly on the floor laughing at the news. I still think of that today, when family and friends are falling away. The twin impulses to cry and laugh; the sublime and the ridiculous.

My eleventh grade French teacher, Mary Boyd was small, with dark curly hair, a captivating husky voice, and a cheerful laugh. Since I was better able to read French than the other students and thus more capable of difficult work, she introduced me to more advanced poets and writers, assigning me special projects. I felt proud to be singled out, and I did well. Miss Boyd's home was in South Carolina, so she boarded the Southern Railway, just as I did, en route to Columbia for Christmas vacation. My parents, already ensconced in their drawing room in SR 40, the Pullman car in which we always traveled, invited her to join them for cocktails.

My father asked Randolph, the porter I'd known all my life, to bring the ice. Then Daddy produced a well-stocked travel kit and mixed his usual dry martinis in a silver shaker. I watched, surprised to see my revered teacher become expansive under the influence of my parents' charm and the strong drinks. They talked and laughed, even using each other's first names, then an uncommon familiarity.

"So you studied in Tours—no wonder your French is so perfect," said my mother. "Will you return to France when this miserable war is over?"

"I hope to, very much. If my friends near Tours are all right. I worry, though. I haven't heard from them lately."

"We go to a village close to Tours," my mother said "But we haven't heard from the caretakers of our house for two years. Last time they wrote, German officers were about to be quartered there. Jean Louis said he'd buried the silver in the garden before they arrived. I dread to think what's happened to them, and to the house."

"That's where my friends live," Miss Boyd exclaimed,

and off we all went to the dining car for an evening of reminiscence.

Back in school, Miss Boyd and I knew each other in a different context—the intimacy of family. She'd make little jokes that only I could understand, or wink at me conspiratorially. She wanted to give me a little push—perhaps she thought that gaining confidence through friendship with a teacher would help me to develop. That spring I was given the lead in a French play and spent extra time in the evenings rehearsing with Miss Boyd. It was different from earlier accomplishments such as riding through pine woods and jumping high fences. My awakening sexual feelings were different, too. When Clare talked one night after lights out about a letter she'd received from a boy she'd met in Maine, I asked, "Do you like him enough to kiss him?"

"Yes! I wouldn't go all the way—but he's fun to go out with. Handsome. Old enough to drive. A good dancer. And he really likes me."

I wanted to ask her what kissing was like. But as comfortable as I was with Clare, I felt shy, and I made a joke instead, a cliché: "I've never kissed a boy. I can't imagine where the noses go!"

Clare laughed. "You'll find out soon. Are you having fun in the play? Paula says you have a crush on Miss Boyd. I used to have a crush on Miss Clayton."

I was shocked. "The piano teacher?"

"Yes, we all did. She'd take my hand to see how far the fingers stretched, and I'd get all shivery. Has that ever happened to you?"

Miss Boyd had asked after the rehearsal that afternoon if anyone wanted to go for an ice cream cone. Sitting next to her in the front seat of her little Ford coupe, I was glad I'd been the only one with time to spare.

"Flora, you're doing so well," she'd said. "I hope you'll continue with your French next year. We can have a tutorial—just you and Celia. We'll read Colette, Baudelaire, some war poetry—It will be fun. Not like a class."

"That sounds wonderful. Thank you, I'd love to," I stumbled along, wishing my heart would stop racing.

"Good, good," said Miss Boyd, turning off the motor, putting a friendly arm around my shoulder. I leapt from the car, escaping both her level gaze and her disturbing hand. Then wished I hadn't.

I wanted to confide in Clare, but it was too difficult to talk about my feelings. I knew I didn't need to be ashamed, and yet I was. A terrible stigma was attached to any rumor of being attracted to a woman. And although nothing had happened, or ever did, I felt a strong attraction to Miss Boyd. I'm sure that many girls, perhaps most girls, have such feelings. But I was scared of my strong emotions and urges. Being both innocent and ignorant, I did a good job of hiding them.

Secrets seemed to permeate my life, then and later, beginning with my longing for my mother. I was full of fears about riding, about popularity, about school. I'd had no one to confide in as a young girl, and I'd been taught to be stoic. Even though I was sixteen, I found it hard to acknowledge the sexual feelings awakened in me when I danced with a boy. Clare had the courage to be curious, and to experiment. I saw this, but I didn't have her assurance.

Growing up in the frenzied atmosphere of wartime, we idealized love. Deciding that it would be delightful to marry each other's brothers, we started correspondences with these heroes overseas. Classmates at Harvard, both in the exclusive Porcellian Club and experienced lady killers, Bim (hers) and Whitty (mine) were sweet to their little sisters, writing letters about their wartime experiences and later arranging dates for us with their desirable friends. Meantime, we languished; dreaming of boys.

Later that year, Clare invited me to spend a week at Orlot, the Chanlers' house on the Hudson. Mr. Chanler mowed the lawns, proudly riding his new tractor, while we raked the grass into sweet-smelling piles. We clambered down to the railroad tracks, looking for arrowheads. Hot and sweaty, we jumped into the dangerous eddies of the Hudson River to cool off. In midsummer, with the family asleep, we danced wildly on the lawn, our white cotton nightgowns floating around us as we sang our desire to the man in the moon.

Clare Chanler was my best friend from ninth grade until she was sixty-four years old. As adults, Clare and I thought of writing about our friendship separately, with the idea of joining our two stories. Even as she wrote suggesting it, she demurred:

> You & I write about our lives at different periods with some bit of overlap here and there, as two friends—two people noticing what was going on, only I'm not sure about that idea. I don't collaborate easily.

The more mature Clare had become sure of herself as an artist. Her strong will vied with her warm affection; her impulse to share with her need to be independent.

I was with her in her hospice room when she died. Her cancer had spread, but even after a brain seizure she held onto a kernel of herself.

"Let's get on with it, shall we?"

As she had in her life, she wanted to get on with the business at hand. When I asked if her father and Nan, her childhood nurse, both of whom had died, were close by, she added her grandmother to the constellation of those she loved.

"They're all working together. Time working in the positive sense instead of the other."

She sang lovely, wordless songs.

And then she was gone. I held her long-fingered hands as they slowly grew cold, her almond-shaped nails turning blue. I wasn't afraid.

She once wrote me,

> I seldom miss people and places—because I feel I am with the people and at the places all the time. There is only one place and one person and one time, and yet there is all this infinite variety, too.

I think of that as I mourn my beloved companion, my husband Sydney. But I'm still too material. Unlike Clare, I want the actual person. I want to touch, and see, and I want to hear a voice.

When I think about my life, Clare is entwined in it—growing up, and keeping in touch during our years of marriage and children. We seemed to reflect each other in a mysterious dance, each with our three siblings, our two husbands, our four children, our similar yearnings. When I write, I'm aware of her—my letters to her were my first real writing—talking to myself as well as to Clare. When I look at her paintings, constructions, and books, when I read again her letters, her presence is palpable. I can hear her melodious voice. As I work on this memoir, I'm in a house overlooking Somes Sound on Mt. Desert Island in Maine, near the place where I once stayed with Clare in her grandparents' house. In the blue water, in the rocks with gray-green lichen, the hills, the blueberries and the salt air, Clare is near me.

I turn the pages of a book she made. A multitude of white figures dance through the shimmering bits of flotsam that make up our world:

> *For some time*
> *it was not clear to me*
> *what was going on*
> *and it was only later*
> *that I realized*
> *I was in the middle*
> *of a celebration.*
> *I found that*
> *just when*
> *I was able*
> *to join the dance*
> *and take my place*
> *the whole thing*
> *was coming to an end.*

PART IV: GROWING UP

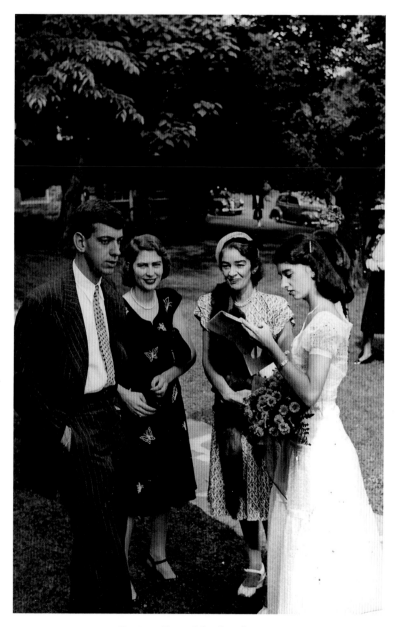

Garrison Forest School graduation:
with Whit, our cousin Syvie Szechenyi Szapary, and my mother

CHAPTER 19

Coming Out

It was 1946. The war was at last over. I'd graduated from school. I was coming out in the summer, and yet I was still in many ways a child.

The male members of our families—various cousins, my Uncle Sonny and Doc's three sons—had joined the Army, Navy, or Air Force. Pam's summer love, Jack Bergamini, joined the Marines and was killed in the Pacific. Whit was home from the Air Force, on his way back to Harvard, and in love with one girl after another. He introduced me to many of his friends—undoubtedly at our mother's bidding—and that was, at last, the beginning of a life that included boys. The mostly older people I began to meet seemed to like me. Astounding! Deep down, I wasn't really part of the group of sophisticated party goers who drank, smoked, and already looked a little weary despite their seeming gaiety. The war they shared had marked them forever.

I had slimmed down, and I had a good haircut. My mother had bought me a number of beautiful dresses, made for me by Hattie Carnegie or Monsieur Tappe of Bendel's. At Mainbocher, I was measured for a headless wire and muslin dressmaker's form upon which a lowcut white lace dress with a bustle waited until I appeared for the final fitting. A column of black lace with a pale pink, heavy silk underslip was molded first to my surrogate body, then to my own. I was changing from tomboy to woman of the world, however superficially. The sensuous fabrics, the form-fitting bodices, and bouffant skirts made me feel like a butterfly. *Paillettes* sparkled on a multicolored, striped sheath, and a band of tiny flowers circled my chest above a sky blue, sprigged, full-skirted organdy gown. My favorite dress was a joyous billow of watermelon-red silk taffeta, the wide rustling skirt trimmed with black lace. Swirling to Eddy Duchin's waltzes, hopping to Lester Lanin's sambas, I never lacked a partner. I felt like the belle of the ball. Two brothers, Bobby and Johnny White, still in their sailor uniforms, did the hornpipe with me one evening under the full moon by the sea. Dancing without a break at all the debutante parties that June and July, boys I'd never laid eyes on cut in on me. Surprised and flattered, I was thrilled to be teased by Whit's attractive, urbane friends. Movement was all, talk was superfluous. After midnight when the band had departed and there was a breakfast of scrambled eggs and bacon, I dreaded conversation with the dancing boys: what could I possibly have to say to such creatures? I had no idea what interested them, or what we might have in common. I remember going through the alphabet for subjects, trying to avoid the silences that seemed to afflict only me. I watched the prattling, laughing girls with envy. How I longed to be like them, even as I retreated into my shell. Budding friendships never progressed beyond the dancing I so enjoyed. Oddly, I felt out of place; out of touch with them and with myself. "Why are you so serious?" one of Whit's friends asked, without much interest in the answer. "That's how I am," I'd have liked to say. "You're so much more experienced than I am—you must have some ideas." But how could I even think of confronting him, when, like many of these men, he, too, perhaps had friends or brothers who had lost their lives in the war. Their wildness, their hilarity, even their excessive drinking were understandable to me.

Despite modest flutters of desire, like the shivers that warn of an impending illness, nothing further developed that summer. I remained pure. From running along piney trails, fly-fishing in Adirondack streams, galloping over Aiken fences, and studying for SATs, I emerged into the world of my grandparents and parents.

For twenty years, those elegant dresses hung in a series of small crowded closets, reminders of my dancing days, and of the miserable terror of being a wallflower—having power, losing power, and, in the end, humiliation. Seldom did I have occasion to wear them after that first coming-out summer. (The words coming out have a very different meaning now.) Those ballgowns were historical remnants of the days when American heiresses were traded to the highest bidder: a European princeling whose wealth needed replenishing, a British aristocrat whose ancestral castle was tumbling down. Fortunately for me, my fortune was no longer large enough, nor would my parents have been prone to that kind of gambling, as much as they enjoyed every other conceivable game.

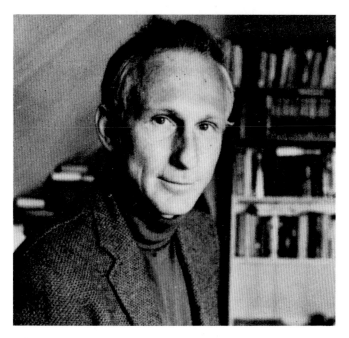

David, 1971

CHAPTER 20

Summer Love

The war interrupted our summers on the lake.

Everything had changed, except for the Adirondacks themselves. Still wild and lovely, they waited for us to return and resume our happy, uncomplicated August lives.

Had I changed, along with everyone else? Impossible not to have changed, but in fact I was not as different as I'd have liked to be. I'd read a lot more books. I'd lost most of my puppy fat. I had tons of energy and was raring to go—but where?

It was six in the morning, August 1st, 1946, at Camp Togus; dark and still, a few stars were reflected in the lake's calm surface. A loon's call broke the silence. I felt my way to the door of my cabin on the way to the lake to skinny-dip in the moonlight. If I turned on the light, the new generator would start and everyone in camp would awaken.

Climbing the stairs after my swim, I remembered that it was the day of our lesson at Squirrel Point with Doc Bergamini. There was an addition to his family that year. His nephew.

He had a strangely accented voice—was it English? Not quite, but close. Since David Bergamini had spent much of his adolescence in Japanese concentration camps in the Philippines, his accent could be anything—even Japanese.

He had high cheekbones in a thin face; the promise of a smile; penetrating blue eyes. His face was angular, slightly crooked, appealing, with a quizzical expression, and a beguiling smile that sometimes included a wink. His sandy hair and freckles appealed to me. When he turned and caught me staring at him, my eyes dropped before his unwavering blue gaze. He was vaguely exotic and cerebral, not like Pam and Whit's male friends who were always on the go, having fun and making noise.

A year or two younger than his classmates at college, David was far ahead of them in many ways. He'd read more widely and absorbed more advanced math and physics. He was already planning his future. He had the assurance of someone much older, perhaps because of his experience in the camps. He was more comfortable with girls, too—certainly with me—than the boys my age that I'd met. He was eager for the future.

It was David's turn to crank the ice cream freezer, and he took over from me, smiling. "Move over, Flora, I'll have this done in a jiffy!" His voice was like a caress. I was instantly smitten, although my fever took a while to register. Despite being seventeen—eighteen in a month—I was remarkably innocent about boys. But I was intrigued, and longing for experience.

Ice cream done, we sank the salt-rimmed container into the cold sawdust of the ice house until lunch time. Doc gave us our Sunday emergency medical training. We were having a lifesaving lesson that day.

"Who wants to be the victim? Okay, Lev, jump in the water. Pretend you're drowning."

Loud groans while Lev sank with much waving of hands.

"Hub," David's uncle shouted to the oldest of his three

sons, "get right in there. Quick! Yes, that's right, pull him to shore any way you can. Don't let him drag you down—grab his hair."

Shrieks of pain from Lev.

"Good, you've saved him. Out of the water, all of you. Flora, lie down on the dock. David, she's full of water, unconscious. How would you do artificial respiration?"

Sitting on my back, he pressed my ribs hard. In and out, in and out. It hurt, not that I'd let him know it. I didn't want him to stop.

"Okay, okay, enough," said Doc.

David, a month younger than I, was already a sophomore at Dartmouth on a full scholarship. I was only slightly aware of his brilliance. He entered my life as a trout slips into a river, perfectly balanced in the current, graceful and adroit. Like the water itself, I was open to him. While he enjoyed having fun, he also spent time reading and talking seriously. I was drawn to the intellectual quality of his conversation.

"Flora, did you know that Shintoism has been abolished in Japan? It's the end of emperor-worship. The emperor was regarded as a god in Japan, so he's really responsible for the war. His commands were always obeyed, and he could have stopped it. Most people don't believe that. They think he's just a nice fellow who loves his garden, but believe me, they're wrong."

"Is that important now?"

"He still has enormous power over his people. After the United States leaves, the same people who started the war will run the government."

David's intense views were not limited to politics. George Orwell's *Animal Farm* had been published in 1945. A satirical allegory of the Russian Revolution, it was particularly directed against Stalin's regime. We'd both read it, but unlike me, David agreed strongly with its message. I thought Stalin had helped us to end the war, and I didn't understand the danger of his tyranny, or his ambitions.

"Don't you see?" asked David. "It suited him for the Allies to win. He has no interest in peace. He's planning to conquer the world. And he's ruthless. He'd do anything—he'd even blow us up."

He had many facts to bolster his views, and his intensity was compelling. He certainly convinced me.

*

While I'd been marooned in the middle of my family's large enclave in Old Westbury, limited for male company to the Polish workers on my Uncle's farm and the soldiers billeted in our stables, David had been leading a very different life. He was born in Japan in 1928, two years after Hirohito ascended the throne. His father, an architect, and his mother, a teacher, were missionaries who had moved their family to Hankow, China, in 1937, shortly before Japan attacked and slaughtered 140,000 people in Nanking. Later, David's meticulously researched book, *Japan's Imperial Conspiracy*, described, in the context of Japan's long history, Hirohito's responsibility for that terrorist attack and many others, especially during World War II. At ten, David had watched with his father from the sacred Chinese mountain of Lushan as Japanese soldiers conducted a reprisal raid against a Chinese farm village below, bayoneting and burning the villagers. Horrified, he writes in his book of the savagery with which these soldiers tortured and raped: "The gentle, thoughtful, courteous, good-natured people among

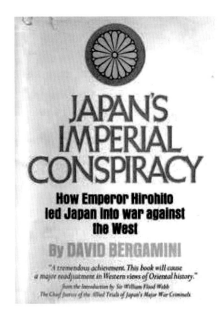

Japan's Imperial Conspiracy, *cover*

whom I had grown to love in boyhood were now transformed, hideously and most puzzlingly."

Two years later, David and his family were evacuated from China by the Japanese. Once away from the war zone, he "found with surprise that the Japanese soldiers were the same cheerful, considerate people that [he] remembered." In the Philippines at the end of 1941, David and his family were moved into a Japanese concentration camp with some three hundred other Americans. Here is part of his account:

> Eventually we settled into a former U.S. Army Post. There we learned to grow thin on two bowls of rice and one serving of vegetable stew a day and became accustomed to living communally on one six-by-three-foot oblong of barracks space apiece. One day a Japanese guard approached our Executive Committee, suggesting that arrangements might be made for opening a school in the camp. Like most of the adult internees, the members of the committee anticipated a short war.

[285]

Preoccupied with immediate problems of survival, they paid little attention to the suggestion. The guard, however, was persistent. He approached one of the older teen-age boys in camp and offered to help get books. Finally he loaded five of us into a truck, covered us with a tarpaulin, and secretly drove past his own guardhouse to Brent School where we had studied before the war.

We found the doors sealed with notices which announced: "Property of the Imperial Japanese Army. Looters will be shot." We broke the seals, loaded the truck with school books, and took them back into the concentration camp. Finding that our assumed birthright of an education might be denied us, most of us read those school books dog-eared in the years which followed. As a result, only one of the score of high-school-age internees lost much educational ground because of the three years in camp, and two of us actually managed to gain a year. After five hours on a work gang each day, our stomachs empty, we had little strength left anyway for anything but reading. I remember lying on my bunk with a geometry book, slightly dizzy as usual before the afternoon meal, puzzling over the fanatic belief in education which gave Japan a literacy rate of over 99 percent and which had prompted our guard to conspire with us in getting the books.

At war's end, after a month and a half in new and appalling conditions, sleeping on the concrete floor of a prison hospital near Manila, starving on a diet of chicken corn, weeds, and snails, the captives learned that the powers in Tokyo, rather than surrendering prisoners, had ordered their execution. By a miracle of timing, they were spared:

I was grateful for their bureaucratic propriety. They had let us live because our executions were not scheduled for another twenty-four hours.

*

David Bergamini's older cousins, across Forked Lake, were

bright and interesting. One would later become a distinguished doctor; another, a Russian scholar and professor; the third, an economist. David dreamed of becoming a writer. His ambition was both compelling and repelling, like a magnet with positive and negative ions. I was drawn to his ready conversation. It was only later that I wondered how much energy and time he'd have left for love.

One perfect day followed another, that summer of 1946. David and I swam across the lake, meeting in the middle to talk while we floated lazily side by side. We were never at a loss for words—ideas, opinions, judgments, the stories of our lives. We hiked through the woods to Salmon Lake, up steep Salmon Mountain to the top of the fire tower, my fear of heights finally dissolved by the joy of his company. We played cribbage against Lev and fire watcher Bill Tuey, shouting our delight whether we won or lost. In an Old Town green canoe, one late summer midnight, we lay on our backs while Northern Lights streamed above us in a quickening of the whole universe. We were dizzy with awe, and silent for once. Suddenly David rolled closer, his mouth near mine—and I turned away. "But why?" he whispered gently. The moment gone, we paddled home, wordless under the eloquent stars.

The next day, I left for Northeast Harbor, Maine, to sail with Clare on her parents' brown-sailed cutter, *Frenchman*. Her handsome, charming brother was on board, with other friends. It was a wonderful cruise with delightful company, but I could only think of David. Why was I so silly, so immature? I was dying for kisses—and I'd rejected him. Would he speak to me again? Would we ever see each other again? I wrote to him, ostensibly to ask if he'd meet me in New York to return a blue sweater I'd lent him one windy day on the

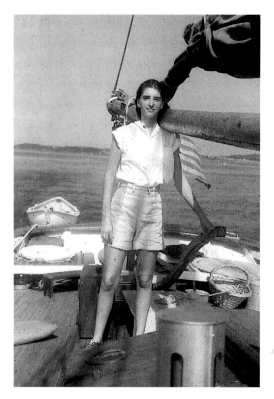

On the "Frenchman," 1946

lake. A friend of Clare's brother arrived from Northeast Harbor to join ship in Eastport, bringing the Chanlers' mail. When he handed me a letter from David, I was stunned. Oblivious to the hoots of the crew, I ripped it open: David had my sweater, yes—but did I imagine he'd ever let go of it? Not a chance. But meeting in New York, yes, definitely. His precise hand conveyed affection in a spare fluid prose.

In New York, in September, we finally kissed. Over-whelmed by first passion, I would have given myself to him entirely, but David was cautious, warning me of my parents' disapproval. Since I imagined myself, by the mere fact of my lineage, to be a prize, I was surprised to learn that his parents, too, objected to our romance. They knew I was out of their league socially, he said, and they were too proud for that. They expected a lot of him, and they didn't want anything to distract or upset him. David had a scholarship to Dartmouth, and he hoped to become a Rhodes scholar. His parents feared my parents' condescension and rejection. They'd already lost one son, and now they feared that I'd soon discard their remaining beloved and brilliant boy. A flighty rich girl would only lure him from accomplishment and success, and then break his heart.

Years later, my father said, "I remember when your mother and I looked out our window and saw you and David walking down 86th Street hand in hand, and we cringed. We were terrified."

Yet they hardly knew him. They certainly would never have dreamed that his family shared their dread of our romance. Or do I underestimate my parents? Perhaps,

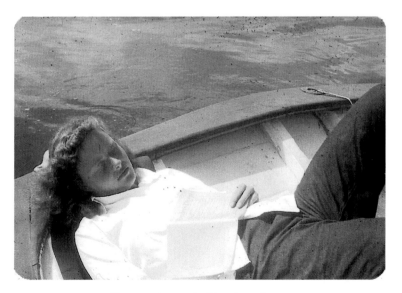

Clare napping on the "Frenchman", 1946

looking at David and me, they saw a different level of intensity than they'd noticed when my sister Pam and his brother Jack had had their brief romance. Maybe they sensed my longing for a long-term commitment. Reluctantly, I understood that David's plans would require all the effort and concentration available to him, ultimately taking him across the seas. I understood that I was a distraction he couldn't afford.

On a rare visit to his family during the long Thanksgiving weekend, David came to New York from Connecticut, and I took him to the opera to hear *La Bohème*. We sat in the box at the Metropolitan Opera house that my grandmother had taken every year, and her parents before her. Now, because of the increased expense, my parents did not want the constant responsibility of filling it, so they had it only for every other Saturday matinee. (My grandmother once invited an artist friend, Guy Pene du Bois, to an evening performance. "But Mrs. Whitney," he said, "I have no evening clothes." "How much would they cost?" she asked. A moment passed as he considered. "Five thousand dollars." She laughed and gave him the money.)

My parents had given their eight tickets to some of their regulars; among others, my father's brother, Uncle Larry Miller, and the publisher Tim Coward. As surrogate hostess, I knew I must sit in the front left-hand corner of the box, with the two other women to my right; David was in back with the other men. We couldn't easily talk, and, as much as we wanted to, we couldn't escape to the little curtained-off coat room in the back of the box. I loved having the occasion to share, however briefly, a family tradition with David. Although this was his first time at the opera, David and his family knew and enjoyed recorded classical music, and he appreciated Puccini and the quality of the singing in *La Boheme*. (In later years, he dove deeply into the theory and history of the music he loved.) That day, he caught on quickly to the customs of the opera box—the formal seating, the hanging-up of our coats, the attendant locking the door to the box—smiling at me mischievously as we maintained a discreet distance from each other.

After the opera, Tim Coward and I returned to Long Island in my parents' town car, driven by their chauffeur William Scott, a cheerful and capable Scot. He'd been with my mother since she was a young woman, when he was under strict instructions to see that she returned home safely—and alone. He'd taught her to drive, and was now doing the same for me; he knew all about each of us, having driven us, too, to parties and late night excursions. I trusted and respected Scott completely. Nevertheless, as was customary, I closed the glass window between the front and back seats of the big black Lincoln. While he drove, I brooded over the brevity of David's and my time together, unable even to hold hands or kiss goodbye.

"You're so quiet," Tim said. "Anything wrong? Did you want to bring your young man to the country with us?"

"I would have liked that," was all that I could say. I wasn't as shy as some people thought. For my eighteen years, I had a certain self-confidence about my accomplishments and increasing attractiveness. Still, except for my few intimate friends, especially David, I found it hard to talk about myself or my feelings.

"Then why not? Couldn't he come?" Tim asked.

"Mummy and Daddy wouldn't like it. They don't approve of David and me. What do you think? Did you like him?" Heart pounding, I waited for his answer.

"Yes, he seems a nice fellow. Parents are anxious about such things—they'll come around eventually." A casual enough response, but I took it as a blessing.

"Won't you say something?"

He didn't promise anything. "If there's a right moment," he said.

And so David and I continued our romance that fall and winter. We talked occasionally on the telephone—long distance was a rare and expensive treat—and we wrote increasingly passionate letters. We seldom saw one another. I never met his parents; he rarely saw mine. We arranged dates at modest restaurants; a Childs or an Automat. We went to a museum—anywhere we didn't have to spend much money. Except for the evenings my parents were away, when we sat on the white built-in sofas overlooking the East River, talking and kissing, we were frustrated but happy.

My first semester at Barnard College was stimulating, even exciting. My classes and papers, the new ideas I was hearing, gave me more to share with David. I also relished making friends who were different, both economically and ethnically, from those with whom I'd grown up. New York itself became an extraordinary laboratory. Our professor sent us across the city searching out the art and architecture we were to write about, starting me on a lifetime of discovery. Only four years earlier, as a novice city-dweller in the ninth grade at Brearley, I was so focused on feeling miserable that I'd been oblivious to the glories of New York.

The dancing parties continued, seeming more and more irrelevant to what I naively began to think of as real life.

I considered the whole apparatus of society superficial, including the time-honored exclusionary tradition, dating back to the early years of the twentieth century, of the Four Hundred. The numbers had increased, and the Social Register in its black cover was published each year with additions and some deletions. Divorces in particular sometimes caused banishment; sometimes not. (Later, politically liberated, I wrote a letter asking for my name to be removed from its pages, but not until I threatened a lawsuit did my name disappear.) The children of the fortunate hundreds are listed under their parents' names as Misses or Masters. After marriage, women join the Married Maidens section, with the names of their spouses appended to their own. Men have their own listing, including their clubs and wives.

It never occurred to me not to go to those parties, no matter how bored I was, and I remained oblivious to the reality that I myself was steeped in convention. Perhaps, too, the exclusive, elegant rituals made me feel important in a way that I needed to feel. My life in Aiken and Long Island had been more isolated. Yet, comforting as that solidarity could be, I understood that membership in that exclusive group implied a complacent conviction that my tribe was better than any other tribe—and that assumption I rejected.

And then, one day that same year—November, 1946—I went to a cocktail party at Clare's house and met Michael Henry Irving. Well liked by my family and his friends, a classmate and clubmate of Whit's, a Dupont and a descendant of George Washington Irving on his father's side, he was far more acceptable to my family than David Bergamini. We saw each other at dances, at dinners, at lunch. He came to Westbury for the weekend, warmly welcomed by my parents. We took the train to the Adirondacks for New Year's weekend with my mother; her old suitor, Carnes Weeks, Whitty, and his future wife, Francie Cheston. We cooked and played poker and Murder in the Dark. Everything seemed effortless, uncomplicated. On the way home, Mike asked me to marry him. I was overwhelmed—happy—and I said yes.

In a few short weeks, and seemingly without a thought, I'd given up David for my future husband. Perhaps I feared that the heat David and I generated would cool. Perhaps I needed my family's approval more than I realized. My new love fit into my life perfectly. He'd gone to St. Paul's, which was the prep school of my father, and brother, Lev. With his Harvard degree behind him, he'd served in the Navy, and was beginning to work in U.S. Lines, a New York shipping firm. He was ready for marriage. Ready for life.

I felt ready, too, as young as I was. I could hardly wait for us to have our own home, make our own meals. Wearing my fiancé's emerald ring, I dropped out of Barnard, took cooking lessons, and shopped for my trousseau. Everything else, including David, flew from my mind and heart.

A year and a half later, on a scorching Sunday in June, 1948, heavy with my first baby, I was playing cards with my parents at their house in Long Island when the phone rang. I answered. It was David. We hadn't been in touch since I'd written to him more than a year earlier to tell him of my decision. Feeling awkward and guilty, I made small talk: how was he, what was he doing? He'd written a book. A novel. It would be published soon.

"What is it about?"

"You."

I was too stunned to speak.

"Yes, it's about an enchanting witch." His voice was still a caress. "And you?"

I told him my news, and heard a shocked gasp.

"Already? You're so young."

Actually, I was not only feeling young, but trapped, and a bit scared. The enormous belly I'd been carrying around would soon become a person, for whom my husband and I would be responsible. I was not at all sure I was up to it. All my insecurities were returning. The time with David seemed like a dream of irresponsible bliss. Not that I admitted any of this to him. I'd made my choice. And I was happy with it. Mostly.

The book, *The Fleet in the Window* was published later, in 1960, by Simon and Schuster. It was the story of a young boy like David, in the Philippines during World War II. A beautiful, rich girl, Enid, plays sexual games with the hero, Peter, who loves and desires her. Enid flirts with the enemy, too; although naïve, she does not betray Peter, who is delivering messages to the guerillas, but she is ready to exchange her body for escape from the war.

Looking back, I see that, like Enid, I'd been looking for an escape from my predictable future. David represented a different, more intellectual path, whose social elements were based on religion and community. In my world, where the Social Register listed who belonged and who didn't, family background and custom were all that mattered. Before meeting Mike that year, I accepted David's invitation to the big winter weekend at Dartmouth. Would I have discovered there more about myself—realized my immaturity, my need for time, education, and experience? Perhaps. I didn't go, because I was already engaged to Mike before the weekend took place.

David maintained the discipline he'd learned in camp all his life. He worked intensely and successfully, writing books on a variety of subjects—the philosophy of science, mathematics, time, and history. Novels, too. He had a wonderful family. He seemed physically and psychologically robust—but today I wonder. He died in his fifties.

How superficial my own childhood and adolescence seem when I think of David's life.

*

I've often felt guilty. As a child, I recited these words from the Episcopal Book of Common Prayer: "We have followed too much the devices and desires of our own hearts. . . . We have left undone those things which we ought to have done; And we have done those things which we ought not to have done; And there is no health in us." When I failed to be good, I felt beyond redemption. Hard on myself and others. Judgmental. I find it more possible, now, to regret some of my actions, rather than indulge in the useless, destructive emotion of guilt. According to the American Heritage Dicitonary, regret is "a feeling of disappointment or distress about something that one wishes could be different." Regret is awareness of the self and the past. It implies the possibility of change.

Reflecting now on my life, I remember those I've loved and hurt. David was the first. After more than thirty years of marriage, when my husband Mike and I separated, I failed to express my reasons any better than I had with David. I hurt the fine man with whom I'd shared most of my life. I'll always be sorry that shame and guilt held me in frozen silence when I needed to be open and honest, both with myself and with Mike. Today, I'm trying to face my perpetual difficulty with confrontation, stemming, I believe, from childhood, when I was taught to hide my problems and feelings. Awareness helps me to better understand and accept myself and others as the flawed humans we can't help but be.

*

Twenty-five years later, when Mike and I moved to a small Connecticut town by the sea, we discovered that David was a neighbor. I wrote him a note and we met again, although this time with our families. He seemed the same—older, of course—but still intense, with his blue-eyed gaze and seductive smile. He still teased me about the too frequent exclamation points in my letters; still laughed about his uncle's first-aid lessons. I enjoyed being with him, and I was grateful that he didn't seem to resent the uncivil way I'd treated him so long ago. David's wife, Penny, a bright, earthy, humorous woman with a finely-tuned irony and wondrous patience, became a friend immediately. They had two boys and two girls, as did Mike and I, and their younger son Jack was in our younger daughter Fiona's class at the local high school. But their friendship is Fiona's story.

CHAPTER 21

Loss

Married and with a baby, I felt closer than I had since childhood to my English nurse, Miss Sligh. I knew that she and her husband, Basil Grant, had been ideally happy. In 1950 when he became ill, they moved to New York to be near the doctors he needed. When I visited them in their tiny, cluttered apartment, it was my first experience of death.

Basil lay in bed, gray and wasted. His eyes held a terrible blankness. Frightened, I tried to talk to him and to comfort Anne, as I now called my old nurse, but words didn't come easily to me. I was not only sad, but embarrassed. One platitude after another gushed from me. I couldn't wait to return to the fresh air outside the stuffy room. I wish that I'd been able to express genuine feeling—the acceptance of finality, and love. Perhaps I could have prayed with them. As a child, even as a woman, I'd been protected by adults from learning first-hand about illness. As a child, I'd learned that it was good to shoot birds and to kill fish and chickens for the family table, but I had no experience of human death. If children were close by, our parents whispered the word cancer to each other. We grew up ignorant of catastrophe. Through our elders' example, we learned to deny the existence of illness and death. When Mimi, my sister's little daughter, died of a brain tumor when I was in my twenties,

I could barely tell Pam honestly and openly of my distress and my love. As much as I longed to, I couldn't even embrace her. I was embarrassed. I'm ashamed to remember that. Customs have changed, almost all to the good. Adults tell children much more now. Parents—my own grown children, for example—want their offspring to understand the natural cycle of life and death.

So many I loved are dead now. I like to think of them as they were when we were happy together: my father, painting in his cabin in the Adirondacks; my mother, swimming in Forked Lake. Every July 29th, we celebrated our mother's birthday at Camp Togus. As many as thirty of us could sit— and often did—in roomy chairs around the long pine table in the paneled dining room. Sometimes it was cold and rainy, even in summer, and the fireplace, built with enormous rocks, blazed at one end of the room.

For our mother's birthday, the four of us—my sister Pam, my brothers Whitty and Lev, and I—would transform her armchair at one end of the table into a throne from *A Midsummer Night's Dream*, festooned with flowers, ferns, and vines. Paddling to the lake's far reaches that morning, we had picked slippery stems of sweet-smelling pink and white water lilies, and arranged them in Chinese export bowls. We'd searched the woods for moss; pale Indian pipes with waxy, nodding flowers; yellow and black mushrooms; scarlet deer berries; and tiny shoots of princess pine to create a miniature forest. using a mirror as a lake. Each of us used the talents we possessed to make a different treasure. With bits of feathers, deer fur, tinsel and twine, I made my best dry flies, resting them on cotton from our Johnson & Johnson first aid kit in a little box I made from white birch-bark. Fishing dry was my mother's favorite way to lure her quarry.

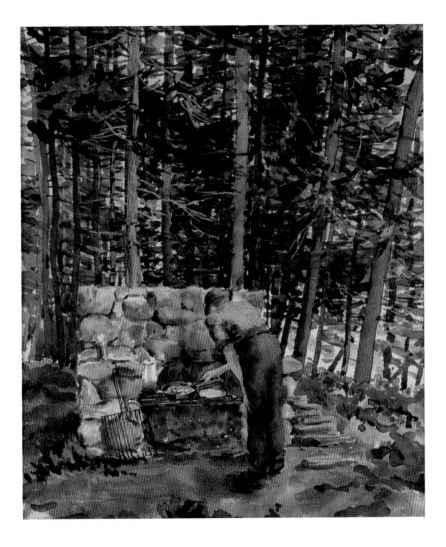

Louis cooking steaks at Togus, by my father

We adored her. We tried endlessly to please her, to be singled out and praised by her. "Darling," she'd gasp as she opened each present, "how marvelous, how beautiful. You didn't! Oh, thank you so much, I just can't believe it."

Sometime in my twenties, with four young children, I began to consider the morality of fishing and of shooting birds. In the Adirondacks, in Aiken, I'd never had any doubts.

Fly fishing with my parents, casting a tiny black gnat across a still pool, waiting for the trout to leap to it, its weight bending the slender bamboo rod in half as the hook was set, was a ritual act. The fish leaped again and again, its glistening, speckled body flashing in the dawn light, until at last, exhausted, it was brought in, netted, and placed under lily pads to keep it cool. Only when cleaning the trout was I uncomfortable, conscious of its beauty and vitality, now extinguished. And extinguished by me.

Later, I tried to remember how I'd felt when I'd killed birds. Exhilarated? Triumphant? Mature? All of these things. Yet also a little sad; an uneasy feeling I'd quickly brushed aside. Certainly I felt satisfaction. After all, hitting a live target was not easy—I'd practiced diligently for months. Not one of my friends in school could accomplish that. I came to understand that the birds' death, as that of the fish, represented the few precious hours I had with my mother. When I finally gave up shooting birds and, still later, catching fish, the lives of small creatures had come to seem too precious to destroy, even for my mother. I'd accepted my feelings about her, and no longer needed to gain her attention as I once had done. She had raised me much as her mother had raised her, with a dependence on carefully chosen surrogates. I came to realize that she loved me much as Gamoo had loved her, and, by sharing her own involvement with the museum founded by her mother, the Whitney Museum of American Art, I discovered a way to be close to her at last.

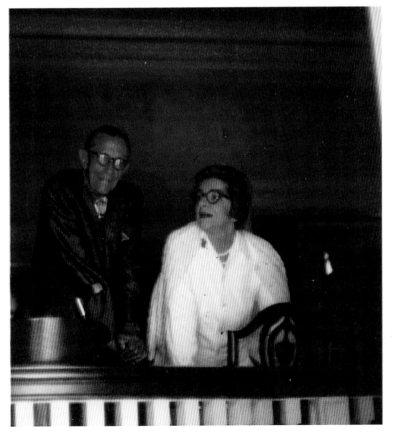

My parents, 1969

CHAPTER 22

Aiken Revisited

What am I now that I was then?
May memory restore again and again
The smallest color of the smallest day:
Time is the school in which we learn,
Time is the fire in which we burn.

DELMORE SCHWARTZ
"Calmly We Walk Through This April's Day"

In 2001, Sydney Biddle, my second husband, and I had been married for twenty years. He had never seen the dream house of my Aiken childhood. We decided to visit Joye Cottage.

There were conflicting reports about its redecoration; people either loved it or hated it. I was determined to keep an open mind. Approaching my mid-seventies, I hoped to continue to explore the new in art, literature, theatre, music—why not a renewed Joye Cottage? (*Make it new*—cried Ezra Pound.) In that spirit, I set out to see how Joye Cottage's new owners had changed the house. Driving to Aiken past the familiar jack pines and cotton fields, I wondered, too, whether I'd discover other things from my past.

Today, most of Aiken's streets are paved, but Easy Street, in front of the house, retains its soft red clay. We parked in the driveway. There were the same small yellowish pebbles, the same embracing wings of the house, the same flight of painted blue-gray steps off to the right, leading to the wide verandah.

The front door looked exactly the same as it had in the early seventies, when I was last there and my parents appeared in the doorway with welcoming halloos and hugs. The current residents, our hosts, Steve Naifeh and Greg Smith, greeted us. We took off our shoes—as they'd asked when they opened the door—and padded along the polished wood.

We followed them into the hall, where a few handsome Far Eastern sculptures sat on polished round tables. My father's chronometer was gone, with its message of precision soothing to him. Although I used to think my parents' lives were ordered and predictable, I understand that they, too, had been vulnerable to disorder and suffering.

The living room was dazzling white. In my time, from the 1930s to the 1970s, and for about fifty years before, when my grandparents and great-grandparents had lived there, rich colors suffused the walls and floors, sofas and chairs. The furnishings and the accompanying multitude of objects had reflected the taste of generations—flowers, silver, textiles, porcelain, paintings, books, guns, clocks, electric trains and an extinct bird in a glass bell had filled the sixty-odd rooms. Now, save for a few recent works of art, everything was plain. No trimmings. Lots of space.

Light poured through uncurtained windows. A piano stood in the same corner where we once practiced our endless scales and exercises; the peak of my achievement Schubert's *Moment Musicale*. (Lev now has that piano in a house he's built in Florida reminiscent of Joye Cottage.)

Steve and Greg's piano faced the porch, not the wall of books that I remembered. Judging by the locked French doors and the few little tables and hard chairs scattered on the broad expanses of the verandahs, once intrinsic parts of the living room, the porches weren't much used. But there was a card table similar to ours in the far corner of the living room, and I instantly pictured my parents sitting on the rosy window seat, playing Canasta or pasting photographs into their albums. The past appeared before my eyes, even if the gleaming white walls and spare furnishings challenged the memories teeming with color. Shiny blue brocade covered the small firm sofas and chairs. Where J. D. had once stood by my father's cornstalk blind, there was a Japanese screen. The room felt cool. It was quite beautiful. I complimented Greg and Steve, noticing—for the first time—the intricate, newly accentuated moldings of the ceiling, fireplace, and denuded windows, as well as the stairs to Pam, Whit, and Sis's rooms. All designed, they told me, by Stanford White— that, too, was new information for me. Past the living room, my parents' bedrooms and the dove room were unrecognizable. Through the diamond-paned windows of the long hall to my former bedroom, I glimpsed my old school across the street. It was not a school any longer, but someone's home.

Steve led us through a nearby door. Once it led to the dark, scuffed stairway winding to the cramped rooms with undersized windows where my mother's tiny French maid, Josephine, had washed, ironed, and slept. The gloomy, damp spaces were gone, replaced by a wide, well-lit, carpeted stair opening to a large windowed bedroom and a huge bathroom—who'd have guessed that so much space existed under the eaves! It was inviting in its airiness, with views over tall trees to the lawn. It was their best guest room.

"We sleep in all the different bedrooms," they told me. Their permanent bedrooms, however, were in what I formerly knew as the spooky wing, down a flight of stairs near my parents' bedrooms. Except for my father's studio at the end of the hall, opening onto the garden and pool, the wing had once been dark and forbidding. Now, it was full of light, like the rest of the house.

I wondered if the changes merely signified a change in fashion. Did Steve and Greg's vision of my home capture its original spirit? In my ancestors' time, Victorian excess had been the principal motif. My mother, putting her own sunny mark on the house she'd inherited, had added bright splashes of yellow, purple, and chartreuse to rooms already filled with color and objects. Today the house is stark; it is one of the two greatest differences between then and now.

Joye Cottage will always define home to me. As perhaps it does for its current owners, too. They have taken extraordinary measures to recreate what had utterly deteriorated, copying bronze sconces from the front hall and installing them everywhere, as well as restoring kitchen cabinets, bathroom fixtures, moldings, mantels, and even bits of furniture. Everything they have added is well-crafted and appropriate. Although the walls are white, in each room a different Scalamandre fabric on a bed, chair or sofa floods the eye with color. Ancient sculptures, Japanese screens, a few paintings and drawings, make exquisite additions to the newly pristine rooms. Trying for detachment, I told the new owners how I admired what they'd done. (Was I being insincere? Reverting to the over-politeness I learned in these same rooms as a child?)

The second great difference is in the number of occupants. No one was cooking in the huge, magnificently equipped kitchen. Everything was immaculate. Who was keeping it so well? Who was making dinner? There were no enticing smells. No food at all.

In a side wing, my mother's once-gaudy New Room contained banks of desks with computers where a few scholarly-looking men and women were quietly at work. Steve and Greg write books. They continually update volumes listing the best doctors and attorneys throughout the country. The books are commercially successful. In 1990, their biography of Jackson Pollock won a Pulitzer Prize.

In the warm, sunny fall afternoon, Sydney and I toured the Hitchcock Woods where I'd spent much of my childhood on various horses. The woods were the same. No cars, except for the open jeep of the generous botanist who'd offered to show us around. A few riders. The same sandy *manege* where Captain Gaylard had drilled us in British cavalry maneuvers. There were the very same lines of Aiken fences where I'd jumped, always excited, often terrified

As we drove through the beautiful woods, I wondered about the effect of all those rides. Did they influence me in some far-reaching way? Of course they did. In ways both good and bad. Gaylard's discipline, the concentration he demanded, and the constant challenge to learn more and to do better, helped me in all that I subsequently tried to accomplish. The assurance I gained through riding carried me through many a bad patch. As I'd grown older, however, I'd held onto the belief that if I could control my environment as I had once controlled my horse, all would be well. Sometimes I tried to manipulate a spouse, a child, a friend or a business associate—which was not good for relationships. At the same time, I made unrealistic demands on myself, trying for perfection in the kitchen, the garden, the nursery, the bedroom. When I couldn't live up to my goals, I became frustrated and dejected. My own children taught me, by example, that perfection is an unworthy and unattainable goal. Their example, their tolerance and love, have been indispensable to any growth I've achieved.

In the woods that day, I felt almost as I once had so long ago on my best days—eager, nervous, my lithe, young body alert yet at ease. Sand River, Cathedral Aisle, Lover's Lane, the horseshow grounds, all, all still there. Happy as I was to be in the Hitchcock Woods, my mind was drifting as we bounced along the soft forest roads back to Joye Cottage. The woods were full of memories, but they didn't have their previous magic. Perhaps because they hadn't changed. Joye Cottage, transformed, had a more powerful impact than the unaltered lovely woods. Perhaps nature, in the end, does not touch me as deeply as human creations.

As a child, often alone, I longed for the companionship and play that my grandchildren take for granted. Taught by my English nurse to be stoic, and never, never to complain of boredom (or anything else), I learned to amuse myself. My friends were the characters I found in books. When a beloved horse or a dog was in pain; when David Copperfield was beaten; when Beth in *Little Women* was ill, I wept. I was terrified for days by *The Hound of the Baskervilles*. I rejoiced when Robin Hood stole from the rich to give to the poor. I developed my attitudes from books, as I did later from other forms of art. Like many bookish children, writers and artists formed my life.

Later that day, we had dinner with a friend whose brother had been killed a month earlier in the World Trade Center. She told us of a memorial service, of her work in New York with the Red Cross. Later that night, CNN brought the news of the bombing of Afghanistan to our bedroom. At the end of our trip to Joye Cottage, when we flew home, the National Guard was patrolling the airport.

The world and Aiken at last seemed entwined, unlike when I lived there as a child.

In many ways, revisiting Aiken was a blessing. So much came back to me. The longing for my mother; the frustration of being a powerless child; the happiness of food, school, my friend Marianna, my teachers, my horses, my dog. There had been a sense that the life we had would last forever.

My identity, embedded deep within me, reaches like the roots of a tree to Aiken. Circumstance has modified, but not quite obliterated, that early self. The changes in Joye Cottage are parallel to the changes in me—I'm glad to discover that we both have a capacity for transformation and for growth.

Until our visit, I had imagined Joye Cottage as it used to be, in all its complicated glory. I was sure that I remembered everything, but now, I understand that my vision is blurred. Ubiquitous white has cooled my image of reds, yellows, blues and browns; flattened the corners; and illuminated warm shadows. The house's current look has become a kind of encroaching microbe, invading the membrane of my memory.

I'm grateful that my home has been so lovingly cared for. Its very survival seems a miracle. It isn't a restoration, but a new creation. And why not? It's the new owners' home, not mine. So why don't I feel happy? My appetite for the new seems to have evaporated. Perhaps I'm not, after all, that old lady I envisioned: eager, curious, ever-young, with open mind and eyes. The aesthetic of purity doesn't suit what I know is the disorder of life. The truth is I want *my* Joye Cottage back. Just as it was. I want to be that innocent, dreamy child again. I want to have a second chance.

Does change always imply loss? Well, that depends on one's perspective. In the middle of my life, I found a new romance, a new job, a new home. A glorious future lay ahead. All would be well. Better, actually, than before. Yet faced with unwelcome change, how differently I now feel. When people took actions I abhorred at the Museum that I loved and once led, I was ready to fight.

Although I know that change is inevitable, even desirable, seeing Joye Cottage again touched a raw nerve. As memories flooded my mind and heart, some devil in me wanted to splash red mud on the gleaming floors, spill chili on the spotless Viking stove, and rumple the covers in what was once my bedroom. The transformation of Joye Cottage brought home a sense of loss. Time passing. People passing. Everything passing.

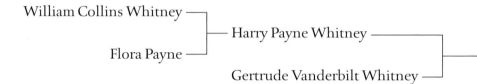

William Collins Whitney ——┐
                          ├── Harry Payne Whitney ————————┐
Flora Payne ——┘   ├──
                          Gertrude Vanderbilt Whitney ——┘

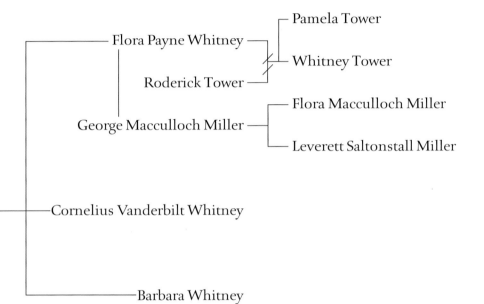

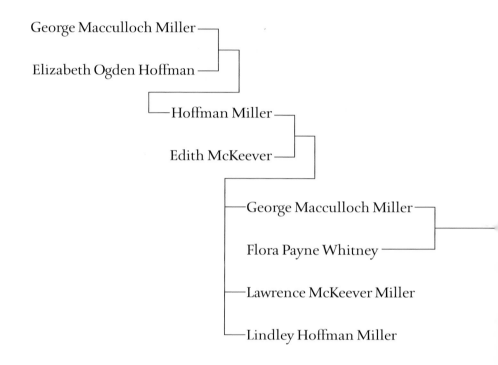

George Macculloch Miller ─┐
Elizabeth Ogden Hoffman ─┘
  └─ Hoffman Miller ─┐
     Edith McKeever ─┘
        ├─ George Macculloch Miller ─┐
        │ Flora Payne Whitney ──────┘
        ├─ Lawrence McKeever Miller
        └─ Lindley Hoffman Miller

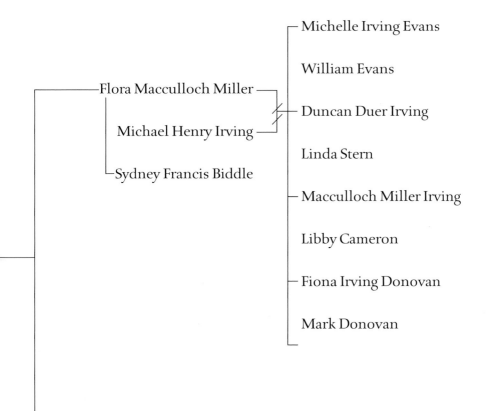

Flora Macculloch Miller
Michael Henry Irving
Sydney Francis Biddle

Michelle Irving Evans
William Evans
Duncan Duer Irving
Linda Stern
Macculloch Miller Irving
Libby Cameron
Fiona Irving Donovan
Mark Donovan

Leverett Saltonstall Miller